A PICTURESQUE TALE OF PROGRESS

By Olive Beaupré Miller

Assisted by Harry Neal Baum

NEW NATIONS

PART I

THE BOOK HOUSE FOR CHILDREN
CHICAGO

COPYRIGHT 1931, 1935, 1949 THE BOOK HOUSE FOR CHILDREN
COPYRIGHT IN GREAT BRITAIN AND IRELAND AND IN ALL
COUNTRIES SUBSCRIBING TO THE BERN CONVENTION.
REGISTERED AT STATIONERS' HALL. ALL RIGHTS RESERVED

SIXTH PRINTING, 1949

PRINTED IN U.S.A.

CONTENTS

I
THE BREAKING UP OF THE ROMAN EMPIRE: 11

II
BARBARIANS INVADE THE WESTERN EMPIRE: 61

III
THE EASTERN, OR BYZANTINE EMPIRE: 90

IV
A NEW POWER ARISES IN THE EAST: 120

V
THE FRANKS: 142

VI
THE MEDIEVAL CHURCH: 177

VII
THE VIKING ADVENTURERS: 207

VIII
LIFE IN THE FEUDAL AGE: 237

INDEX: 253

MAPS AND CHARTS

161—395 A.D.
THE BREAKING UP OF THE ROMAN EMPIRE: 18

ABOUT 450 A.D.
THE EMPIRE OF ATTILA: 70

843 A.D.
DIVISIONS OF CHARLEMAGNE'S EMPIRE: 209

161—305 A.D.
ROMAN EMPERORS FROM MARCUS AURELIUS TO DIOCLETIAN: 45

305—565 A.D.
ROMAN EMPERORS AFTER DIOCLETIAN: 59

THIS COVER IS A MINIATURE *of Charles the Bald, king of the Western Frankish Kingdom and grandson of the great Charlemagne. Charles was ambitious and active, but he was not strong enough to maintain order.*

The king, however, had been well educated by his mother, and his court was the home of many scholars, for he was truly a patron of learning. He had a large library of manuscripts, and thus it is only fitting that we find a miniature of Charles the Bald in his imperial robes and jeweled crown, taken from a medieval illuminated book made in the monastery of St. Emmeram for the king about 870.

The stiff, flat figures are clad in rich garments of brilliant colors, and the foreground is filled with glittering gold, so that the whole picture forms a decoration that is highly ornamental.

I
The Breaking Up of the Roman Empire
(161 A.D.—395 A.D.)

The Barbarians of Spain, Britain, Gaul, and Germany

When imperial Rome ruled the world, where could a young man go if his soul burned for strange adventure, if he felt the eager desire to meet half-civilized folk or even to fall in with savages and know the thrill of escaping whole from men who adorned their horses with rows of human heads? He must either turn his face west toward the distant province of Spain, or toward the more barbarous north, where swarms of savage tribes dwelt among forests and marshlands. In the south and east were old, long established civilizations—Egypt, with its ancient culture; Syria, with its markets and its caravans like an army, and Greece with its dreams of beauty—these were old, old, old! Romance in the days of the Empire followed the setting sun or the trail of the lone North Star.

Sailing far to the west, toward the mystic Pillars of Hercules on the edge of the Unknown Ocean, Marcus Julius Paulus, young, romantic, and eager, disembarked from a Roman galley on the fertile coast of Spain. There were prosperous cities there; but these were too Roman for Marcus. Turning his back on the cities, he rode through vineyards and orchards, toward the line of glistening snow-peaks, and the high-lying rocky plateau that ran through Central Spain.

Spanish warriors with tight-belted waists, plumed headdresses, typical little round shields and short spears. The centipede tails of horses show Phoenician influence. (Vol. III, page 127.) I-be′ri-an gold band. Louvre, Paris.

Spaniards of the days when Rome subdued I-be′ri-a. The ladies have long, finely-pleated under-chemises and over-garments laid in folds. Veils or cloaks are arranged on their heads like Spanish mantillas; tassels dangle over their ears. All carry sacred vases. The second figure is a man in pleated tunic and long draped robe. He wears an armlet and necklace like the ladies. The worshiper at the left wears sun, moon and star, with strange designs on her skirt.

As he passed through the rugged mountains, he saw half-naked miners bearing their little lamps, and issuing dirty and sweaty from the famous silver mines; and he passed many native Iberians afoot or on horses or donkeys, riding from town to town down the rocky mountain roads. Sometimes he met a slow-paced, solemn, religious procession, women bearing sacred vases in ceremonial fashion, or perhaps a husband and wife who bore between them a vase. And some of these solemn votaries wore symbols of the gods they worshiped, a moon, a star, and a sun dangling in gold on their breasts. They were serious folk, these Iberians, of the short, dark, Mediterranean race, like Cretans and Egyptians. No wasting a smile on a stranger! They passed the young traveler coldly with a proud and haughty reserve.

Nevertheless, they showed that they were still barbarians by the number and size of their ornaments. Who ever saw such huge chains, such necklaces with pendants, such bracelets, armlets, ear-rings, fringes, tassels, and jewels! The studied grace and simplicity of a well-draped Roman toga made no appeal to barbarians. Look at the number of pleats, the elaborateness of the folds, the tunics and overtunics, the cloaks and flowing veils! And Jove! what enormous head-dresses! The higher the rank of the lady, the taller the height of the mitre, till some of these grand Spanish dames seemed scarcely able to support the overwhelming weight of their rank! Marcus perceived one woman in floating red veils and cloak, who wore what appeared to be a pair of golden chariot-wheels dangling over her ears!

Spanish ladies in tall peaked hoods and towering headdresses. Tall mitres represented a higher civil or religious condition. The woman in the huge, round turban sits in a chair, and wears across her forehead a bandeau with short fringe. Dresses are laid in elaborate folds. Stone figures found at Cer'ro de los San'tos, Spain, done in the crude native Iberian style. (Madrid Museum.) See Iberian figures brought to life, page 10. See also Vol. IV, page 40.

NEW NATIONS

The famous bust of the Lady of El'che (440 B.C.). Iberian art at its best. She wears a red veil turned back in three folds over her forehead, and rising high over a frame in the rear. Over this, a crown supports two huge gold wheels with pearls around the rim. Inside these wheels, a plaque holds ten tassels, which dangle over her shoulders, ending in spindle-shaped ornaments. Her collar has three rows of pearls, decorated with urns and plaques. (Madrid.)

Rome was trying to Latinize all these Iberian people. Would she succeed, Marcus wondered? A thousand years before, Phoenicians from Tyre and Sidon had settled in Iberia; later the Greeks had come, and then the Carthaginians; but all this time the natives had stubbornly remained Iberian. Take a statue of Cupid, for instance; the Iberians got the idea from Greece; but what had they done to that charming and dainty little Greek god? They had made him squat and fat, as broad as he was long, a clumsy little gnome forever anchored to earth by a pair of heavy wings!

Phoenician, Greek, and Carthaginian influenced Spanish art only a little. Phoenicians brought the idea of the sphinx from Chal-de′a; but this sphinx is thoroughly Iberian. Minerva, the Centaur, and Cupid came from Greece; but all are transformed by Iberian artists. The clumsy little gnome, meant to represent the charming and dainty Cupid, is amusingly Iberian, and Minerva with her huge goggle eyes has received a tiny round Spanish shield and leather skull-cap, in place of her grand Greek helmet and shield. All these statues are in Madrid Museum.

BREAKING UP OF THE ROMAN EMPIRE

An Iberian priest and priestess with hands extended in blessing. The war-god, a typical warrior, on a strong, stocky Spanish horse, with mouth open in favorite Spanish style. The harness is a bridle of stamped leather. There is no saddle, but a saddle-cloth edged and held in place by twisted braid. The rider holds the head of a wild beast. He wears a short jacket with sleeves, a wide belt, and a collar with four ornaments resembling cockle shells. (Madrid.)

Clumsy, crude, and yet interesting was all their artistic work. They had a war-god on horseback, of whom they made many statues, and Marcus saw large gold brooches whereon this heavenly horseman sat as stiff as a ram-rod, his horse barbarically carved and decorated with circles and geometric designs, as though made by some lively child. On nights when the moon was full, the people worshiped this god by means of religious dances, and Marcus saw their figures moving in stately rhythm, darkly silhouetted in the gleam of silver light that flooded the wide stretch of moor.

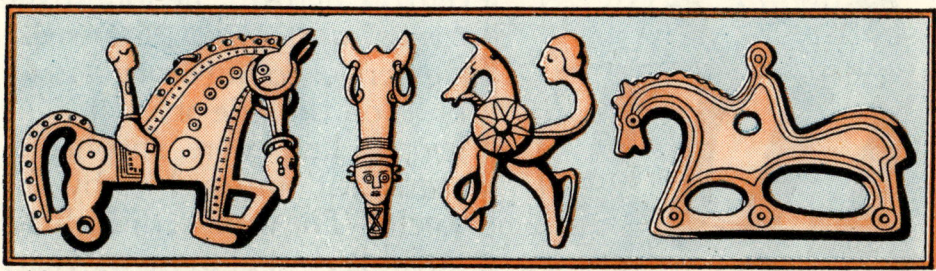

At left and right, the warrior-god, interpreted in true Spanish style, and made into safety pins. Center, a front view of one of these pins, and an artistic bronze figure of the warrior-god with interesting curves in the rearing of the horse and the swaying of the rider's long, thin body, with its long neck and unwieldy head. (Collection Vives, Madrid.) For the great artistic ability of prehistoric Iberian cave-artists, see Vol. I, pages 29, 31, 32, 33, 34, 39. The description of Iberia given here is taken largely from Strabo, a Greek geographer of the age of Augustus.

Spaniards hunting a deer. Pottery found at Am-pur'i-as, Spain. Iberian pottery first bore geometric and floral designs; later, animals and human figures.

Save for fighting with bulls, holding contests in running and boxing, dancing was the chief delight of all the Iberian people. After dinner was passed around, they danced to flute and trumpet, leaping up and crouching low; and in some parts the women danced with the men, taking hold of their hands.

Around the sunny coast-lands, where the people had come in contact with Rome and civilization, Marcus saw towns well-fortified, with truly gigantic walls of enormous, roughhewn stones; but as he left behind the dusty gray olive orchards and the fragrant, flowery vineyards bordering the smiling sea, as he made his way further inland, over the bleak, windy uplands of that dreary central plateau, he found the towns quite unwalled, mere clusters of round stone houses built on the side of a hill. The people here were shepherds, crude and untouched by the world. The women did a little farming; but of industry there was none save the making and painting of pottery.

Bareheaded Iberian soldiers in pleated tunics with round shields, their shoes fastened with thongs. (O-su'na.)

BREAKING UP OF THE ROMAN EMPIRE

Plenty of soldiers appeared; for the Spaniards were fierce little people, by nature given to war. Most of these native warriors carried the characteristic small round Iberian shield, and many had drawn in their waists by means of leather belts, as the men of Crete and Mycenae had done in the ages past. Ye gods! to what wasp-like dimensions they had belted in their waists!

Spanish pottery. A bird struggles in the claws of a monstrous beast; another attacks his back. (Madrid Museum.)

Generally they were bareheaded though some wore a leather skull-cap that fitted close to the head. They were dogged fellows, these Spaniards, intensely rebellious of leadership, and they would not combine in tribes, being more inclined to rob and venture on petty plunderings than to unite in a large and powerful federation. Each little town remained a separate self-governing unit, though some were so small they contained a scanty fifty souls. For two hundred years, Rome had battled to gain control of Spain, fighting the Spaniards piecemeal, subduing them group by group. Yet traveling now in Spain, Marcus saw the Iberian half-civilized at least, and he eagerly longed to visit far more savage lands where the people were stranger still.

Iberian soldier in very short tunic, his waist belted in tight. See page 11. (Stone relief found in Spain; Louvre.)

The Roman Empire, showing Spain, Gaul and Britain; and Rome's neighbors, the Germanic tribes, the new Persian Empire and Palmyra, the desert-kingdom. Gaul reached from the Pyrenees to the Rhine and Danube rivers and contained modern France, Belgium, Switzerland, and western Germany. Gauls were the ancestors of Frenchmen.

North of Spain lay Gaul where Caesar had fought and conquered. There were the real barbarians! Proceeding slowly on horseback, Marcus turned his face northward. Southern Gaul he found stupid, a second edition of Rome, with people in Roman togas gossiping on the streets or crying their wares from shops in his own native Latin tongue. Here were houses with pillared porticoes, Roman baths and theaters, and long lines of Roman aqueducts, lifting their beautiful arches across the flowery fields; but who wanted more of Rome? One could see such things at home.

North, ever north went Marcus. Rude tracks through the forest made long ago by some swineherd or lonely charcoal-burner, had now been widened and strengthened into imperial highways. Marcus met Roman legions or peaceful Roman traders driving their pack-trains northward; yet in spite of these advance-guards of Roman civilization, Northern Gaul was still Gaul, with its native barbaric customs.

A welter of tribes Gaul had always been, a shifting, ever-changing sea of tribe replacing tribe. The Romans had called all the people who lived in this vast land by the single name, Gauls or Celts; but as a matter of fact, there were three distinct races in Gaul. In the south and west, near Spain, were the short, dark Mediterraneans. In the Alps and Central Gaul were the brown-haired, gray-eyed Alpines; and mingled with these two races everywhere in the province were the light-haired, blue-eyed Nordics, who had come down from the North and conquered all of Gaul. Celtic was now a name to be correctly applied only to the language of the land; for the Celtic-speaking Nordics had spread their language and culture to all the tribes in Gaul, so that dark-haired Mediterraneans and brown-haired Alpine highlanders now spoke Celtic in Gaul. As Marcus went further northward, he soon began to see the first signs of the savage—men wearing barbarous trousers! Tunics and well-draped togas betokened the civilized Roman; breeches denoted a savage. In Gaul, in Britain, in Germany the native costume was trousers, at which the elegant Roman turned up his nose in disgust.

A bronze wagon from Gaul bearing mounted warriors in the peaked Gal'lic helmet. Unlike Roman chariots, this wagon has four wheels, and it was undoubtedly on a base like this that migrating German tribes piled their belongings. It has deer's heads, and the antlers of Cer'nun-nus, Celtic god of abundance. (Strettweg, Austria, 550-400 B.C.)

Celtic scenes in Gaul. At the left a priest, perhaps a Dru'id, offers a human sacrifice. In the center are two rows of horsemen and foot-soldiers. Many helmets have animal effigies. The soldiers wear trousers, and bear javelins, and large oblong shields quite unlike the small round Iberian shields. (See page 11.) Trousers characterized all northern barbarians, Briton, Celt, and German. Right, three trumpeters blow long animal-mouthed horns. (One side of a beautifully embossed silver dish of Celtic workmanship, 2nd or 3rd cent. A.D. National Museum, Copenhagen.)

Traveling through the cool depths of the sun-spangled woodlands of Gaul, Marcus saw forest-villages with little round dome-shaped huts made of wicker and thatched with straw, among which long-legged hogs, exceedingly tall and swift, wandered freely about, holding their own for fierceness against any chance attacks by quarrelsome dogs or men. Through occasional open doorways, he saw that the villagers slept on the ground, and ate their meals squatting on straw. Dressed in long breeches and tunics, with a coarse woolen cloak called a *sagus*, they passed him on all the highways looking up at him curiously under their long, yellow hair. Nor did Marcus lack the thrill of feeling that he was here at last among men wholly savage; for he met more than one Gallic warrior with long, bristling, yellow mustache, returning from a foray with a necklace of human heads decorating the chest of his horse.

A Celt in the tall peaked Gallic helmet drives a chariot. From a Celtic bronze pail, 550-400 B.C., now in Vienna.

BREAKING UP OF THE ROMAN EMPIRE

The horned, Celtic god, Cer'nun-nus, with a snake, a deer, a wolf, and other animals. The Celtic-speaking Nordics of France and Britain, who mingled with original dark-haired people, had a culture and a language quite unlike the northern Germanic Nordics who spoke Teutonic, and whose chief god was Woden. Cernunnus is entirely different from Woden. The word Celt actually means a language and culture, not a race; since Celts and Teutons were both yellow-haired Nordics. (Opposite side of same Celtic dish shown on p. 20; National Museum, Copenhagen.)

A tall race these Gallic folk were and the native warriors had weapons commensurate with their size. Some wore the characteristic tall peaked Gallic helmet and others had round leather caps, surmounted with figures of beasts, a crudely carved boar, or a bird. Marcus had thought the Iberians barbarically fond of jewelry; but the Gauls were as ostentatious. They loaded themselves in showy display with necklaces, and armlets; and their dignitaries wore garments exceedingly vivid in color and gleaming with sprinklings of gold. These people were cousins at least to the German tribes of the Baltic, yet they had wholly different gods and a wholly different speech; for while the Germanic tribes left up in the frigid North spoke a pure Teutonic tongue, and worshiped Woden, the one-eyed, the Celtic-speaking Gauls adored Cer'nun-nus, the deer-horned, the Celtic god of abundance.

Two Celts, in the long Gallic cloak or *sagus*, drive a two-wheeled wagon. (Bronze pail, 500-400 B.C., Vienna.)

A barbarous ancestor of the modern Frenchman in typical Celtic helmet, returns to his village with enemy heads swung around his horse's neck. Later these heads will be nailed over the door of his round wicker hut.

Through all Gaul, Marcus found Druids held in the highest honor. These Druids were priests and judges; and whenever they sentenced many men to be sacrificed to the gods, the people believed there would also be a larger yield from the land. Marcus saw these Druids strike condemned men with a sabre and read omens in their death-struggles. He saw victims shot to death and impaled within the temples; he even saw a colossal figure made of straw and wood, stuffed with men, cattle, and beasts, and fired in seething flames as a sacrifice to the gods. On the wicker-huts in the villages, he saw the heads of enemies nailed beside the doors; and men showed him other heads of more important foes embalmed in cedar-oil, while the war-like Celtic chieftains vowed they never gave back those heads, though an equal weight of gold was offered for their return.

Northern Gaul was surely savage enough to suit the most venturesome youth; but there were always other lures to entice a young traveler onward. Across the channel in Britain, the great Julius Caesar had said were wild-men who painted their skins bright blue to make themselves more terrible, whenever they went into battle! Having actually seen the barbaric Gallic collectors of human heads, Marcus now yearned to behold those interesting British savages, who inclined so staunchly to blue. Enshrouded in fog and mist, Britain was the farthest and least known of Roman provinces. Marcus found Roman cities there; but in the wilds of the backwoods the people seemed far more simple and barbarous than the Gauls. The island was covered with forests in the midst of which the Britons fenced off circular places with rough palisades of logs. Here they kept their cattle, built straw-covered huts, made barbaric ornaments of red enamel, and raised fine hunting-dogs. So uncivilized did they seem that although they had plenty of milk, they did not know how to make cheese, and had no knowledge of farming.

Warlike Britons painted blue, showing the mixture of races on the island. Dark-haired Britons belong to the original Mediterranean race now found in Wales and Ireland; blonde warriors, to invading Nordic tribes. Shields, helmets, and ornaments with enameled decorations from contemporary articles, British Museum. See Vol. IV, 75.

Stonehenge, England, a circle of huge stones, erected about 1800 B.C., long before the Druids were in power. Another Stonehenge in northern France, shows relationship with Gaul. (From the model in Salisbury Museum.)

As a rule the Britons seemed taller and less yellow-haired than the Gauls. Originally of the short, dark Mediterranean race, they had, like the people of Gaul, adopted the Celtic tongue through various Nordic invasions; and the last of these Nordic invaders, called the *Brythons*, or *Britons*, had given the island its name. The swarthy faces of the Sil'u-res, along the borders of Wales, indicated the crossing of Iberians in older times; but those people opposite Gaul greatly resembled the Gauls. Their language was similar and Marcus saw among them Gallic ceremonies, and ruins of ancient stone circles, like old stone circles in Gaul.

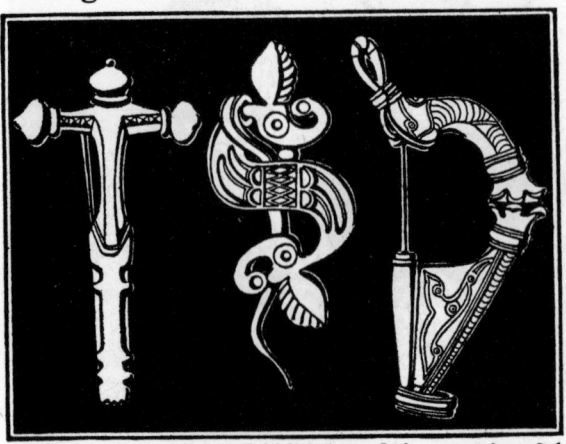
Broaches with characteristic British designs. Left, a cross-bow, 3rd century. Center, an enameled S-broach, shaped like a dragon, Right, a silver-gilt, harp-shaped broach, 139 A.D. (British Museum.)

The Druids, once as powerful in Britain as in Gaul, were almost suppressed in Britain; yet Marcus managed to see their secret and terrible rite of plucking the mistletoe. In the moon-lit depths of an oak-grove, tables were spread for a feast; two white bulls were led forth into the pale white light, and a Druid, clad in a long white robe, ascended the stately oak, cut the sacred mistletoe with a gleaming golden sickle, and handed it down to other venerable white-clad priests who received it with awe below.

British urn of yellow ware with a human face, painted in brown. (4th cent. British Museum.)

In the moonlight they sacrificed victims and offered prayers to their god. So powerful were these Druids, that on their Island of Mona had centered all the stubborn British resistance to Roman rule. Julius Caesar had never conquered the land; and the noble chief Ca-rac'ta-cus, most heroic of British rebels, had led the Romans a merry chase until he was captured and sent away to be shown with his wife and daughters in a triumphal procession at Rome. Thenceforth the Island of Mona remained a refuge for rebels and a gathering place for Druids, until the year 61, when Sue-to'ni-us, the governor, crossing from the mainland, came and attacked the island, ferrying his troops across in crude, flat-bottomed boats.

A Briton in trousers drives a 4-horse chariot, followed by hunting dogs. (Cup, 135 A.D.) Hunting with dogs was a favorite British sport.

Ornaments and weapons of the ancient Britons. Left to right, two enameled bronze bridle bits; a bronze harness ornament with red enamel decorations; an iron dagger with a bronze hilt capped by a little old man; bronze armlet with red enamel decorations; and an iron dagger with a cut-out bronze handle, and sheath. All in British Museum.

Wild was the savage resistance,—men barbarically armed densely lining the shore, Druids uttering curses, women with streaming hair, clothed in black like furies and holding torches in their hands! Terrified, the Romans stood paralyzed at the sight, until, exhorted by their general, they broke through the spell of their fear, advanced, and defeated the Druids, burning them in the flames of their own sacrificial fires. Then Suetonius cut down the groves and tried to suppress the Druids; but the Britons, taking advantage of his absence from the mainland, rose under Bo'a-di-ce'a, a widowed British Queen. The Romans had grossly insulted and robbed this courageous woman and riding now in her chariot before the British lines, with her hair floating out on the wind and her two young and beautiful daughters, injured by the Romans, lying at her feet, she cried aloud for vengeance. The Britons stormed and massacred, burned and harried the land until Suetonius, hurrying back, defeated the raging troops, while Boadicea took poison and so escaped Rome by death.

BREAKING UP OF THE ROMAN EMPIRE

For Marcus, Britain remained the climax of his adventures; for he dared not visit the German tribes in their primeval forests and fen-lands around the cold gray Baltic. There ended the frontier of Rome; yet there lay a threatening volcano, seething with restless life, wild tribes forever expanding, forever pushing each other, and ejecting streams of invasion into the Empire itself. These blue-eyed, light-haired giants who before 100 B.C., had pushed their Celtic-speaking cousins west across the Rhine, had remained pure-blooded Nordics, clinging to their Teutonic tongue and worshiping Woden, the All-Father. The Romans called them *Germans*, which meant in Latin, *genuine*, indicating that these tribes were held to be genuine Nordics, while the Celts of Gaul had degraded through intermarriage and ease. To study the German peoples, Marcus, returning to Rome, soon lost himself in reading the *Germania* of Tacitus.

Gigantic, blue-eyed Germans with flowing hair and beards. Many Germans wore beards, but Britons and Celts wore only mustaches. Right, a spearman in tight-fitting trousers with upper body naked. Center, a chieftain in long war-mantle. Left, a common warrior in short knee-trousers. Trousers characterized all Nordic barbarians.

A German, wearing trousers and armed with an axe, attacks a mythological creature. A Germanic bronze buckle made during the 4th cent. Museum, Stockholm.

"Personally," wrote Tacitus, "I agree with those who hold that in the peoples of Germany, has been given the world a race untainted by intermarriage with other races, a peculiar people and pure, like no one but themselves; whence it comes that their physique, in spite of their vast numbers, is identical: they have fierce blue eyes, red hair, and frames exceedingly tall.

"There are some varieties in the appearance of the country, but broadly it is a land of bristling forests, and unhealthy marshes. It is fertile in grains, but unkindly to fruit-bearing trees, and though it is rich in flocks and herds, these are generally undersized.

"The gods have denied the people gold and silver, whether in mercy or wrath, I find it hard to say. One may see among them silver vases given as gifts to their chieftains, but treated as of no more value than earthenware. Although the border tribes, for purposes of traffic, treat gold and silver as precious metals and collect certain coins of our money, the tribes of the interior continue to practice barter in the simple, ancient way.

"Even iron is not plentiful among them. Few have swords or lances, and their spears have a small iron head.

A bronze buckle of Germanic workmanship. It shows a man flanked by two beasts. 4th-6th cent. Stockholm.

There is no bravery of apparel among them; their shields only are picked out with choice colors. Few have breast-plates and scarcely one or two at most have metal or leather helmets while their horses are conspicuous neither for beauty nor speed. Their warriors have cries by the utterance of which they inspire courage and as the object they seek is a certain volume of hoarseness, a crashing roar, they bring their shields to their lips, that the voice may swell to a fuller and deeper note by means of the echo.

A German warrior on horseback wearing an eagle helmet, and accompanied by ravens and a snake; possibly the Germanic god, Woden. From 4th-6th cent. bronze.

"The battle line itself is arranged in wedges and the strongest incentive to courage lies in this, that neither chance nor casual grouping makes the squadron or wedge, but family or kinship. Close at hand, too, are their dearest, whence is heard the wailing voice of woman and the child's cry. Here are the witnesses who are in each man's eyes most precious; here the praise he covets. They take their wounds to mother and wife who do not shrink from counting their hurts. Further they conceive that in woman is a certain uncanny and prophetic sense; they neither scorn to consult them nor slight the answers they give.

German warriors wearing boar helmets. The boar was sacred to the god Frey who fought ice-giants. (See p. 231.)

Early German religion. Left, stone figure of a priest with a long pointed beard. His hands are clasped and his long robe, tied with a girdle, falls to his feet. (Stuttgart.) Right, reconstruction of an exquisite bronze model of the sun-chariot which the Germans believed was drawn across the sky each day. The sun disk itself is of gold. (Copenhagen.) Not until later when they learned from the Romans, did the Germans make images of their gods.

"Of the gods, they give a special worship to Woden, to whom on certain days they count even the sacrifice of human life lawful. Apart from this, they deem it incompatible with the majesty of the heavenly host to confine the gods within walls, or to mould them into any likeness of the human face; they consecrate groves and coppices, and they give the divine names to that mysterious something which is visible only to the eyes of faith. They suppose that the gods accompany them on campaigns. Totems, in fact, and emblems are fetched from groves and carried into battle.

"To divination and the lot they pay as much attention as anyone. Divination by consultation of the cries and flights of birds is well-known, but their special divination is to make trial of the omens and warnings furnished by horses. In the same groves and coppices are fed certain white horses, never soiled by mortal use; these are yoked to a sacred chariot and accompanied by a priest and king or other chief of the state, who observe their neighing or snorting.

On no other divination is more reliance placed; for the people regard the priests as the servants of the gods but they look upon the horses as their confidential friends.

"On small matters the chiefs consult; on larger questions the community. They meet, unless there be some unforeseen and sudden emergency, on days set apart when the moon is new or at the full. It is an affectation of their freedom that they do not meet at once and when commanded, but waste a second and third day by tardiness in assembling. When the mob is pleased to begin, they take their seats carrying arms. Silence is called for by the priests, then a king or a chief is listened to in order of age, birth, glory in war, or eloquence, with the respect which is accorded wise counsel, rather than with any regard for position, authority or rank. If the advice tendered be displeasing, they reject it with groans; if it pleases them, they clash their spears. At this assembly it is also permissible to lay accusations and to bring capital charges. At the same gathering, are selected chiefs who administer law through the cantons and villages.

German tribesmen in council meeting. The men all have trousers and wear long, flowing cloaks. Seated in a circle, those in the upper row seem to be listening to the argument between the two men standing at the right. The lower row look toward the man leaving. The council is guarded by armed horsemen. (Column of Marcus Aurelius.)

German knives. Center and right, two views of a handle in the form of a woman with large earrings, carrying a dish. Left, a more simple handle. Both knife blades are decorated with engravings of a ship, the one on the right showing shields of the warriors. 200 B.C.

"The custom is that no youth takes arms until the state has endorsed his competence; then in the assembly itself one of the chiefs or the young man's father or relatives equip him with shield and spear; this corresponds with them to the bestowing of the toga with us, and is youth's first public distinction. This means rank and strength for a chieftain, to be surrounded always with a large band of chosen youths—glory in peace, in war protection. When the battlefield is reached, it is a reproach for a chief to be surpassed in prowess; a reproach for his retinue not to equal the prowess of its chief; but to have left the field and survived one's chief, this means lifelong infamy and shame.

"Many of the high-born youth voluntarily seek those tribes which are at the time at war; for rest is unwelcome to the race; besides, you cannot keep up a great retinue except by war and violence, for it is to the free-handed chief that they look for that warhorse, for that murderous and masterful spear. Banquetings together with certain rude but lavish outfit take the place of salary and the material for this free-handedness comes through war and foray.

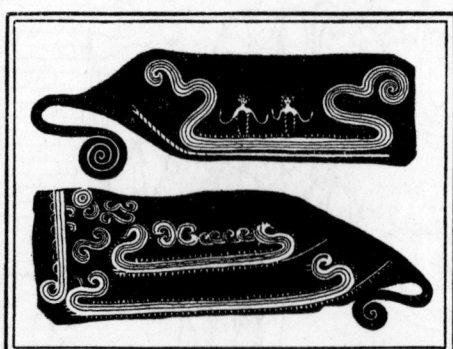

Early representations of German ships, illustrating their inherent love for the sea. Two bronze knives, or razors with designs of ships on the blades. Both ships curve upward at each end, like later Vi'king ships. The upper ship has two men in it. Both from the early Bronze Age.

You will not so readily persuade them to plough the land and wait for the year's returns, as to challenge the enemy and earn wounds; and when they are not making war, they spend much time in hunting, but more in idleness; creatures who eat and sleep, the best and bravest warriors doing nothing, having handed over the charge of home and hearth to women and old men.

"It is well known that none of the German tribes live in cities, that even individually they do not permit houses to touch each other. They live separated and scattered, according as spring-water, meadow or grove appeals to each man. They lay out their villages not after our fashion with buildings adjoining and connected; but everyone keeps a clear space around his house, whether as precaution against fire or merely ignorance of building. They have not even learned to use quarry stones or tiles; the timber they use for all purposes is unshaped and stops short of all ornament or attraction though certain buildings are smeared with a stucco, bright and glittering enough to be a substitute for paint. To make a refuge for winter, they dig pits in the earth, and pile dung on the roof.

A German urn formed into a head with ears at the side; the cover is a cap. Its decoration shows a rude drawing of the 4-wheeled wagon in which Germanic tribes migrated. The wagon is drawn by two horses and is driven by a man; nearby are three men, and a shield. (Danzig.)

The early Iron Age tribes in eastern Germany used urns formed into faces for burial purposes. This vase is decorated with a 4-wheel wagon drawn by two horses. (Berlin.) The two urns on this page belong to the period about 500 B.C., before contact with Rome.

A German village. The houses are dome-roofed, circular dwellings of rushes bound together. A tall, dignified chieftain stands aloof watching the destruction by the Romans. (From the Column of Marcus Aurelius at Rome.)

"For clothing all wear a cloak, fastened with a clasp, or, in the absence of a clasp, with a thorn. The richest men are distinguished by the wearing of breeches. They wear also the skins of wild beasts, the more distant tribes particularly, since they cannot depend on traders for clothing. Women have the same dress as men, except that they often wear long trailing linen garments which are striped with purple.

A fight between half-naked, German spearmen in trousers, and fully-clad, Roman archers. The Germans are retreating; one man is astride his plunging horse, his short mantle spreading out behind. (Column of Marcus Aurelius.)

"The marriage tie with them is strict; you will find nothing in their character to praise more highly. They are almost the only barbarians who are content with a wife apiece. As for dower, it is not the wife who brings it to the husband, but the husband to the wife—oxen, a horse and bridle, a shield and spear or sword; it is to share these things that the wife is taken by the husband and she, herself, in turn brings some piece of armor to her husband. She is thus warned by the very rites with which her marriage begins, that she comes to share hard work and peril; her fate will be the same as his.

A German warrior with spear and shield, astride his horse. A German gravestone. (Halle.)

"There is no arena with its seduction, no dinner-tables with their provocations to corrupt them. No one laughs at vice there, no one calls it 'the spirit of the age.' For the girls there is no hot-house forcing. They pass their youth in the same way as the boys and their stature is as tall. When they reach the same strength they are mated and in the children the vigor of the parents is reproduced.

"No race indulges more lavishly in hospitality and entertainment. To outdrink the day and night is a reproach to no man. Brawls are frequent, as is usual with heavy drinkers, and for drink they use the liquid distilled from barley and wheat, while their diet is wild fruit, fresh venison, and curdled milk.

German gravestone showing the god, Odin, on a six-footed horse. Below a boat, carrying men.

"Their shows are all of one kind whatever the gathering may be; naked youths, for whom this is a form of professional acting, jump and bound between swords and upturned spears.

"Their slaves are not organized like ours. Each slave remains master of his own home. He owes his master stated amounts of grain, cattle, or clothing; but other services of the household are discharged by the master's wife and children.

"In burial there is no ostentation; the single observance is to burn the bodies of notables with special kinds of wood. To each man his armor; to the pyre of some his horse is added, while the tomb is a mound of turf. So much in general we have ascertained concerning the Germans as a whole."

Such were the neighbors of the Roman Empire and the wildest of the Roman provinces in the days when Marcus Paulus sought to know somewhat about them. The Germans as a whole, however, were divided into countless tribes,—the Angles, the Saxons, the Jutes, the Franks, the Burgundians, the Alemanni, the Lombards, the Vandals, the Goths. To name all the wild German tribes would have been a task to set a naughty Roman boy put in the corner for punishment; but as Rome grew weaker and weaker in her luxury and her wealth, these fresh young German tribes, unspoiled by vice and luxury, were increasing most alarmingly in numbers and in strength.

German cloth and actual trousers of a 4th cent. German found in a grave at Torsberg. (Museum, Kiel.) The name *Franks* survives in *France*; and the French name for Germans is still *Alemands* from the tribe of *Alemanni*.

The Barrack Emperors

After Marcus Aurelius, the history of Rome read like an ugly dream. Com′mo-dus, his cruel and drunken son, was murdered by his own household; the good old gentleman, Per′ti-nax, attempting to put forth reforms, was murdered by the Prae-to′ri-an Guard, who held a public auction and sold the Empire to the highest bidder. Sep-tim′i-us Se-ve′rus, commanding the legions on the Danube, defeated this jaunty purchaser, and by a harsh rule and murders, restored order for a time; but his two sons hated each other; Car′a-cal′la, the elder, murdered Geta, the younger, and all his life was pursued by half-crazed, remorseful hate of all connected with Geta.

The cruel, dissipated, and degenerate Com′mo-dus (180-192 A.D.), who followed his wise father, Marcus Aurelius. He believed he was Hercules born again, and is here shown with the lion's skin draped over his head and shoulders and with the club of that ancient hero. (Bust. Palazzo dei Conservatori, Rome.)

In the end, he too was slain. There followed a terrible time of civil war and intrigue. The Praetorians set up their favorites, one after another, only to have them murdered. Then leaders of provincial armies, seeing that the throne lay open to whoever had the strongest soldiers, began to proclaim themselves Emperor, —a Carthaginian warrior, a high-priest from Syria, an Arab sheik, a Moor! And because these men owed their elevation solely to the army, they were called the *Barrack Emperors*. In a space of fifty years Rome had twenty-six emperors, of whom twenty-five met their death by murder.

And during this time of horror, the strong Germanic tribes began to invade the Empire. The Goths took to their boats, and laid waste Northern Greece. Other bands broke through the line of forts along the Rhine and Danube.

The East too, now arose. Under the vigorous leadership of a family called Sas-sa′ni-ans, the Persians overthrew their once-powerful overlord, the King of the Parthians, established a new capital at Ctes′i-phon on the Tigris, and stood forth as champion of the East, to make an attack on Rome. The incompetent Emperor Va-le′ri-an, having vainly marched against Sapor, the King of this strong New Persia, was vanquished and taken prisoner. It was said that Sapor placed his foot on the poor old Emperor's neck whenever he mounted on horseback, and that when Valerian died, he kept his skin, stuffed with straw, exposed to public view.

New Persia triumphs over Rome. Emperor Valerian in chains, kneels in supplication before the victorious King Sa′por on horseback, 260 A.D. Sapor wears the dome-shaped crown of Persia, and full flowing trousers, the folds of which are carved in beautiful parallel curves. (A Sassanian relief, Naksh-i-Rustum.) The first great Persian Empire was overthrown when Da-ri′us III was conquered by Alexander of Macedon. After the division of Alexander's Empire, Persia became subject to Parthia, or Pontus, one of the smaller nations carved from the Macedonian Empire. The second Persian Empire was established by Ar′ta-xerx′es, who overthrew the Parthians in 226 A.D. It lasted till the 7th cent. A.D., when Moslems overthrew the last Persian King Chos-roes′.

A Sassanian King of Persia hunting lions. One lies dead, and the King stands before the Queen and the prince as he stabs another. Compare this wonderful animal sculpture with the Assyrian, Vol. II, p. 78. (Sor Mashhad.)

The Story of Zenobia, The Great Queen of Palmyra

While the East still trembled before the awful name of Sapor, the Great King received a gift—a train of camels laden with gifts sent by one Od'e-na'thus, a senator of Pal-my'ra, that luxuriant, palm-shaded, oasis which bloomed mid the barren stretches of the rocky Arabian Desert. A caravan-center of trade between the Persian Gulf and the Mediterranean Sea, Palmyra was rich and opulent, with splendid temples and palaces, a little neutral republic, that in the days of Trajan had been absorbed by the Empire, and now for a hundred and fifty years, had flourished as a colony.

"Who is this Odenathus?" enquired the haughty Sapor, as he ordered the splendid presents cast into the Euphrates. "Let him fall prostrate before our throne! Otherwise swift destruction shall fall upon him and his race."

Pressed by such an extremity, Odenathus met Sapor; but he met him with an army! With soldiers gathered together

Worshipers in a Pal'my-ren'i-an temple, dedicated to three Syrian gods, Zeus-Baal, Yarhibal, and Aglibal, and showing the Graeco-Syrian civilization of Palmyra in the 1st century. At the left are three priests, standing beside an elaborately ornamented seated woman; worshipers with leaves are at the right. Below are three children worshipers. (Fresco from a temple at Dura in the desert, 140 miles from Palmyra, recently discovered by Dr. J. H. Breasted.)

from the villages of Syria, and the Bed'ou-in tents of the desert, he hovered around the Persians, harassed them and plundered their treasures, till the Great King had to retreat in haste across the Euphrates. To reward the avenger of Rome, the Senate then gave Odenathus the title of Augustus, and formally entrusted to him the government of the East, which, without their sanction, he already possessed.

Now the wife of Odenathus was the beautiful Ze-no'bi-a, a dark-haired, heroic woman whose fine eyes sparkled with fire. Descended from Cleopatra and the Ptolemies of Egypt, she had the courage of a man; she went to war with her husband, and by his side she hunted panthers, bears, and lions across the sands of the desert. To Zenobia's prudence and fortitude, Odenathus owed much. Twice they pursued the Great King to the very gates of Ctes'i-phon.

But it chanced that Od'e-na'thus, angered with one of his nephews, who had insolently darted his javelin ahead of him in the chase, took the youth's horse away, and imprisoned him as a punishment. Soon after, the outraged young man murdered his royal uncle in the midst of a great entertainment. The authority which the Senate had given to Odenathus ended with his death, but Zenobia, disdaining to ask the sanction of the Senate of Rome, assumed on her own authority, the title Queen of the East, exacting, like the King of Persia, an abject adoration, and blending with the popular manners of genial Roman princes, a rich oriental pomp. Her soldiers conquered Egypt, the land of her own forefathers. She obliged a Roman general who had been sent out against her, to retreat in hot haste into Europe, and soon Palmyra stood forth the haughty rival of Rome.

Ruins of Palmyra today. The grand triumphal arch and temple of Mal'ak-Bel, the sun-god. This enormous temple, covering over 14 acres, combines the Roman arch with the Greek column. In its court of 374 columns, 70 feet high, Zenobia, bare-armed and helmeted, reviewed her troops or held court. (From a photograph.)

The beautiful, dark-haired Ze-no'-bi-a, Queen of Palmyra; brilliant, courageous, a fitting descendant of the famous Cleopatra. (Coin.)

The Emperor Au-re'lian (270-275), conqueror of Zenobia, brave, manly, generous in victory, a capable soldier and leader. (A coin.)

But now the days of chaos in Rome were ended for a time. A line of five good emperors was to give comparative peace to the land so long misruled. The worthy Claudius having died, Au-re'lian was now emperor, the warlike son of a peasant, who had risen from a common soldier to the throne of the Empire itself. Distinguished for matchless valor, good judgment, and rigid discipline, Aurelian, though he had yielded the distant province of Dacia to the Vandals and the Goths, had put an end to the Gothic War, and chastised the Al'e-man'ni, who, inflamed by their eager youth, had just invaded Italy and traced a line of destruction from the Danube to the Po. Seated on his splendid throne in camp near the great Black Forest, Aurelian by his manly grace, and majestic, dignified figure, taught the wild barbarians to revere not only the prowess but the person of their conqueror. Having overcome the Germans, and recovered Gaul, Spain, and Britain out of the hands of a rebel, he advanced on Palmyra at last.

Zenobia came to meet him, animating her armies by being present in person whenever they went into battle. But in spite of the courage inspired by the sight of her gleaming helmet, her unwieldy heavy-armed cavalry was defeated in two battles. Then as far as the frontier of Egypt, the nations subject to her joined the standard of Rome, while Aurelian straightway sent Pro'bus, the bravest of his generals, to possess himself of Egypt. Zenobia fled to Palmyra, preparing for vigorous resistance, and declaring with fiery courage, that if conquered, she would die.

Pursuing her over the desert, Aurelian was constantly worried by flying troops of Arabs, who swooped down on his baggage, and successfully slipped away from the slow pursuit of his legions. Arrived at last at Palmyra, he pressed the attacks in person, and was himself wounded with a dart.

"The Roman people," Aurelian wrote home, "speak with contempt of the war I am waging against a woman. They are ignorant both of the character and the power of Zenobia. It is impossible to enumerate all her warlike preparations."

Aurelian soon offered the Queen advantageous terms of surrender; but his proposals were rejected with obstinacy and insult. The firmness of Zenobia was supported by the hope that in a short time famine would compel the Roman army to retreat across the desert; and that the Kings of the East, especially of Persia, would come to her aid against Rome. But Aurelian met and cut off the paltry assistance sent Zenobia from the East, while from every part of Syria, a regular succession of convoys safely arrived in his camp, to which Probus now added troops victorious in Egypt.

Left, a gentleman of Palmyra in elaborate mantle and cap (Rome). Right, a rich Pal'my-rene' lady, bedecked in costly jewels. (Boston Museum.) Two gravestones again showing a mixture of Greek and Oriental culture.

Zenobia resolved to fly. Mounting the fleetest of her dromedaries, she had already reached the banks of the Euphrates, about sixty miles from Palmyra, when she was overtaken by the pursuit of Aurelian's light horse, seized and brought back a captive to the feet of the Emperor himself.

Aurelian would have treated the captured city kindly, but no sooner had he turned his back, than Palmyra rebelled again, and the Emperor, returning in anger, executed many of its citizens. Then making his way to Rome, he celebrated his triumph. Twenty elephants, four royal tigers, two hundred curious animals from the North, the East, and the South, all the wealth of Zenobia, honored the great Aurelian. There followed behind his chariot envoys from Ethiopia, Arabia, Persia, Bactria, India, and China, all in their singular dress, long trains of German captives, and best of all, Zenobia, beautiful and pathetic, no more the fiery heroine but only a drooping woman marching in fetters of gold.

Zenobia in chains walks in Aurelian's triumph.

His pride thus satisfied, Aurelian, in all kindness, gave Zenobia a villa at Tiv'o-li, and there the Queen spent the rest of her days as a humble Roman matron, who doubtless sincerely mourned when she heard that Aurelian was dead, murdered at the instigation of certain dishonest officials, afraid of conviction and punishment. So ended the struggle of Zenobia against the great Aurelian.

Diocletian, (285—305 A. D.)

Aurelian was followed by Tacitus, Probus, the good old man Carus, and his sons; then the army raised to power Diocletian, the strong Commander of the Body-Guard.

Diocletian saw that to guide and oversee such a vast and varied empire needed more than one man's time, so he chose a fellow-emperor, his comrade-in-arms, Max-im'i-an, to guard the Rhine frontier, while he protected the Eastern border.

He himself liked the East better than the West, so he settled at Nic'o-me'di-a in Asia Minor, proposing from there to rule Egypt, Asia and Thrace. Maximian, as co-emperor, was to live at Mi-lan' in Italy, and rule Italy, Africa, and Spain. Moreover, each of the Emperors was to choose an assistant to be his Caesar and successor. Diocletian chose his son-in-law, Ga-le'ri-us, to whom he entrusted the care of the Danube and Euphrates frontiers; Maximian chose Constan'tius, who was given Gaul and Britain. Diocletian and Maximian were to rule for twenty years, after which they were to retire and hand over the power to their Caesars, who in turn were to choose successors to follow them in time.

ROMAN EMPERORS from MARCUS AURELIUS to DIOCLETIAN (161-305)

MARCUS AURELIUS (161-180), last of the "five, good emperors." Beginning of barbarian attacks upon the Empire.

COM'MO-DUS (180-192), his dissipated son, murdered

"BARRACK EMPERORS" (193)
  Pertinax (193), murdered after three months.
  Julianus (193), bought the throne.

SEP-TIM'I-US SE-VE'RUS (193-211), a stern general, restored order.

CARACALLA (211-217), his son, murdered Geta his brother, and was himself murdered.
  Macrinus (217-218)
  E'la-gab'a-lus (218-222)

ALEXANDER SEVERUS (222-235), a weak ruler, grand-nephew of Septimius.

"PHANTOM EMPERORS" (235-268), many ruled for only a few days.
  Maximus (235-238), Gordianus I (237), Gordianus II (237), Gordianus III (238-244), Philippus (244-249), Decius (249-251), Gallus (251-253), Aemilianus (253), Valerian (253-260), Gallienus (260-268).

Claudius II (268-270), an able general, began restoring the Empire.

AURELIAN (270-275), a great general, brought order and security.

Tacitus (275), a senator, elected by the Senate

Florianus (276)

Probus (276-282), a vigorous general

Carus (282-283)

Numerianus (284)

Carinus (284)

DIOCLETIAN (284-305), reorganized the Empire.

Each of the four sections, governed by the Emperors and Caesars, was called a prefecture, and had over it a prefect. Under each prefect were three or four vicars who governed a diocese or group of different provinces, and under each vicar were placed a number of provincial governors. These officials were arranged in regular grades, as in an army, each officer under the control of the one above him. In this way, Diocletian hoped that the Empire would be well governed, and that wars over the succession would from now on cease.

Yet, though he granted power and responsibility to his co-rulers, Diocletian never ceased to regard himself as sole Emperor of the mighty Empire. In his splendid Eastern palace he wore a priceless crown; his robes were of purple and gold; his officials fell prostrate before him as they would before a god, and he brooked interference from no one. The last shadow of the ancient Republic had vanished altogether. No longer had the Senate or people even a vestige of power.

Constantine, the First Great Patron of Christianity
(323 A.D.—337 A.D.)

When Diocletian willingly, and Max-im′i-an most unwillingly resigned the imperial purple, their places were filled by the Caesars. Con-stan′tius continued to rule Britain, Gaul, and Spain. He was a merciful man, temperate, and amiable. Instead of imitating Diocletian in his Eastern pride and magnificence, he lived with all the modesty of a simple, Roman prince; and the people of his provinces, loving him sincerely, reflected with anxiety on his declining health and the tender age of his children, the issue of his second marriage with the daughter of Maximian.

Con-stan′tius, ruler of Britain, Gaul, Spain.

BREAKING UP OF THE ROMAN EMPIRE

The stern temper of Galerius was cast in a different mould. He it was who urged Diocletian to give up his toleration of the growing sect of Christians, and to try and wipe them out. During this persecution, Constantius, humane, and kind, protected the Christians in his provinces; but Galerius was intolerant, haughty, jealous, and proud. He hoped when Constantius died to make himself sole ruler of the Empire.

Helena, the inn-keeper's daughter, mother of the man who became the Emperor Constantine.

As the health of Constantius declined, he longed once again to see his eldest son, Con'stan-tine, from whom he had long been parted. Constantine's mother, Helena, was the daughter of an humble inn-keeper, who kept a public-place where the young Constantius had lodged during earlier soldiering days; but when Constantius had been raised to the lofty rank of Caesar, he had divorced this Helena, and married Maximian's daughter. Since that time young Constantine had never seen his father. He had remained in the East serving in the Eastern wars; but now Constantius wrote him, urging the youth to come to him, stating with pathetic yearning how he longed to embrace him once again before he died. But this did not suit Galerius. Galerius feared lest Constantius should name the young man his successor, and he detained Constantine with every sort of excuse. When at last consent was wrung from him, Constantine left by night, and reached the port of Bou-logne' in the very moment when his father was boarding his ship for Britain. They embraced each other with joy, and went together to Britain; but no sooner had Constantius defeated the wild Caledonians, than he died in the palace at York. His devoted soldiers at once hailed Constantine as emperor.

Max-en'tius, son of the retired Augustus, Max-im'i-an. (Roman coin.)

Constantine, alert, vigorous; a real soldier and organizer. (Roman coin.)

Tall and majestic in figure, brave and agreeable, the young man had always been trained to war, to action, and to command. Although quite unlettered in books, he was a capable soldier, energetic and strong. Hearing of his promotion, Galerius was in a rage; yet all he could do at present was to acknowledge Constantine as the ruler of Britain and Gaul.

And now there was trouble in Rome. No more was that haughty city the capital of the world. The Eastern Emperor chose to live at Nic'o-me'di-a; the Western ruler for years had held his court in Milan. Privileges which had exalted Italy over the other provinces, now no longer existed. For five hundred years, Roman citizens had not had to pay any taxes; now they were numbered and taxed just like common provincials. Max-en'tius, son of the old, retired Emperor, Maximian, took up the cause of Rome. He easily persuaded his father to reassume the purple; and the two made alliance with Constantine, who married the old man's daughter. Galerius retaliated by raising two of his friends to the lofty rank of Caesar; and now six emperors claimed the distracted Roman Empire. Plots, intrigues, and battles, followed one another, until Galerius died and Maximian, caught in a plot to seize the throne of Constantine, was forced to strangle himself. Then Constantine and Maxentius strove for the throne of the West. Maxentius had proved so tyrannical and full of every vice, that Rome, which had long regretted the absence of the Emperor, had now for years lamented the presence of her sovereign.

The Romans appealed to Constantine, and he determined to fight. Leading his troops in person he twice defeated the hosts Maxentius sent against him; but while Constantine showed such valor, Maxentius remained at home concerned with nothing but pleasure. Soldiers who had served his father obliged him to see his danger. A large force was straightway collected, but Maxentius had no intention of leading that force in person. A stranger to the arts of war, he trembled with fear of the contest. The circus soon resounded with indignant cries against him. Shame at last forced him to fight, and he marched with a mighty army to take his stand against Constantine at the village of Sax′a Ru′bra, which lay some nine miles from Rome. The crucial conflict had come, the crisis of the whole struggle.

Constantine felt the strain. His heart and spirit yearned to be upheld in that moment by a power he might know was divine. The gods meant little to him; but the faith displayed by Christians was a vital, living thing. In that age, so debased and vicious, Constantine loved virtue; he loved the clean lives of Christians, the humanity of their aims; his father had befriended them in the days of persecution. Of what they believed he, as yet, understood very little. He felt only honest sympathy with their spirit and confident faith; and while he fitfully slept, concerned for the following day, he saw in a dream the figure of Jesus, bidding him use the Christian sign on his banners during the battle and confidently declaring: "By this sign thou shalt conquer."

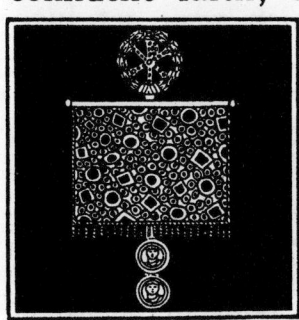

A *lab′a-rum*, bearing the Christian symbol, XP, the first two letters beginning the Greek word for *Christ*.

A medallion showing the Emperor Constantine with a *labarum*, bearing the Christian symbol, XP.

Battle of Mil′vi-an Bridge showing the army of Max-en′tius throwing themselves in the Tiber. (Arch of Constantine.)

So Constantine used that symbol. He felt in his conflict with baseness the cross represented a spiritual force upholding the victory of good. And he routed the host of Maxentius, who threw themselves in the Tiber. Maxentius, himself, blindly fleeing over the Milvian Bridge, was forced into the river, where he drowned by the weight of his armor. His body, sunk deep in the mud, was found on the following day.

The Romans now received Constantine with joyous acclamations. He put to death certain members of the family of the tyrant, but otherwise showed great humanity in dealing with his foes. A general Act of Oblivion quieted the minds of the people, and the famous Edict of Milan granted religious liberty to Christians and all others, giving everyone the right to worship as he chose. Three years later Constantine erected his arch in Rome, to commemorate this event, but alas, in these degenerate days, no sculptor could be found capable of adorning it; so the Arch of Trajan was stripped of its most elegant figures, which were set into Constantine's Arch with the necessary new ornaments fashioned in crudest style. Roman art was already dead.

The triumph of Constantine as sculptured on the Arch erected to commemorate his victory over Max-en′tius.

Henceforth, Constantine visited Rome only to celebrate the tenth and twentieth years of his reign. Perpetually he traveled, inspecting the provinces. For a time his mind fluctuated between the gods and God. Until he was forty years of age, he had worshiped the gods of Olympus. The medals, which issued from his mint, were impressed with the figures of Jupiter, of Mars and of Apollo. To blot out the habits and prejudices of more than half a lifetime was indeed a difficult task. Moreover, he was not a scholar, he was not an abstract thinker; he was a man of action, a simple, unlettered soldier with plenty of human faults.

Coins showing the gradual change of Constantine's religious beliefs. Upper left, Constantine and the reverse of same coin, showing the pagan god, Mars, but issued in the same year as the battle of Mil'vi-an Bridge, when he turned for help to Christianity. (312 A.D.) Lower left, the pagan goddess Victory, issued by Constantine three years later. People, even so-called Christians, clung so tenaciously to this goddess that the Christian fathers had to leave her in men's hearts and merely change her name, calling her the Angel of Victory. The last coin, showing the XP of Christianity, was not minted until 333, four years before Constantine's death. Constantine accepted as much of Christianity as he could understand, but he had his father deified and was himself called a god after his death. In the history of Christianity it is always necessary to separate between the claim a man makes to being a Christian, and the actual spirit of Christianity which he manifests in his life, as judged by the ideals taught by Jesus himself.

Nevertheless, he esteemed the moral purity of the Christians, while he saw that the cause of goodness derived no support whatever from belief in the wanton, tricky, quarrelsome Olympian gods. He saw that Christianity offered fine standards of human conduct and gave men a confident faith that all the power of God upheld and maintained what was good. Christians were still small in numbers compared to the mass of people; but among a degenerate race, they alone stood forth with a living and vigorous spirit, a germ of life and growth. He saw that Christianity would expand, while the gods of Olympus already were as dead as the spirit of their worshipers. Slowly he assented to as much of the teachings of Jesus as he was able to grasp.

Gems engraved with Christian symbols. (British Museum.) During the first three centuries when Christianity was not officially tolerated within the Roman Empire, it was dangerous to make pictures of Jesus and necessary to represent Christian ideas by symbols understood only by Christians. Left to right: gem engraved with shepherd's crook, fish, and olive-branch; gem with anchor, doves, palm-branch and fishes; the good shepherd; dove on fish with olive-branch and monogram XP; the crucifixion, one of the earliest departures from symbol to a real picture.

But Li-cin'i-us, an appointee of the former Emperor Galerius and the only co-ruler now left to dispute the control of the Empire, soon showed he had not been sincere in recently agreeing to the Edict of Milan. Secretly he oppressed and persecuted the Christians, till Constantine, forced to fight him, publicly declared himself the deliverer of the church.

By this time objections to fighting which had marked the early Christians, were rapidly abating. A generation before, on a public holiday, a Christian centurion had thrown away his arms, loudly crying out that he renounced forever the use of carnal weapons and would fight no more with the sword, but would serve Jesus in peace. Nevertheless, the bishops now used their great authority to enforce the carrying-out of military oaths, and to excommunicate soldiers who threw away their arms. Christians fought boldly for Constantine. They looked on him as a hero inspired by the Lord of Hosts. Sight of their sacred symbol gleaming on banners and helmets fired them with an enthusiasm terrible to behold. Licinius was defeated and committed suicide,—and Constantine, left sole Emperor, exhorted all his subjects to imitate his example and embrace Christianity.

Peter and Paul, with a small figure of Jesus between them. Jesus is beardless, like a Greek and not a Jew. (Glass work of 3rd-5th cent.)

Christian subjects quaintly pictured in color on a bowl of transparent glass. The four scenes show Jonah in a ship with three men, and above, a dolphin; then a sea-beast pictured as a monster swallows the prophet. Jonah's legs project from its jaws,—but in the next picture he is vomited forth head first; Jonah lying beneath the gourd tree. Each scene is a medallion in blue and green glass on a white bowl. This 3rd-5th century bowl also bears other colored medallions of Biblical scenes. It was found in Co-logne', but is now in the British Museum.

Bishops and Christian teachers, little qualified by dress or manners for residence at a court, now sat at Constantine's table, and accompanied him on the march. In the midst of constant labors, he studied the Scriptures at night. In church he contented himself with a seat below the sanctuary, and humbly agreed that the Emperor, heretofore regarded as a god, held a spiritual rank less honorable than that of the meanest deacon. At last, he altogether disclaimed the gods of Olympus, refusing to lead a procession which offered the public vows to Jupiter Capitolinus. Nevermore, he proclaimed, should his person or his image be seen in a pagan temple.

Moreover, with the fresh simplicity of an inexperienced child, this vigorous, unlettered soldier promised to everyone who would become a Christian, a holiday garment of white with twenty pieces of gold, as though one could change his convictions for any price whatever! Under his encouragement, Christianity now flourished. The church was carefully organized with patriarchs, bishops, vicars, after the system Diocletian had applied to the temporal government. In one year 24,000 people were baptized in Rome alone!

A Christian family. Husband, wife, and little daughter dressed like her mother. Note the symbol XP. (3rd-5th cent. glass, British Museum.)

A silver treasure chest, known as the Casket of Projecta, which shows plainly how little the teaching of Jesus had influenced many of the wealthier Romans, who called themselves Christians simply because Christianity had become fashionable, but without having had any real change in heart. The upper panel pictures Venus in the center seated on a shell dressing her hair. Tritons support the shell, and one holds up a mirror. Back of each Triton is a genius, one holding a basket of fruit, the other a box. Despite this purely pagan scene, the words immediately below the panel are: "*XP Secunde and Projecta live in Christ.*" In the lower panel, the bride is seated upon a cushioned chair with a high back, holding a fillet for her hair and a cosmetic box. Attendants hold up a mirror and another box. The panel is decorated with rosettes, doves, and fruit. The casket was found on the Esquiline Hill, Rome, where it had probably been buried at a time of barbarian invasion. (4th-5th century; now in British Museum).

Warriors and traders spread Christianity abroad, and missionaries carried their faith to the most remote barbarians. But how much actual change of heart, how much honest acceptance of the ideals and teachings of Jesus, such wholesale conversions meant, remained for the ages to tell. Real moral and spiritual change in a man's inner heart and mind, come about only through honest, sincere, and humble conviction, through true satisfaction of mind. To this no man can be forced, nor influenced, nor bribed. The earlier Christians were honest; while they clung to a faith unpopular in the midst of persecutions, they were deeply and truly sincere, but now that the faith was fashionable, many pretended conversions meant no real change of heart.

They meant only changes of name, old pagan beliefs and attitudes, disguised with Christian names. Moreover, no sooner had Christians been given freedom of worship, than trouble arose in their ranks. It was now three hundred years since Jesus had been on earth, and taught in Galilee. He had offered men a knowledge of God as a loving and merciful father; he had offered them a great ideal, a body of simple principles whereby they might live together with the greatest mutual joy. He had said: "These things have I spoken unto you that your *joy* may be made full." And he had commanded simply: "If ye love me, keep my commandments." Yet now men came arguing, quarreling, breaking his chief commandment: "I command you, love one another!"

A very early representation of the crucifixion, and the death of Judas. At the left, Judas in the usual Roman costume of a tunic and pallium, hangs from a tree; below him is the purse, from the mouth of which fall the pieces of silver. At the right, with an expressionless face, is Jesus nailed by his hands only, to a cross with expanding ends. His feet are side by side and are unsupported; around his loins is a narrow loin cloth, and at the back of his head an engraved nimbus. On the border of the panel above his head is a plate with the inscription REX IVD. To the right stands a soldier in the act of piercing Jesus' left side with a spear; on the left stand the Virgin Mary and the apostle John. Jesus is beardless like a Roman. (Ivory panel 5th century. British Museum.)

Christians no longer talked about how they ought to live to keep their hearts, their thoughts and deeds obedient to the commandments of their loving master, Jesus. They talked about what they believed concerning the nature of Jesus;—was Jesus God they wondered; was he of the same essence, the same substance as God; what exactly was the Trinity?

A certain bold presbyter of Alexandria, A'ri-us by name, said that Jesus was the son of God, the only-begotten son, but still the son who had not always existed, as had God. Alexander, Bishop of Alexandria, violently opposed Arius, and excommunicated him. Jesus, the bishop said, had always existed like God and was actually of the same substance. Indeed Jesus was the same as God. Soon all the East was aflame over this abstruse question.

At first the Emperor Constantine treated this argumentation as any simple-hearted soldier might have been expected to treat it. He thought it most unimportant. He lamented that Christian people who had the same God and the same religion, should be divided by such petty distinctions, and he seriously recommended to the clergy of Alexandria, the example of the Greek philosophers who could maintain their arguments without losing their temper, and assert their freedom without violating their friendship.

But as the quarrel persisted, he ordered the bishops to settle it by convening at the Council of Ni-cae'a in 325 A.D. Constantine himself often appeared at the meetings, seating himself with modesty on a low stool in the hall. It was agreed by this Council that Jesus and God were one and the same, or as Ath'a-na'si-us and other Orthodox Christians said, God and Jesus were *Ho'mo-ou'si-an*, and not only they themselves, but all Orthodox Christians must believe this. To think that God and Jesus were *Ho'moi-ou'si-an*, instead of *Homo-ousian*, constituted a heresy, and to be a heretic became far more dangerous than to remain a pagan.

Arius was banished into a distant province; his disciples were branded with odious names, and the Emperor, having at last imbibed the spirit of the fight, declared that those who resisted the divine judgment of the Council, must prepare for immediate exile. Thus the very Christians, who had labored to free themselves from pagan persecutions, now in their hour of triumph turned the lash on those sects which did not agree with them. Human nature had triumphed over the spirit of Christ.

Turning from all these quarrels, Constantine found relief in carrying out his dreams of building a fine new capital. After due consideration of all existing cities, he chose the town of By-zan′ti-um to be the new center of the world. A poor little place it was; but Constantine, looking beyond the poverty

One of the earliest representations of the Madonna and Child adored by the Wisemen; below, Mary on a mattress, the child in swaddling clothes in a manger, with Sa-lo′me extending her withered hand to touch him. (A 6th century ivory carving from Syria.) The Madonna was not much represented in art until after the furious quarrels of Nes-to′ri-ans and Orthodox Christians. Nes-to′ri-us, patriarch of Constantinople, was excommunicated (431 A.D.) and driven into the desert for saying: "Let no one call Mary the mother of God, for Mary was a human being, and that God should be born of a human being is impossible." This statement was directly opposed to the position taken by the Church, and statues in honor of the Virgin immediately began to appear. The Nestorian missionaries established churches throughout Africa and Asia to the borders of China.

and the squalor, saw the sweep of the Golden Horn, the seven-mile long harbor which shone like a jeweled belt along the north side of the settlement. Across the glittering straits of the Bosphorus and the Hellespont, he saw the green hills of Asia, promising peace and plenty; and collecting an army of workmen, he set the streets ringing with noise.

Soon there arose as by magic, theaters, churches, baths, a splendid imperial palace, the beautiful little basilica known as Sanc′ta So-phi′a, an elaborate Hippodrome, and a Senate House built and equipped just like the one in Rome.

Constantine, in rich Eastern robes, gazes on the city of his dreams, overlooking Sancta Sophia and the Hippodrome.

Constantine invited nobles from Rome and Asia Minor to come and settle in the city. He imported a number of senators to give the new Senate House dignity, and he ordered free grain to be given the poor as it had been given in Rome. On May 11, 330 A.D., the city was dedicated. Constantine wished to call it New Rome, but the citizens themselves called it Constantinople, the city of Constantine.

For thirty years Constantine ruled, the longest reign since Augustus, and during these years his private life knew many deep tragedies. Led to suspect his eldest son of various miserable crimes, he ordered that Crispus should die, and then to atone for that wrong, he further commanded the death of the young man's false accuser, although that accuser was Fausta, Constantine's own wife.

When he felt that death was approaching, the Emperor called his three sons to him. To Constantine he gave Gaul and the West; to Constantius, Constantinople and the East; to Constans, Italy. Then sending for attendants and priests, he put off his purple robe of state, put on a simple white garment, and was humbly baptized at last into the Church whose champion he had been for so many years.

The End of a United Empire

Constantine's sons did not inherit their father's genius for leadership. One after another, they yielded before fierce Germanic invaders until the whole Empire seemed in danger. Then their cousin, Julian, took command of the army, drove the Germans back, and made himself Emperor of Rome.

Now Julian despised the Christians. In Athens, where he had spent his youth, philosophers still walked in the groves of the Academy and taught the reasonable doctrines of Plato and Aristotle. The teachings of Jesus himself, Julian deeply respected; but he hated the quarrels of *Ho'-mo-ou'si-ans* and *Ho'moi-ou'si-ans*, the latter of whom were now lashing their former victors. Julian tried to revive the glory of the gods, but the teachings of Jesus too completely met the needs of men's hearts; and in spite of unworthy followers, these teachings triumphed. On his death-bed Julian cried: "Gal'i-le'an thou hast conquered!"

ROMAN EMPERORS AFTER DIOCLETIAN

DIOCLETIAN (284-305) divided the Roman Empire

THE WEST	THE EAST
Max-im'i-an (285-305)	Diocletian (285-305)
Constantius (305-306)	Galerius (305-306)
Constantine (306-323) Civil War and six claimants to the throne.	

CONSTANTINE (323-337) united the Roman Empire,
but divided it upon his death between his sons.

THE WEST	THE EAST
Constantine II (337-340)	Constantius (337-353) and Constans (337-350)

CONSTANTIUS REUNITED THE EMPIRE (353-361)

Julian (361-363) enemy of Christianity
Jovian (363-364) the Christian

VALENTINIAN I (364-375) again divided the Empire

THE WEST	THE EAST
Valentinian I (364-375)	Valens (364-378)
Gratian (375-383) and Valentinian II (375-392)	Theodosius I (379-394)

THEODOSIUS I (394-395) again united the Empire, but permanent division on his death.

THE WEST	THE EAST
Ho-no'ri-us (395-423)	Arcadius (395-408)
Valentinian III (425-455)	Theodosius II (408-450)
Romulus Augustus (475-476)	Marcianus (450-457)
O'do-a'cer (476-493)	Leo I (457-474)
Theodoric (493-526)	Zeno (474-491)
	Anastasius (491-518)
	Justinus (518-527)

JUSTINIAN (527-565) attempted to unite the Empire.
KINGDOM OF THE VISIGOTHS IN SPAIN (507-711)
KINGDOM OF THE LOMBARDS IN ITALY (568-774)
CHARLEMAGNE (768-814) restores the Western Empire, 800 A. D.

Under Jovian, Julian's successor, Christianity was restored to its former privileged position, and no emperor after Julian ever pretended to worship the ancient gods of Rome. Val′en-tin′i-an and Va′lens were Christians, and their successor, The′o-do′si-us the Great, closed all the ancient temples, threatening death to anyone who sacrificed to the gods. Heretofore, pagan festivals, such as the famous Olympic games, had attracted great crowds every year. But Theodosius stopped the games, and if pagan holidays survived, they were given Christian names. Moreover, Theodosius submitted to well-deserved punishment at the hands of the Bishop of Rome or the Pope as he came to be called; and henceforth the popes at Rome were as powerful as the emperors.

Theodosius was the last ruler who governed the whole Roman Empire. On his death in 395 A.D., the division of land between his two sons became a real division, and the Eastern and Western Empires henceforth remained distinct.

Emperor The′o-do′si-us who first closed all pagan temples, and his sons Ar-ca′di-us and Ho-no′ri-us under whom the Empire was permanently divided into an Eastern and Western Roman Empire. (Byzantine bronze shield, Madrid.)

Wild riders akin to the Huns, a man and a woman. The Huns lived on horseback. (Chinese pottery, about 621 A.D.)

II

Barbarians Invade the Western Empire
(375 A.D.—526 A.D.)

The Huns and the Visigoths

In the year 375, while Valens still ruled the East, Roman sentries on the Danube noted some strange disturbance among the Vis'i-goths who lived on the further bank. Day by day spies reported that the Goths were gathering by hundreds. What could the trouble be? A canoe shot across the stream, bearing Gothic envoys to the Roman border-captains. "The Huns!" they cried in despair. "The Huns are down upon us. Permit us to cross the river!"

The Huns were the bogey-men of Europe! From their home far in the East, under the Great Wall of China, they had swept over the level, treeless steppes of Asia, through what is now southern Russia. Taking the Os'tro-goths, or Eastern Goths, by surprise they had made the whole nation their slaves; and now they were down on the West Goths. Wild, bow-legged horsemen, who lived on the backs of their horses, yellow-skinned, slant-eyed savages, the Huns seemed scarcely human to the eyes of the frantic Goths.

Savage Huns, the bogey-men of Europe, a Turko-Mongolian race, who terrified both barbarous Goths and Romans.

"The Huns are a race savage beyond all parallel," wrote a horrified Roman soldier who lived in those troubled days. "At the very moment of birth, the cheeks of their infants are seared by an iron, in order that the hair, instead of growing at the proper time on their faces, may be hindered by the scars; accordingly they grow up beardless, and without any beauty. They have closely knit, strong limbs; are of great size, and bow-legged. So hardy are they that they neither require fire nor well-flavored food, but live on the roots of herbs, or the half-raw flesh of beasts, which they warm rapidly by placing it between their own thighs and the backs of their horses. There is not a person in the nation who cannot remain on his horse day and night. On horseback they buy and sell, they take their meat and drink."

Never had barbarians so hideous been seen by civilized eyes. Clad in the skins of beasts with fur caps, and foot-gear of cords, they were barbarous bundles of fur, bristling with quivers and lances. Mounted on skittish horses, they sowed terror throughout the world. On the wide, high-lying plateaux of distant Central Asia they had lived in nomadic

BARBARIAN INVASIONS

hordes, peaceful so long as the plains gave them and their horses food. But their domains bordered the desert; sudden inundations of sand destroyed their pasture-lands, and constantly forced them on. Their life was as unstable as the sand dunes of the desert. They had no cities, no houses. They did not even have tents. The women and children lived in the huge, lumbering, cumbersome wagons, the men on the backs of their horses. Advancing away from the wind and the movements of the sand, they wandered wherever they chose, seizing by violence the territories they needed, as swift, as relentless, as invincible as the sand.

Long had they lived on good terms with the emperors of China, till the Chinese grew tired of their raids and built the Great Wall to keep them out. Thus thrown back to the westward, they reached the Danube at last, and the Visigoths lost their heads and fled in frantic fear.

The Great Wall of China, a writhing serpent, winding endlessly over mountains, rivers and gorges, and erected about 214 B.C. to keep out the Huns. It is 20 feet high and so broad that the top forms a roadway 15 feet wide.

What were the Romans to do? Were they to leave the Goths to be destroyed by the Huns, or should they permit these Germans to find refuge in the Empire, from which they had with such difficulty been kept out all these years? The Captains of the Border sent hastily to Constantinople to know what answer they should make to the Visigothic King. Doubtless Valens, the Emperor, knew that whether he said yes or no, the Goths would enter the land; or perhaps he feared that the Huns, if they overpowered the Goths, would threaten the Empire itself. However he reasoned, he sent back word that the Goths should be protected and allowed to cross the river, provided they gave up their arms, and promised to settle down peaceably among the people of the land. The Goths agreed to these terms, and with their families and goods, they poured across the Danube. On rafts and in hollowed tree-trunks, thousands on thousands came. They had entered the Empire at last!

All might yet have been well had the Romans kept faith with the Goths. But Roman officials on the Danube were greedy and corrupt. Instead of feeding the Goths and keeping them peaceful and quiet as the Emperor had commanded, the Romans forced them to pay high prices for their food.

Captive Goths, among them a woman. The men wear ¾ length coats with open collars and scalloped trousers.

Gothic chieftain and wife in a decorated chariot drawn by oxen. ("The Storied Column" of Arcadius.) See p. 148.

They even sold them back the weapons they had given up. But when provisions ran short, and the Roman officials demanded that the Goths give their sons as slaves in exchange for filthy dog-flesh, the starving and angry barbarians took their repurchased weapons and turned against their false friends. They fought at A'dri-an-o'ple. The Goths won a mighty victory, and Valens was killed on the field.

With the might of the Empire thus broken, many barbarian hordes came pouring into the land. Tall, fierce, long-haired Franks drifted across the Rhine into that part of Gaul to which they were one day to give the name of France. The most savage of all Germanic tribes, the wild, untamable Vandals, made their way into Spain, wreaking such havoc as they went, that to this day the word *vandal* means one who destroys. As for the Visigoths, they marched on Constantinople, but seeing its walls so strong, they gave up attacking the city, and started westward towards Rome. Plundering and destroying, loading themselves with treasures from Corinth, Argos, Sparta, and other ravaged cities, they marched down into Italy under their leader Al'a-ric.

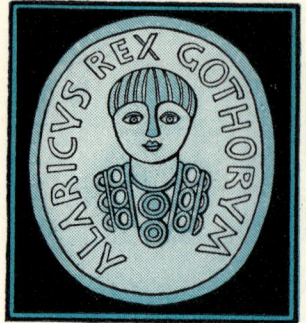

Al'a-ric, King of the Visigoths. A sapphire seal ring. (Museum, Vienna)

Who could now defend Rome? Ho-no'-ri-us, Emperor of the West, son of the great The'o-do'sius, was a poor, faint-hearted creature, who retired to his poultry farm in the city of Ra-ven'na as soon as he heard tidings that the Goths were in Italy. For eight or ten years the Visigoths lingered in Northern Italy, while Honorius, finding Ravenna in the midst of her great mud swamps, more easily to be defended than the ancient city of Rome, made Ravenna his permanent capital. Then Alaric marched on Rome, thus deserted by her ruler. The Visigoths overcame the feeble resistance of the Romans and triumphantly entered the city in 410 A.D. But though they plundered and murdered, they believed themselves to be Christians and so spared the Christian churches. Moreover, Alaric himself forbade them to burn the buildings; for already intelligent Germans realized that they wished to preserve the civilization of Rome.

Soon after this, Alaric died. To provide their beloved leader with a tomb no Roman could violate, the Goths turned aside a stream, and in the river-bed they placed the body of Alaric, armed and completely mailed, upright on his horse, and surrounded with spoils of Rome. Then they turned back the stream, and slew the slaves who had done the work, that no man but Alaric's followers might know his last resting place. How little had Christianity as yet changed the heart of the Goths! This was surely the burial of a mighty heathen chieftain rather than a Christian king.

In time, the Gothic hordes marched north again through Italy and southern Gaul into Spain. There they set up a kingdom, while the Vandal settlers in Spain crossed the seas to Africa, seized Carthage as their capital, and turned themselves into pirates, the terror of the Mediterranean.

BARBARIAN INVASIONS

St. Augustine's "City of God"

Rome, the "Eternal City," taken! Rome, the symbol of everything unchangeable and firm! How could such a thing be? Worshipers of the old gods cried out in their mental agony, that the gods had forsaken Rome, because Rome had forsaken them. See how much the new Christian God cared for the city of Rome! Christians could find no answer. Why had God permitted the city of Rome to fall? Augustine, Bishop of Hippo, a Roman town in North Africa, answered this question in a book which he called *The City of God*.

Rome had grown wicked, he said. She deserved no better fate than Sodom and Gomorrah. Rome was but a city of this fleeting world, subject to decay like everything made by man. The true City of God was not earthly Rome, but the Heavenly City, where men no more sinned or died—the promised home of all who accepted the faith of Jesus. Augustine's book brought comfort to thousands of anxious Christians and was studied as much as the Bible for many hundreds of years.

The City of God, from a manuscript of the 15th century, showing how long St. Augustine's book was read. Though St. Augustine himself plainly represented the City of God as a glorious home of the spirit, his readers made their conception as material as the brick and stones of Rome. Thus in this picture, the upper enclosure within the solid stone walls, represents Heaven, where the saints with halos around their heads have already been received. Seven sections of the circle below show those who are preparing themselves for the Heavenly City by exercising Christian virtues, or excluding themselves from it, by committing one of the seven deadly sins. (Saint Genevieve Library, Paris.)

The Beginning of the Dark Ages

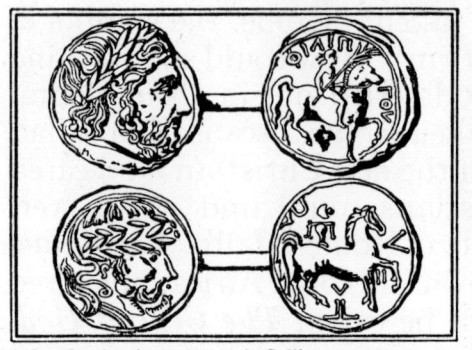

A fine Greek coin, and a crude Gallic attempt at copying, showing how quickly art degraded in the West.

Terror-stricken Italy now had a brief period of peace, but elsewhere in the West, all was in direst confusion; for the Roman legions had been withdrawn from Britain and the Rhine to meet the forces of Alaric, and the way was thus left free for further inroads of barbarians. Even under the Romans, Saxon pirates had often swept down on the shores of Britain, sacrificing to Woden a tenth part of their captives, and vanishing as swiftly and as suddenly as they had come. But now with Britain defenseless and Roman troops withdrawn, Angles, Jutes, and Saxons came and remained in Britain. Burgundians crossed the Rhine and established a kingdom in Gaul under their leader, Gund'o-bald.

"Nations innumerable and most savage have invaded all Gaul," wrote St. Jerome, about 420 A.D. "The whole region between the Alps and the Pyrenees, the ocean and the Rhine, has been devastated. O wretched, wretched Empire!"

The coming of the barbarians brought chaos to the provinces. Trade and manufacture ceased. Learning was halted abruptly. Roman law gave way to the rough and ready justice of the savage conquering tribes. Civilization ceased, and Western Europe entered on a period of darkness and ignorance, which came to be called the Dark Ages. Nevertheless, these German tribes brought new life and vigor to the lands which they had seized, and from them were to emerge not a single conquering people, enforcing their will like Rome on a mass of half-slave provinces, but those independent nations, which are the nations of modern Europe.

Attila, "The Scourge of God"

In the year 451, the most fearful of all barbarians threatened to swallow up the dying Western Empire. The Huns were marching on Rome! These savage and merciless Mongols were sweeping down on Italy, ravaging and destroying. And this was no mere urge for grasslands; this was a well-planned movement for the actual conquest of Rome!

At'ti-la, King of the Huns, short, squat, swarthy, broad-chested, the terrible "Scourge of God," led the threatened attack, inspiring in his savage followers a wild and fanatic enthusiasm which inflamed their natural lust for destroying, burning, and ravishing. Though the Huns were hard to control, and followed individual leaders in numerous little groups, Attila came of the foremost tribe, whose chieftain was King of the Huns. When Ru'gi-la, his uncle, was king, Attila, twelve years old, had been sent to Ravenna as a hostage; for the Romans, fearing the Huns, purchased a shameful peace with the payment of tribute-money, exchanging hostages with them. Thus, while the Hunnish boy prowled like a sullen, ill-tempered, caged beast through the perfumed rooms at Ravenna, A-e'ti-us, the Roman lad, who was one day to fight against Attila, grew up, a hostage to the Huns, living in the circle of wagons, the jumble of leather tents around a wooden palace, which was Rugila's capital-city.

The youth, At'ti-la, a sullen hostage at the Roman court, tries to rouse his fellow hostages to attempt an escape.

Attila was stifled by the over-powering luxury which dazzled the other hostages. Accustomed to mare's milk and tough, half-raw meat, he spat forth the dainty dishes served in the Emperor's household. Some day he would crush this soft, luxurious Rome, whose young men trembled with fear at the martial sound of a trumpet, whose armies were hired barbarians! He would subjugate the Huns, assemble under one leader all the scattered tribes between the Volga and Danube. He would bring under his control the Slavic and Germanic peoples, whether as vassals or allies. With these he would conquer Europe; then, rich in the treasures of Rome and the splendid Constantinople, he would hurl himself upon Asia, crushing Persia, China, and India! From the China Sea in the East, to the Pillars of Hercules in the West, he would rule a vast Hunnic Empire, as Emperor of the world! Still working over his plan, still dreaming his lurid dreams, he returned to the rude, Hunnish capital when he had grown a young man. He must see that all was made ready before his uncle should die.

Europe and Asia about 450 A.D., showing the enormous Empire of Attila, completely overshadowing both Eastern and Western Roman Empires. His influence extended from Europe to the Great Wall of China on the east.

Meanwhile, the young Roman, A-e'ti-us, rose to high posts of honor in the Empire of the West. On the death of the Emperor Ho-no'ri-us, Theodosius II, the Emperor of the East, gave the western throne to his nephew, Valentinian III, a childish little fellow whose mother, the Empress Pla-cid'i-a, ruled the court at Ravenna to accomplish her own selfish aims. Placidia

Val-en-tin'i-an III, the boy-emperor of the Western Empire; his mother, Gal'la Pla-cid'i-a, who ruled for him; and that great and honest general, A-e'ti-us, who defeated Attila. Ivory diptych, 400 A.D. (Monza Cathedral.) On the death of Theodosius (379-395), the Roman Empire was divided, never to be united again. The East fell to his son, Arcadius (395-408). (See page 90 for following rulers.) The West went to another son, Honorius (395-423) who, after some confusion, was followed by Valentinian III (425-455). After Valentinian followed many puppet-emperors with German chieftains as real rulers. The last puppet emperor was Romulus Augustulus (475-476). Then the German, Odoacer (476-493) seized the throne and was followed by Theodoric (493-526).

feared and disliked the young high-steward, Aetius. He had too honest a hatred for incompetence and intrigue. He loved the Empire too well, with too little care for the interests of any official or any ruler who did not serve the Empire. In 424 A. D., he raised a Hunnic army and aided John the Usurper, a man who would, he believed, clean up corruption in government, reunite the two Empires and restore the glory of Rome. But defeat met this attempt; Aetius fled the land, and not until he had raised a second Hunnic army, did he defeat Placidia, make her restore him to power, and wipe out the intriguers who sucked the life-blood of the land.

Neighbors of the Huns, Scyth'i-ans of Southern Russia, the first occupants of the Russian steppes. The Huns adopted Scythian costume when they did not wear stolen finery of Persians, Turks, or Chinese. The engraving from this Scythian silver vase from Kul-O'ba shows hillocks and graceful flowers, typical scenery of the steppes. A Scythian chief, leaning on his staff, listens attentively to a messenger. Another Scythian strings his short bow.

Soon after this, Rugila died, and Attila, aged forty, became the King of the Huns. His brother, Bleda, shared his power, but Bleda was more interested in hunting over the steppes, than in ruling a Hunnic Empire, and at an opportune moment, Attila had him killed. And now the sullen Hun was free to pursue his plans. Constantinople should furnish the funds. She should double her tribute-money, and buy her prisoners back at eight gold pieces each!

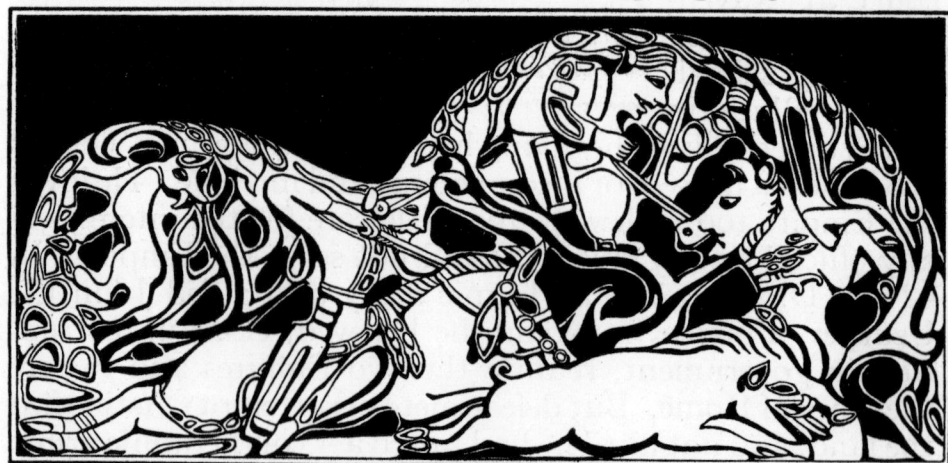

Hunters like Attila's brother, Bleda, in the wilds of Russia. One horseman in tight trousers and short tunic, his hair and huge moustache floating in the wind, pursues a boar at a wild gallop, drawing his bow as he rides. Another rider has climbed a tree and clings wildly to his plunging steed. At the left a dog prances on his hind legs. (A beautifully inlaid gold ornament from Siberia, now in the Museum of the Hermitage at Len'in-grad in Russia.)

BARBARIAN INVASIONS

One Scythian examines a comrade's sore tooth, while another binds up a wounded leg. Scythians, Sar-ma′tians, and Slavs of Russia wore long-sleeved coats of fur or leather belted at the waist, and trousers of fur or leather. Beautiful designs were pricked in the leather. Pointed, narrow bonnets of camel's-hair, or fur caps were the national head dress. The Huns were destroyers, making nothing, but stealing from their neighbors. (See Vol. II, p. 235.)

Attila's demands were excessive and made with arrogant pride; but Constantinople had no army able to meet the Huns; her envoys had to agree. Thus with Roman money, Attila consolidated the scattered Hunnic tribes, gained control of the Germans and Scythians, the Sarmatians and various Slavic tribes who dwelt on the Russian steppes, and so he established a vast and powerful military empire which reached from Central Asia as far as Central Europe.

A more peaceful Russian scene. Under a beautiful tree, a much mous-ta′chioed cavalier rests his head on the knees of a woman who wears a tall tiara. Nearby, his servant holds the sturdy steppe ponies. The tails of the horses are braided, and their short manes stand up like brush. The cavalier's quiver hangs on the tree. The saddles are of rush or wicker and the strap hanging from them is to attach the game. (A Siberian gold ornament. Len′in-grad.)

Moreover, the course of events provided him with a strange and most ridiculous weapon for worrying the Romans. Early in his reign, the little princess Ho-no'ri-a, sister of the boy-ruler, Valentinian III, found herself shut up and kept almost a prisoner in the palace at Ravenna, because she was far too flirtatious for a well-conducted princess. With the crazy sentimentality of sentimental youth, she wrote to Attila, sent him a ring, and begged him not only to free her but to take her for his wife! The offer meant nothing to Attila. He already had several hundred wives; one more or less did not matter; but the crazy offer of the princess gave him a fine excuse. Henceforth, he based his demands on his rights as her promised husband! So hateful did he make himself, that the minister of Theodosius sent Vi-gil'as, an interpreter, on the pretense of an embassy with secret instructions to kill him.

After a lengthy journey, the envoys reached a Hunnish camp, littered with wagons and tents, where they found the great chief's pavilion swarming with savage attendants clad in dirty but gorgeous garments evidently stolen from the Persians and Chinese.

A Turkish noble in such finery as the Huns stole. Note the man's two little sons. (Votive flag, Chinese Turkistan.)

Chinese robes such as the Huns stole. China, with its age-old culture, never touched the West. (4th cent. painting.)

Under a canopy held by girls, Attila approaches the wooden houses and tents of his capital city in Central Hungary.

Attila himself, sallow and with deep-set eyes, sat on a wooden stool in garments strikingly simple. Receiving the envoys curtly, he answered none of their questions, but obliged them to follow at his heels through forests, plains and marshes, till they came to his capital city in the wilds of Central Hungary.

When Attila entered the city, he was met by girls carrying in pairs, a canopy of white linen. In addition, other young girls, marching in groups of seven, greeted him with songs of welcome, while he rode between lines of his subjects.

"O this magnificent capital of the Huns!" wrote Priscus, a secretary who accompanied Vi-gil'as on the embassy. "Lest I shame the truth, it is a mixture of tents and wagons, at the center of which rises a sort of village surrounded by a stockade. Attila's palace, naturally, occupies a commanding site. It is the chief object of the village, hugged by the quarters of his wives and his body-guard. Viewed closely, it turns out to be a curious structure of polished boards, the roof supported by columns forming a kind of gallery.

Though of wood, like all the better buildings of the 'city,' it contains, nevertheless, baths of stone and marble like those of Rome. As for the builder of the baths, he was a prisoner, a Greek architect. The poor fellow had expected to win his freedom as payment for his work. His reward, instead, was the job of keeping the baths in running order; and as they are something of a marvel to the Huns, the chances are that this will turn out to be a life job!

"A man, whom from his Hunnic dress I took to be a barbarian, approached and addressed me in the Greek for 'Hail!' I was taken aback, for most Huns by adoption use, if any tongue besides their own, either Gothic or Latin. This man, however, resembled a well-to-do Hun, being well-dressed, and having his hair cut in a circle after the Hunnic fashion. Having returned his salutation, I found myself quizzing him as to his former life. This earned a smile, and the admission that he was a Greek by birth, a Hellene who had gone as a merchant to Vi-mi-na'ci-um on the Danube; but the city fell a prey to the Huns, and he was stripped of his wealth. Owing to his large fortune, he was allotted to O-ne-ge'si-us, Attila's chief-minister, in the division of the spoils. He had served his master faithfully, fighting in battles under him, and with the spoils of war, he had at last purchased his freedom, having now married a Hun.

"This was not all he told me. He offered the highest possible tribute to primitive society by insisting that he was far better off among the Huns than he had ever been under us Romans. 'It is,' said he, 'the simple life with none of your trimmings, the wholesome life a man has the right to expect, secure from injustice, exactions, insults from the powerful, the burdens of taxation, and the delays and corruption of law courts.' Whereupon, he proceeded to paint a horribly gloomy picture of civilized society, fervently thanking his lucky stars for having been saved from its tyranny.

"When the hour arrived, we went to Attila's palace with the embassy from the Western Romans. Standing at the threshold of the hall, I could see Attila on his dais, his seat a bench covered with furs and rugs of many hues. The Huns did not rise to greet us. As we entered, each of us was given a cup which we must empty as a salute to the King. This done, we proceeded to our places to the left of the royal table. All the seats were ranged along the walls of the room. Attila sat at the center. Behind him was a couch, and from it steps led up to his bed, which was covered with an embroidered coverlet, such as Greeks and Romans use to deck bridal beds. The places on the right of Attila were held chief in honor; those on the left, where we sat, conferred far less distinction. As for Attila's sons, they sat, not near him, but at the extreme end of the room, their eyes fixed on the ground out of deference to their father. When all were seated, an attendant handed Attila a wooden cup filled with wine. He took it, saluted O-ne-ge'si-us first, and then guest after guest in their order of precedence. In acknowledgment, the guest so honored, rose and might not sit down until the King, having emptied his cup, returned it to the attendant. All the guests then honored Attila in the same way, saluting him and draining their cups; but the King did not stand up. When this ceremony was over, tables, large enough for three or four, were placed next to the table of Attila. A luxurious meal, served on silver plate, had been made ready for us, and for the barbarian guests; but Attila ate nothing save meat on a wooden trencher. In everything else he showed himself temperate; his cup was of wood, while to the other guests were given goblets of gold and silver. His dress was extremely simple, and conspicuous only for its spotlessness. He avoided ostentation. His sword, the latchets of his shoes, and the bridle of his horse, were not adorned like those of the other Huns, with gold or precious gems.

The saturnine Attila, conspicuous for his simplicity, sits at the banquet among his followers, who are elaborately clad in garments and jewels stolen from Chinese, Persians, Scythians, or Turks. Further to the right sit Gothic and Slavic allies. Roman guests in togas, and Byz'an-tines in rich mantles, are assigned seats on the left. Zer'con, the dwarf, performs before Attila, but though the assemblage are greatly entertained, their leader is unmoved.

"When evening fell, torches were lit, and two minstrels came before Attila, chanting songs they had composed to celebrate his victories. After the song, a half-crazed Hun, by uttering outlandish words, made the company laugh. Then Zer'con, the Moorish dwarf, entered and he threw all save Attila into uncontrollable laughter by his dress, his voice, and his words, a most ridiculous jumble of Latin, Hunnic, and Gothic. Attila, however, remained unmoved during these antics, never by word or act betraying the smallest smile."

After the banquet, Attila stunned his guests with surprise, overwhelming Vi-gil′as by revealing that all along he had known of his plot to murder him! Nevertheless, the Hun scornfully refused to take the life of a servant as satisfaction for the crime. He sent the envoys home in disgrace, arrogantly demanding the head of the prime-minister! And while the unfortunate minister lived in deadly fear lest his sovereign should purchase peace with the price of his unworthy head, Attila decided that the time was ripe at last for him to attack the Empire. The only question was, which should he attack first, Ravenna or Constantinople?

The matter was settled for him. In the year 450 A.D., Theodosius II died, and his sister, the Empress Pul-che′ri-a, married the warlike Mar′ci-an, who was thereby raised to the throne as Emperor of the East. When Attila demanded the usual tribute money, Marcian replied that Constantinople owed the Hun nothing whatever, and that, henceforth, any claims Attila made, would be met by iron, and not gold!

Marcian, the forceful warrior, whom the Empress Pul-che′ri-a married, has the audacity to defy the astounded Hunnish ambassadors and to refuse to purchase peace with gold. Thus repulsed, Attila turned to attack the West.

Rebuffed by this unexpected and courageous attitude, Attila decided to concentrate all his forces against the Western Empire. Though many years had passed since Ho-no'ri-a crazily wooed him, the grotesque old Hun now demanded that Valentinian III should send him his promised wife, and with her, yield up as dowry one-half of the Western Empire! Valentinian prepared for war.

In 451 A.D., the hordes of Attila suddenly appeared along the Rhine! The sound of his host advancing was like the roar of the sea! Wild cries, and wilder songs surged above the stamping of horses. An intolerable stench of leather, combined with grease and sweat, arose from the fur-clad horsemen. The Burgundians tried to stay them. Worms, Wen'disch, Spires, and Mainz were destroyed as object lessons. At last, the savage Hun appeared before Orleans.

A-ni-a'nus, the Bishop of Orleans, determined to resist. The city was besieged, it faced starvation and death, but the stout-hearted bishop escaped and made his way to A-e'ti-us, sole support of the Empire in these trying and terrible days. With his small Roman army, Aetius had now advanced to Arles, where he was urging Theodoric, the King of the Visigoths, to join him against the Huns. Orleans could hold out for another fifteen days only, so the bold bishop said, but Aetius swore to arrive before the last day had passed! The bishop returned to his flock; and the Huns had already occupied the suburbs of the city, when watchers on the ramparts beheld a dust cloud in the distance. Aetius had kept his promise! The banners of Romans and Goths soon appeared from the dust. Surprised by their sudden appearance, Attila raised the siege. Repassing the Seine, he took up his stand on the great plains of Cha-lons'. Here was now to be fought a most important battle, a struggle for the defense of western civilization, a struggle to preserve all that mankind had gained in its long, slow struggle upward.

Warriors, like the Huns, riding skittish ponies. Russian figures, from a private collection, and the Museum of Ti-flis'.

But Aetius adopted tactics most painful to the Huns, the trying tactics of waiting. The Huns were unaccustomed to controlling themselves with patience. They had difficulty, too, in controlling their restive horses. Occasionally a group broke forth, making a senseless sortie. Three o'clock! Sharp commands! A long, sustained, rhythmic cry! The Huns were in action at last! Soon the Roman lines became a living wall, over which came roaring the vast wave of the horde, crested with axes and javelins. It came to a hand-to-hand struggle! But arrows, lances, and lariats cannot be used at close quarters, and stone-headed axes have no effect on helmets made of bronze. Attila exposed his person with the rashness of a private soldier, but only the approach of night saved him from total defeat. Retiring to their circle of wagons, the Huns fortified their camp. Attila ordered the saddles and harnesses of the horses to be heaped in a funeral pyre. If his entrenchments were forced, he meant to fire the pile and fling himself into the flames; for no foe should ever boast that he took the old Hun alive!

But his enemies passed the night in equal anxiety. Three hundred thousand dead covered the plain of Chalons, and beneath a heap of slain was found the body of The-od'o-ric, the Visigothic King, who had fought like a hero, and fallen covered with honorable wounds. Great was the Roman loss!

After his defeat by A-e'ti-us at Cha-lons', Attila withdraws the remnant of his host to a fortified wagon circle. There he prepares a pyre of saddles and horse-furnishings, on which to sacrifice himself if about to be taken captive.

Attila, meantime, faced his foes like a lion brought to bay. His instruments of martial music, loud and animating, incessantly sounded defiance; the troops who advanced against him were destroyed by showers of arrows. Nevertheless, in spite of all this noisy display, Aetius saw that the Hun was in truth completely defeated. He sent the Visigoths home and desisted from the attack. Attila then began his slow retreat to the Danube. The Western Empire was saved, and Aetius led his victorious army back home to Ravenna.

Attila did not, however, give up his plans for conquering the world. The very next spring he set out again, ravaging and destroying. Fleeing before his hosts, the Venetians, a Nordic tribe, who had settled in Northern Italy, sought shelter on little islands in the lagoons of the Adriatic, there starting the city of Venice. Everywhere people fled!

Aetius recruited and trained a second army for defense; but Leo, the aged Bishop of Rome, trusting only in God, put on his stateliest robes, and went forth to meet the wolf who threatened his precious flock. Harmless in his simplicity, venerable in his gray hair, he stood before the grim Hun and pleaded so bravely for mercy, that Attila, deeply impressed, withdrew his horde from Italy without attacking Rome.

This was his last attempt at conquering the world. He was now over sixty years old; moreover, rebellion was brewing among his German allies and even among his Huns. Returning northward, he conquered a rebel German tribe, seized the chief's fair daughter, the golden-haired Il-di'co, took the maid to his camp and forced her to be his bride.

Il-di'co, the beautiful golden-haired German maiden, is forced to become the bride of the ugly old Hun, Attila.

The marriage was celebrated at Attila's wooden palace. Worn out with feasting and drinking, the ugly old Hun, very weary, retired to his marriage chamber. Next morning he did not appear. Continued silence from his room alarmed the attendants on guard; they decided at last to enter, and there they found Attila dead on his bed,—a sudden hemorrhage had killed him,—while the trembling Ildico, saved from the hideous, hated old man, crouched in a corner terrified and hiding her face in her veil.

Attila's body, lying in state under a silken canopy, was exposed in the midst of the plain, while chosen squadrons of Huns wheeled around it continuously, gashing their faces with wounds, and chanting a funeral song. Surrounded with spoils and plunder, his remains were buried at night, and almost immediately the vast Hunnic Empire broke up. As for the Roman Aetius, he was shortly afterward murdered by order of Valentinian, and so did he meet his reward for saving the Roman Empire from the hideous host of Huns.

A barbaric, gold ornament from Siberia, such as were buried in Attila's tomb. In this bizarre creature the animal's horns have been turned into heads of birds of prey, with long curved beaks, and other weird beasts form his body.

BARBARIAN INVASIONS

The Fall of Rome, in 475 A.D.

When Valentinian died, murdered like Aetius, Vandal pirates from Africa under their fierce King, Gen'ser-ic, sailed from their stronghold at Carthage, marched on Rome, and took it! For fourteen days the Vandals stole and slaughtered and plundered. Finally, loading their ships with the spoils which Rome in past years had taken from all the world, they set sail for Africa, losing most of their treasures in a terrible storm at sea. German generals of the army, hired barbarian soldiers, now seized the power in Rome.

Vandal bronze-gilt buckle with a man fighting a lion, showing the primitive workmanship of this destructive tribe. Found in Algeria, once the Vandal territory in Africa. (British Museum.)

Count Rik'i-mer set up and pulled down four powerless puppet emperors. There was chaos in Italy. The last of the puppet emperors was a little boy called Romulus. And because he was only a helpless child, and yet bore the honored name of Rome's wolf-suckled founder, the soldiers mocked him and called him Rom'u-lus Au'gus'-tul-us, or "Little Emperorkin Romulus." Then the German giant, O'do-a'cer, King of the Her'u-li, seized the little Augustus, stripped him of his purple robes, and sent him to a country villa, while he made himself ruler of the West.

Zeno, the Eastern Emperor, having his own hands full, could not now take time or money to wage war with Odoacer; so he gave him the title of "Patrician," and bade him govern Italy as a subject of Constantinople. Thus, the year 475 saw the final fall of Rome before a barbarian chief. For fourteen years, Odoacer ruled Italy firmly and wisely. Then came the great Theodoric, the King of the Ostrogoths.

The harbor of Ravenna, new capital of Italy, stronghold of O'do-a'cer. (Mosaic. S. A-pol-li-na're Nu-o'vo, Ravenna.)

Theodoric the Ostrogoth
(488 A.D.—526 A.D.)

The-od'o-ric had been sent, when a little fair-haired lad, as a hostage to Constantinople. At first he had hated the crowded streets, the oppressive rooms of the palace; but during the ten years he had spent at the court of Constantinople, this child of shepherds and hunters had learned the meaning and dignity of civilization and order; he had learned to enjoy the busy, varied life of a Roman city, its public shows, its baths, its stately courts of law, its constant hum of life. Indeed, when he was sixteen, and returned to his father's home, he was more Roman than Goth, and was filled with a great ambition to become the mighty champion of Roman civilization. Nevertheless, he was also a typical German warrior, gigantic and impetuous, harrying the Eastern Empire; and he had a great ambition to conquer Italy. Forthwith, he thus addressed Zeno: "Direct me to fight Odoacer. If I fall, you will be relieved from a costly and troublesome friend; if, with God's help, I succeed, I shall govern the land in your name!"

Theodoric. (Coin, British Museum.)

Now Zeno had never really approved of Odoacer; perhaps if Theodoric fought him, both these troublesome leaders would manage to kill each other! At any rate the Goths would leave the Eastern Empire. Zeno agreed with pleasure that Theodoric should take his whole people and conquer Italy. Thus after a wearisome journey, the Os′tro-goth′ic warriors with their host of women and children, at last saw the snow-capped Apennines and the gently rippled, blue waters of the smiling Adriatic. Years of fighting followed, till Odoacer found himself besieged within Ravenna and forced to admit the Ostrogoths within the city-walls. Then during a banquet that followed, Odoacer was stabbed by command of Theodoric, who declared himself King of the Romans and Goths in 493 A. D.

O′do-a′cer. Probably a likeness. (Coin)

Straightway, Theodoric began to copy the gorgeous and elaborate ceremonies to which he had been accustomed in his boyhood at Constantinople. To the plain-spoken, hard-hitting Goths, this elegance seemed ridiculous; but with the outward semblance of an ancient Roman Emperor, Theodoric put on the mind and vigor of ancient Rome.

The palace of Theodoric. A mosaic, showing the influence of Constantinople. (S. Apollinare Nuovo, Ravenna.)

He rebuilt ruined cities and preserved the fine old monuments of Roman civilization. Order and plenty returned to Rome and to Ravenna. Not for many years had Italy been so well governed. Senators once again retired to their country villas during the winter season. Agriculture revived, iron and gold mines were worked; marshes were drained and cultivated, and roads were cleared of robbers.

"During the reign of Theodoric," declared a Catholic bishop, "so great was the happiness of Italy that even the wayfarers were at peace. For he did nothing wrong. So did he govern the two nations, the Goths and Romans, as if they were one people. Belonging himself to the A'ri-an sect, yet he ordained that the civil administration should remain for Romans as it had been under their Emperors. He attempted nothing against the Catholic faith."

The Consul Bo-e'thi-us, father of the philosopher. (Ivory diptych, 487 A.D.) Throughout the Middle Ages, men studied the *Consolations of Philosophy* by Boethius, and King Alfred, the Saxon, even had it translated into English.

The only great blot on the name of Theodoric was the execution of Bo-e'thi-us, the Roman philosopher, whom he first entrusted with the position of consul, and then cast into prison. Confined in the tower of Pa-vi'a, Boethius wrote his *Consolations of Philosophy*, while he was awaiting death. From earthly affairs, he ascended the heights of thought in search of the Supreme good; he explored the meaning of chance and destiny, of fate and free will, of time and eternity; and his book survived to bring comfort to many in the darkest times to come.

Tomb of Theodoric at Ravenna. Theodoric wished his body to lie in a mausoleum with a mighty dome like that of Augustus at Rome, but the knowledge of how to build a dome had been lost in Italy, and his bewildered architects were compelled to curve a mighty piece of solid stone and erect that for a dome. (From a recent photograph.)

In the fullness of time, Theodoric died, and was buried with barbaric splendor in a tomb which he had built outside the walls of Ravenna. But the kingdom he had established, the strong, united Italy, was not to endure. Theodoric left no son, but a daughter and little grandson. The Goths split into factions, demanding a man for their leader, while the Romans, forgetting the misery, the poverty, and chaos, from which Theodoric had saved them, cried out against the Goths, those Arian heretics far worse than the heathens!

However, Am'al-a-sun'tha, daughter of Theodoric, continued to rule for her son until the little boy died. Then she chose her cousin, The-od'a-had, to be co-ruler with her. But Theodahad imprisoned her on a lonely island in a lake, and when she sent for help to the Emperor of the East, Justinian, Theodahad put her to death. Justinian then decided that the time had arrived to wipe out the shame of more than fifty years' submission to German kings; he dreamed of reconquering Italy and restoring the prestige of Rome.

III

The Eastern, or Byzantine Empire

Justinian and Theodora, the Circus-girl Empress
(527 A.D.—565 A.D.)

Since the death of The′o-do′si-us in 395 A.D., and the division of the Empire between his incompetent sons, Ho-no′ri-us and Ar-ca′di-us, the two halves of the Empire had remained absolutely distinct. Though the Eastern half still called itself the Eastern Roman Empire, it was in reality Greek in its civilization and language, and in its ceremonials it was thoroughly Oriental. More properly it was called the Greek or Byzantine Empire, after the name of the city where Constantinople arose. While the Western Empire was breaking up into different Germanic kingdoms, the emperors at Constantinople, the sallow and sleepy Arcadius, his son Theodosius II, the warrior-emperor Mar′ci-an, and those three very capable rulers, Leo, Zeno, and An-as-ta′si-us, had kept the Germans at bay and maintained their realms intact.

Jus-ti′nus, the successor to the able Anastasius, rose from the ranks in the army. Once he had journeyed to By-zan′ti-um, carrying his wordly goods in a bundle swung from a stick. He could still scarcely sign his name when he found himself Emperor of the East. Most actual matters of government were left to Proclus, the quaestor, or to the Emperor's nephew and adopted son, Jus-tin′i-an.

Justinian was not like his uncle, a crude, uncultured peasant. Born after his uncle and father had attained to positions of standing, he had been educated as the heir of a wealthy house. A trustworthy, business-like man, a staid and practical personage his subjects thought him to be. But, when he was past thirty-five, he suddenly and deliberately scandalized the world! He declared his intention of taking to wife the dancer, The-o-do′ra, the star of the comic stage!

Who had ever heard the like? A man of his position to marry a common actress! There was actually a law which forbade a member of the Senate to make a marriage with an actress. And who was this Theodora? A gutter-child, a circus-wench! Her father had been keeper of the bears for the party of the Greens in the circus; but one day the beasts killed her father. Left penniless and destitute, her mother, with three little daughters, was turned out by the Greens. With an eye to dramatic effect, the mother took her children, dressed in white as suppliants, and brought them up from the dressing-rooms to the sanded arena of the circus on a day when the games were in progress. While the mother appealed to the public, the second child, a mite of a thing, flung out her thin little arms in tragic supplication. This was Theodora, a finished dramatic artist at the immature age of five! Mingled applause and laughter greeted the efforts of the group, but in the end the Blue leader promised his help to the widow, and the family was given employment.

Amid the excitement of games in the Hippodrome, the circus-girl, Theodora, and her mother beseech assistance.

Scenes from the circus in the days of Theodora. Behind the semi-circle sit the spectators. In the plaque to the left, attendants irritate a bear, and drive him on two men who swing from a pole in baskets. Below, an acrobat balances himself head-downward on a stick, while a second bear attacks a youth. Two young attendants watching the performance, peek around the doors through which actors enter the arena, ready to slam the doors quickly if the bears become too obstreperous. In the plaque to the right, a lion, a bull, a pony, and three bears fight with each other, or with gladiators, while jugglers toss up disks. Christianity put an end to the more bloodthirsty gladiatorial combats of the circus, and introduced the jugglers, acrobats, and mimics of the modern circus. (Ivory plaques from the bottom of Byzantine consular diptychs, 517 A.D., and 506 A.D., Cluny Museum, Paris. See illustration p. 93.)

Thus Theodora and her sisters grew up in the circus, in daily companionship with charioteers and jockeys, gladiators and acrobats almost as brutish as the bears.

Co-mit'a, the elder sister, became a graceful dancer. An-as-ta'si-a played the flute, but the beautiful Theodora posed in living statues or sauntering out on the stage, appearing not to notice the audience, she twisted her body, puffed out her cheeks, and imitated well-known citizens till the audience roared with laughter. Speedily she became the favorite of Constantinople. She had taught herself to read and write; she was a jolly companion, intelligent, quick of wit. Many young aristocrats were captivated by her. Justinian, however, was the only one of her lovers who really wanted to marry her. His mother tried to dissuade him; his uncle, the Emperor Justinus, threatened to disinherit him; but Justinian only persisted. He secured a repeal of the law which prevented a man of his rank from marrying an actress, and before Justinus died, he had wedded the fair Theodora, and induced the old man to bestow on her the title of Patrician.

Thus the girl of the streets found herself Empress of the East, and on a fine Easter morning in the year 527, she and her husband came in state after the coronation in the Church of Sancta Sophia, to receive the homage of the people in that same Hippodrome, where she had once begged for aid. In the splendid imperial box, surrounded by a brilliant assemblage, the former slave of the public, now held both friends and foes in the hollow of her little jeweled hand. But instead of losing her head at this sudden change of fortune, Theodora began to prove herself as clever at playing the Empress as she had been at playing the fool. Justinian called her "My sweetest charm," and "Most honored wife"; and many a time her quick wit, sound judgment, and common sense helped him in grave difficulties.

Justinian himself, was a hard and suspicious master, intolerant in religion, unscrupulous in politics, sleepless, stern, and strict. All night long he sat alone over his state papers or paced the dark halls in deep thought. Nevertheless, his efforts, his abilities and ambitions, built up a powerful empire. Under him Constantinople reached new heights of magnificence.

The Byzantine consul, Ar'e-o-bin'dus seated at the games in the circus (506 A.D.). In his elaborate consular robe, which boasts two embroidered saints on the band down the front, he sits on the consular throne, holding in his left hand the sceptre, and in his right, the napkin which the consul always dropped as a signal for the games to begin. This carved ivory plaque formed one half of a consular diptych (dip'tik), two leaves of ivory hinged together and made when a man became consul, to present to important people. Below the figure of the consul were always carved circus scenes, to remind people of the consul's role of providing the public games, or with figures of men pouring money out of sacks to signify the generosity of the new-made consul. The circus scene at the right, on page 92 forms the bottom of this plaque of Areobindus. (Cluny Museum, Paris.)

Justinian and his court. A brilliantly colored mosaic in the new style of Byzantine art: figures flattened to form a design of many long parallel lines, the spectator made to feel keenly the magnificence and austerity of the court.

Byzantine Life and Art

The Byzantines loved color, beautiful clothes, fine houses. They loved the circus, the baths, the theaters, and the shops. Fashionable young men, wearing garments entirely different from the simply draped Roman toga, now appeared in embroidered tunics, and long elaborate cloaks, with jewels in shoes and girdles, their dark hair cropped and curled, and their whole persons breathing the perfume of ambergris and musk. As they walked in the public squares, each one was followed by a slave carrying a folding stool, in case his master should chance to feel the need of a rest. Sometimes they rode on horses, or white mules with gilded trappings, while the ladies went abroad in gaily painted wooden carriages, drawn by three or four mules, impressively harnessed abreast.

The Empress Theodora and her ladies, also flattened to form a design. The new notes in Byzantine art are feeling, color, and design. These mosaic portraits (pages 94 and 95) were ordered for the Church of San Vitale in Ravenna.

Byzantine houses gleamed with brilliantly colored mosaics done in that new style of art which came to be called Byzantine. The Greeks had sought to express the perfection of outward form, the beauty of a perfect body exactly as it was; but they had made little attempt to get beyond outward form, to find the soul of a thing, to make the observer *feel*, to arouse in him the love, the joy, the laughter, the hate, the horror, or the pity, caused not by outward form, but by the inward meaning which the artist sees in his work. Moreover, the Greeks had loved the pure classic white of marble; they had never responded keenly to the joy of vivid color; and they had been little aware of the beauty of mere design, of flowing, parallel lines, or intricate, interlaced scrolls. They had sought to *depict* rather than to *decorate*.

The new note in art, love of design, as applied by Teutons and Celts to animal forms. Left, a 5th century Gothic lion from Ka-nev', Russia, not pictured realistically as in Greek art, but with various parts of his body seen for the design they form. Second, increased love for new design has dismembered the animal to cover the surface of a 6th century bronze ornament from Vyat'ka, S. Russia. Eyes and jaw are visible, also the tail and a hind leg twisted over the back. Last, a frieze of beautifully interlaced animals of the 7th cent. (Book of Durrow, Dublin.) The Goths, living near the source of this movement in the Scythian-Turkish tribes around the Caspian, passed it on to Europe. Teutonic art long consisted of animal ornament, while in Byzantium, love of design was applied to persons.

Now there came out of the East a new note in the world of art. From two barbaric races, the Scythians and the Mongolian-Turks, there had spread over the West the love and understanding of geometric design. Through Russia, this love of design had spread to the Teutons and Celts, who applied it to animal forms, to dragons and rich serpentines. Through Syria and Arabia, it had reached Constantinople, bringing in its wake a stirring use of color wholly unknown to the Greeks, and the art of glass mosaics in which to express itself. This love of line and color, of flowing formal design, finding in Constantinople the remains of the ancient Greek love for painting the human figure, as well as a Christian demand for Christian subjects in art, was there applied less to fantastic beasts as among the Teutons and Celts, and more to the human figure and outward representation of actual material things. Nevertheless, here too, it retained its aim to decorate rather than to depict, and thus it flattened out objects, using lines of face and body, flowing robes and jewels, merely to form the design, and seeking rather the thrill that comes from beauty of line than accurate representation of any object or thing. It gloried in rich use of color and a search for inward feeling, demanding that the beholder should be made to feel in response. In Byzantine mosaics it reached its highest form.

The Justinian Code

A stranger in the palace early in Justinian's reign, might have opened a certain door and seen a curious sight. At one end of the room a group of men sat at a table heaped with old scrolls of parchment. At the opposite end another group wrote in the new-fashioned way, using square sheets of vellum with quill pens dipped in ink and making not scrolls but books, each of which would be bound between two blocks of wood and called in Latin a *codex*, from the word for "block of wood." What could all this mean? The answer was simple enough. Few lawyers in those days had money enough to buy law books; they had to depend on their memories for a knowledge of the laws. Moreover, many statutes contradicted each other, and some were quite unsuitable to govern a Christian state. Who, in these advanced days, would think it up-to-date to threaten a Christian culprit with the curse of the goddess Ceres? Under Justinian's orders, the Chief Justice and his companions were systematizing the laws. This new Code of Justinian was his great gift to civilization; for it proved to be so good that in time it came to be used in nearly all parts of Europe, and it still forms the basis of the legal systems both in Europe and America.

Early picture of a book; Jesus holding a copy of the Gospels. (Ivory diptych, Kaiser Friedrich Museum, Berlin.) Among the first books as we know them today were Justinian's collection of the Roman laws, that famous code which was his greatest gift to civilization, and which still forms the basis of laws in modern Europe and America. No longer were books written upon rolls, but on flat sheets bound together between two blocks of wood which formed the covers. Such a book was called a *codex*, because *codex* is Latin for "block of wood."

Christianity in the days of Justinian

Justinian's laws showed clearly that enough of the ideals of Christianity had sifted through the minds of the people, so that there was now a greater demand for charity and justice. In the old days a father had been able to do what he liked with his children, even to killing them or selling them into slavery. Unwanted babies were frequently left in lonely places to die. But cruelties such as these were forbidden by Justinian's laws, thus proving that Christian ethics were remolding human thought, and taking men a step forward toward general recognition of the right of all to live and fulfill their natural gifts, the weak as well as the strong. Nevertheless, there were other facts not so complimentary to the Christianity of that day. Justinian himself spent the greater part of his time in arguments on theology, for dogma, creed, and belief had overlaid the teachings of Jesus and almost wiped them out.

A general council of the Church. At such meetings the officers of the Church decided what was true doctrine and what was false. All men were then required to accept these doctrines on pain of persecution or death. No matter which sect temporarily got the upper hand, those who did not believe exactly as they decreed, suffered persecution. A'ri-ans as well as Orthodox Christians and every other nameless little sect that sprang up, tried to enforce their belief on their brother-Christians, as though it were possible to club a man over the head and command him to believe that 2x2 is 4 when you have not made him understand it. (Festival Calendar of Basil II, Vatican, Rome, 963 A.D.)

THE BYZANTINE EMPIRE

The martyrdom of a saint. (Festival Calendar, Basil II.) With steadfast, unfailing courage, under Roman persecution Christians died for their faith; but later Christians were less willing to *live* for their faith, to live each day in accordance with the ideals and teachings of Jesus. Scarcely had Christianity itself been saved from persecution than it persecuted all other faiths. Lecky says: (*History of European Morals*,) "From the very moment the Church obtained civil power under Constantine, the general principle of coercion was acted on both against Jews, heretics, and pagans. They were tortured with every refinement of cruelty and were burnt at a slow-consuming fire to enable them to think of the charity and humanity of the Church of Christ." In Alexandria in 415 A.D., a mob of Christians fell on the beautiful, virtuous, and intelligent young pagan woman, Hy-pa'tia, head of the School of Ne'o-pla-ton'ic philosophers. Socrates, the church historian says: (Hist. Eccl. VII:15) "She was torn from her chariot, dragged to the Cae'sar-e-um (then a Christian church), stripped naked, done to death with oyster-shells, and burnt."

Whether a man was an A'ri-an, an Orthodox Catholic Christian, or something else with a long and unpronounceable name, he was determined that everyone else should believe exactly as he did. The tyranny of self-will and religious persecution took possession of human nature. All sects alike were to blame. No one seemed to think of checking up his conduct with the standards given by Jesus. The question everywhere asked was not what sort of a life do you live, but what do you believe? And problems of belief concerned the most abstract questions with little relation to life,—did Jesus have a divine nature only, or did he have two natures, one human and one divine? Did he suffer on the cross, or was he a spirit, a supernatural being, a phantom, who could never suffer? Over such questions men fought with violence and fury while Justinian, himself, stoutly persecuted all heretics.

Christianity in those days presented a sorry picture to the genuine lover of Jesus, and the simple truths he had taught. It is one thing for a man to say he is a Christian, and another thing to be one. Obviously the only test by which to judge how much of a Christian anyone is, is to check up the life one is living with the standards offered by Jesus. Jesus himself had based all his teachings on two commands simple enough for a child to understand: "Thou shalt love the Lord thy God with all thy heart and with all thy soul and with all thy mind," and "Thou shalt love thy neighbor as thyself." He had fought for a simple faith as against the crushing complexities of Jewish religious forms; yet now forms appeared again to be of supreme importance, and the Roman's inborn love of organization and government was organizing Christianity, refusing the individual's right to seek the truth for himself, and demanding, as in temporal government, the implicit obedience of men to those of higher authority.

As Christianity came into fashion, men willingly called themselves Christian; but not so are men's hearts changed. Their hearts are never changed, until they are wholly *convinced*. The people clung to their ancient gods, their ancient forms of worship. Mithra, Adonis, Isis,—the tales men had known of these gods colored their Christian faith. Men did not so much change their hearts as they changed the names of things. They gave up the names of their gods, but not the gods themselves. Over all of Christendom, pagan sacred places were turned into Christian chapels; hundreds of shrines to the Virgin stood on ground once sacred to goddesses and nymphs; statues of Jupiter and Apollo became Saints Peter and Paul; and figures of Isis, the Queen of Heaven, holding Horus the divine babe, were used to represent the Madonna holding the infant Jesus.

In the early Christian Church there had been no festivals, no holy days, and no Sabbaths; for as Chrys'os-tom said:

"The whole of time is a festival unto Christians, because of the excellency of the good things which have been given." However, the old pagan festivals could not be suppressed, and it became necessary to give them a Christian signification. The clergy, for example, could not prevent their people from celebrating each Spring a holiday in honor of the yearly resurrection of At'tis and A-do'nis, pagan gods of vegetation; so, says Socrates, the church historian, they agreed to continue this custom by giving it a Christian meaning, especially as it came at the season when Jesus himself had risen. Moreover, the Anglo-Saxons held the month of April sacred to *E'os-tre*, goddess of the teeming life that bloomed anew in the Spring; and her great festival which gave its name to the English *Easter* was celebrated by the exchange of colored Easter eggs, the egg being the heathen symbol of the beginning of life. The Venerable Bede, an English historian, quotes a letter from Pope Gregory, in which the Pope declares that the policy of the Church is not to suppress pagan feasts but adapt them to Christian ideas; and Bede frankly states that in England the Easter feast is simply "the old festival observed with the gladness of a new solemnity."

Silk cloth, 6th cent., with the twin gods, Castor and Pollux, showing how love of the old gods still lingered in men's hearts. For further discussion of this subject, see *Paganism in our Christianity* by Arthur Weigall. The letter from Pope Gregory, preserved in Bede, is in *Ecc. Hist.* Chap. XXX. Facts concerning Eostre, Saxon goddess of Spring, and the custom of celebrating her feast by exchanging Easter eggs are from Guerber's *Myths of Northern Lands*.

Stern, ascetic churchmen. Much of the joyous confidence of early Christians had been lost in the perverted belief that holiness or salvation was attained by an austere repression of all natural desires and affections. They had lost sight of the fact that Jesus had taught not repression, but selection. As men select which of the thoughts that come to them are good to express in speech, so they are obliged to select which of the desires that come to them are good to express in action. (Mosaic, Church of St. De-me′tri-us, Sa′lo-ni′ka, 7th cent.)

Even the date of the birthday of Jesus had never really been known. Christians at first selected January 6th as a suitable date for the celebration; but December had been the month of the greatest of all pagan feasts, the jolly Saturnalia, when people feasted with every sort of noisy merrymaking, and according to Vergil, celebrated by hanging a tree with toys. Moreover, December 25th was the birthday of the sun, the day when ancients believed the days began to grow longer. A Catholic Christian wrote: "The reason why the fathers transferred the celebration from January 6th to December 25th, was that it was the custom of the heathen to celebrate on the same December 25th, the birthday of the sun, at which they lit lights in token of festivity, and in these rites the Christians also took part." (Creder, in Zeitsh. Hist. Theol. III, 2, p. 239, 1833.)

The joy of these ancient festivals rightly survived in Christianity, for Christianity was indeed a religion of deepest joy; but many pagan beliefs likewise survived with the joy. Many still thought to purchase everlasting life, as the pagans had purchased favor, by outward worship and creed rather than with the sacrifice of a purified humble heart, unselfish love and affection. Fear of hell-fire and damnation if they failed in worship or creed was prevalent among Christians, and that austere fear of all natural joys which is called *asceticism.*

THE BYZANTINE EMPIRE

Even before John the Baptist's time, men had thought they could come nearer God if they sought Him in the wilderness, away from worldly pleasures. These men had left their homes and lived in caves or dried-up wells, eating roots and berries, and never washing their bodies, believing that the body instead of being governed, "kept under" as Paul had said, and made to be obedient only to wholesome desires, was to be despised and tormented, so that the soul should be free. Jesus himself had said in praying for his disciples: "I pray not that thou shouldest take them out of the world, but that thou shouldest keep them from the evil;" nevertheless, many people now followed the example of the hermits and took themselves out of the world, especially to the deserts of Egypt and the waste-lands of the Nile. Some were sincere and genuine seekers after God, but many were merely frauds who sought to win notoriety or to get food and money from pilgrims. Simeon, nicknamed Stylites, lived for twenty-eight years perched on the top of a pillar said to be fifty feet tall.

Anchorite like Simeon on his tall pillar. Such men made suffering seem good; they never washed, wore haircloth shirts, ate little; and the fame of their holiness spread through the world. (Calendar of Basil II.)

Removal of the remains of the forty martyrs to the Church of St. Irene, Constantinople, in the presence of Justinian. Two church officials sit in a chariot bearing a box of relics, and the streets are thronged with people, while spectators crowd windows. Justinian greatly reverenced relics of holy-men. (Ivory carving, 6th cent. Cathedral, Treves.)

"For twenty-eight years," wrote The-od'o-ret, who had himself seen this uncombed and unwashed pillar-saint; "Simeon remained fasting for forty days at a time. For the first few days, he stood and praised God. After that, when through emptiness he could no longer stand, he would sit to perform divine service, and on the last days, even lie down." What little food he ate, was put in a basket, and tied to a rope which Simeon lowered from his perch.

Often a group of hermits agreed to live near each other for the sake of company. Each had his own little cave or hut, but all met together to hold their services on Sundays. Then, as the little community grew, one of their members was chosen to be the head of the settlement. He was called *abbot*, or *father*, and the others were known as *monks*, from a Greek word meaning *alone*, while the whole group of caves or huts was called a *monastery*.

A school friend of the Emperor Julian, a man by the name of Basil, drew up a set of rules for a monastery which he founded; and his rules proved so satisfactory that they came to be used in time in almost all parts of the East.

THE BYZANTINE EMPIRE

Basil said that monks must always obey their abbot; they must give up all personal belongings and promise never to marry; they must work for the sake of others, and not spend their days in merely trying to save their own souls. His monks taught the youths of the neighborhood in the quiet of their shady gardens or the long cool stretch of their cloisters; they gave alms to the poor, looked after orphans and sick folk, and began to collect and copy ancient manuscripts. It was also the monks who acted as missionaries, boldly carrying Christianity through forests, swamps, and mountains to Russia, Britain, Germany, and even to far-off China. And in carrying their faith abroad, they willingly bore all discomforts, risked all dangers and even met death. They felt that they had to offer the world the promise of eternal life and trust in a God who was good, with an equal chance for all men to enter into that joy, provided they accepted certain set beliefs and led lives of genuine goodness. And though their faith was overlaid with doctrines and difficult creeds and still half-buried perhaps in ancient pagan beliefs and absolute demands for obedience to organization, the faith that inspired them was genuine. In spite of all their mistakes, Christianity was spreading through them, its demand for love and compassion, for mercy, purity, justice, unselfishness, devotion, and service to mankind.

Silk cloth, 6th cent. (Vatican Library.) It was missionary monks who brought back to the West the knowledge of silk-making, hitherto a Chinese mystery. Two monks visiting China in Justinian's reign, hid some silk-worm eggs in a hollow bamboo cane, and smuggled them out of the land despite Chinese customs officials. They taught workmen of Constantinople to hatch the eggs, feed the worms on mulberry leaves until the cocoons were spun, then to unwind and to spin the threads.

Justinian the Warrior and Builder

A Persian king hunting boar. Under his crown is a cloth cap to which are fastened streamers, and a ball of pleated cloth over an iron support. His horse's harness is decorated with tassels. (Silver plate, from the private Collection of Count Strogonof.)

Sas-san'i-an king on a camel with a tiny woman perched up behind. He hunts roebuck and, like the king above, wears a short, long-sleeved tunic and long baggy trousers. See pages 38, 40. Silver plate. (Private Collection M. Likhatchev, Kozan.)

Justinian had begun his reign with a large and well-managed treasury, and a large and well-trained army, the backbone of which was not infantry, as in the days of Rome's greatness, but mailed horsemen armed with lance and bow after the Parthian fashion. No more than a year had elapsed before Justinian found himself forced to use both his gold and his soldiers. In 528 A.D., Kobad, King of Persia, declared war upon Justinian. There followed a four-year struggle, bloody and indecisive; but when, on the death of Kobad, Chos-roes', his son, made peace, the terms agreed upon were a restoration of the frontier just as it had been before; so that all Justinian gained by this cruel and costly war was the chance to test his army, and the discovery of a great general in the Thracian, Bel'i-sa'ri-us.

No sooner was the Persian War ended than the Blues and Greens of the Circus started a dangerous riot. Blue and Green were the colors of the two chariot teams which staged regular races in the Hippodrome, and so keen was the rivalry between them, that there had often been bloodshed. The Greens were friends of the former Emperor Anastasius, and favored one of his family, instead of Justinian, for Emperor. They also believed most violently in the Monoph'y-site heresy, while the Blues on the other hand, were Orthodox Catholic Christians and partisans of Justinian.

In January, the parties began a riot in the streets. The Emperor ordered the leaders on both sides put to death, and four were duly beheaded. But the last three were to be hanged, and the hangman twice bungled his task. Twice at the moment of suspension his rope somehow gave way and two of his prisoners, a Blue and a Green, fell to the ground alive. Then the crowd broke loose, seized the half-hung criminals, and thrust them into sanctuary at a nearby monastery.

The hangmen bungle their task and let two rioters fall unhung, thus serving as the immediate cause of the Nika Riot, which proved the heroism of Theodora, and almost cost Justinian his throne. Already Justinian's costly building ambitions, and his extensive wars were overtaxing the people, and exhausting the strength of the Empire.

Soldiers of the time of Justinian, drawn to form a design. A pound weight. 6th century. (British Museum.)

This exciting incident marked the beginning of six days of desperate rioting. The Blues and the Greens united, and taking as their watchword, *Nika*, "conquer," they swept through the city, demanding the removal of John of Cappadocia, the minister of finance, and of the city praefect, who had ordered the executions. The Greens even began to shout that Justinian should be deposed and Hypa'ti-us, a nephew of Anastasius, made Emperor in his place.

The city had almost no soldiers; for the garrison itself had been sent to the Persian War. Bel'i-sa'ri-us, however, took command of such troops as there were, and set out to clear the streets. The rioters stoutly resisted. They set fire to the Brazen Porch before the Senate House, so the Senate House itself caught fire, and the flames, spreading east and north, were driven across the square to the Church of Sancta Sophia. On the third day of the riot the cathedral was burned to the ground; and the flames, spreading farther and farther, at last put an end to the fighting, leaving the rebels in possession of the greater part of the city. Everywhere the mob now searched for the frightened Hypatius, the leader whom they had chosen; but having no wish to rule, he had taken refuge in the palace. Not until he was actually driven out by Justinian, who feared to have him near his person, did Hypatius, in spite of himself, fall into the hands of his supporters. On the sixth day of the riot, he was led to the Hippodrome, installed in the royal seat, and crowned with his wife's gold chain for lack of a diadem.

Meanwhile, Justinian's ministers urged him to fly to his troops at Her′a-cle′a. At Constantinople only the palace now remained in his hands. But Theodora refused to fly, and urged her husband to make one final assault on the enemy.

"If you wish, O Emperor, to save your life, nothing is easier," she cried. "Behold your ships and the sea. But I agree with the old saying: 'Empire is the best winding sheet.'"

Spurred on by his wife's bold words, Justinian ordered a last attack on the rebels. The mob had gathered in the Hippodrome to salute their new leader, Hypatius. Forcing his way through the gates, Belisarius caught the rebels all crowded into the building. Unable to escape through the exits, they fell by thousands before the swords of Justinian's victorious soldiers. Thus ended the Nika Riot.

Forty days after the riot, Justinian started rebuilding the beautiful Sancta Sophia as a monument to his triumph. On the site of the Emperor Constantine's rectangular basilica, the greatest of Byzantine architects, An-the′mi-us of Tral-les′ now built a wonder church. Heretofore, Christian architects had been using two patterns for churches. The first was the round domed church, copied from the celebrated Roman temple of Vesta; the second was the *basilica*, a rectangular church with projecting semi-circular apses copied from the ancient Roman basilica or law-courts. But in architecture as in art, Byzantine genius was bursting to express itself, and Justinian's architects combined a new and beautiful type of dome with a ground-plan shaped like a cross. Where the four arms of the cross met, they constructed a dome more beautiful than any ever built before.

A church with a semi-circular apse behind, copied from a Roman basilica or law court. (Bronze lamp, 5th cent.)

Emperor Justinian upon his throne examining the model of Sanc'ta So-phi'a presented to him by the architect, An-the'mi-us of Tral-les'. From an illuminated manuscript entitled the *Chronicles of Sancta Sophia*, which tells the story of the building. (Vatican, Rome.) Justinian was so greatly interested in building this wonder church that he erected temporary quarters nearby, in order to exercise a closer supervision day by day.

Instead of resting solidly on a heavy round stone wall as in the Pantheon at Rome and so appearing of the earth earthy, the dome of Sancta Sophia was given an appearance of soaring, airy-lightness, by its delicate support; for it rested on two lofty arches and two tall, graceful half domes which rested in turn on piers. So finely poised was this dome that men said it seemed as if "hung by a golden chain from heaven," while forty windows, cut in the rim, let in great floods of light.

"It presents a most glorious spectacle," wrote the historian Pro-co'pi-us, who had watched it grow. "It towers above the city which it adorns, and from it, all Constantinople can be seen as from a watch tower. Within, it is singularly full of light and sunshine; you would declare that the place is not lighted from without, but that the rays are produced within itself, such an abundance of light pours into it. The gilded ceiling adds glory to its interior, though the light reflected upon the gold from the shining marble, surpasses it in beauty. Who can tell of the splendor of the columns with which the church is adorned? One would think one had come on a meadow full of flowers in bloom; one wonders at the purple tints of some and the green of others, the glowing red and glittering white."

Interior of the magnificent Church of Sancta Sophia at Constantinople, built by the architects An-the′mi-us of Tral-les′, and Is-i-do′rus of Mi-le′tus, under the inspiration and guidance of Justinian. Sancta Sophia is a bold departure from the established styles of Greece and Rome. The dominating feature is the dome, 107 feet in diameter, which, instead of resting solidly on a round wall as in the Pantheon and the baths of Rome, is given an appearance of soaring lightness by being lifted up on two open arches and two tall half-domes which in turn rest on piers. Another feature of Sancta Sophia and Byzantine architecture is the larger, heavier capitals on the columns. These were necessary to support the continuous row of arches which the Byzantines used to give buildings lightness instead of the solid, stone walls of Greece and Rome. The capitals were made to appear light and graceful, however, by a delicate all-over, lace-like pattern. The interior of Sancta Sophia was a riot of colored mosaic, gold, and marble.

As the great doors ground on their hinges, and the first beam of rosy light leapt from arch to arch on the day when the church was opened, all the princes and people hymned their song of praise, and it seemed as if the mighty arches were set in heaven itself. The Church of Sancta Sophia represented all that was finest in Byzantine architecture and art.

Justinian was now free to take up a task which lay very close to his heart. It was his dream to reunite under his rule the Germanic kingdoms in Italy, Africa, and Spain, and to end the solemn pretense by which he was nominally acknowledged Emperor in the West, while in reality all the power was in the hands of the Germans. As heir of the imperial Caesars, he would make himself lord of the world!

The Empress Theodora urged him to forget the West. "Leave the barbarians to their conquered ruins," she said, "and do you take thought for Byzantium." But Justinian merely answered that women knew nothing of wars.

Having made Bel'i-sa'ri-us sole commander of the expedition, he sent him with 15,000 men to subdue the Vandals in Africa; and as life beneath the African sun had sapped the ancient fierceness and strength of the Vandal pirates, Belisarius defeated them easily and not only brought their king, Gel'i-mer, a captive to Constantinople, but also brought back the treasures of the splendid palace at Carthage, which included golden vessels from the Temple at Jerusalem and other articles taken by the Vandals eighty-six years before, when they sacked the city of Rome. Justinian then granted his general a most magnificent triumph, and encouraged by his success, he began to think of attacking The-od'a-had, the King of the Ostrogoths in Italy. From her tower in the middle of the lake, where Theodahad had shut her up, the unfortunate Am'a-la-sun'tha, daughter of the great Theodoric, sent messengers to Justinian, telling him of her plight and begging him for assistance. Here was Justinian's excuse. When messengers soon arrived with news that the Gothic King had put his cousin to death, Justinian sent Belisarius to avenge the murdered Queen.

King The-od'a-had with closed crown, jeweled robe, and cross on breast. Portrait coin. (Brit. Museum.)

With an even smaller army than had been given him to conquer Africa, Belisarius conquered Sicily. The-od'a-had was terror-stricken; he wrote to Constantinople offering to resign his crown if the Emperor would guarantee him his life and his private property. Belisarius, nevertheless, crossed safely into Italy, the Goths slew Theodahad and elected as their leader the warrior, Vit'i-ges.

And now Belisarius faced a foe who was worthy of his steel. Greeted by the Italians as their deliverer from the Goths, he made his way to Rome, where Vitiges with his army besieged him for a year. But when a second army sent out by the Emperor Justinian landed in Northern Italy and laid siege to Milan, Vitiges with-

The unfortunate Queen Am'a-la-sun'tha, daughter of the great Theodoric, who was imprisoned and murdered by her cousin, King Theo-od'a-had. (Ivory panel, Florence.)

drew his troops from before the walls of Rome, took refuge in Ravenna, the Gothic capital of Italy, and was there besieged in turn. The flower of the Gothic nation was shut up in Ravenna. If Ravenna fell, the Ostrogoths were lost. In their despair the Goths, admiring Belisarius as a great and powerful warrior, invited him to throw off his allegiance to Justinian, and to become the King of an independent Italy. But Belisarius, true to his trust, refused the proffered crown. Entering Ravenna, he made Vitiges his captive, and with him and the great Gothic treasure-horde from the palace of Theodoric, he sailed for Constantinople to lay his spoils at the feet of his master, the Emperor Justinian.

Meanwhile, Chos-roes' of Persia, seriously alarmed at these conquests, determined to strike at Byzantium, while the best of Justinian's army was still occupied in the West; so he fell on the city of Antioch, and dragged away thousands of captives. Belisarius had to come home to force the Persians to peace. In the midst of such events, a plague broke out in the Empire; all occupations ceased, and the market-place was empty save for the bearers of corpses. Justinian himself fell ill, and never regained his full strength.

Under their new king, To-til'a, the Ostrogoths soon rebelled. For eleven years Belisarius fought in vain to subdue them. Not till a new general, Narses, was sent to replace Belisarius were the Goths at last defeated; so they all moved out of Italy and sought new homes elsewhere. And when Justinian's armies likewise subdued Southern Spain, most of the old Roman Empire had been restored to his rule.

The Emperor now did his best to encourage the Italians to build up their cities again; he himself ordered the erection of public buildings in Rome, and he decorated Ravenna in the new Byzantine mosaics. But the people were all worn out with poverty, war, and pestilence. They had been far better off under the wise Theodoric. It was no kindness to bring them back under the rule of an emperor in far-off Constantinople. Rome now suffered more from dishonest Greek officials than she had ever suffered from the just and well-meaning Goth. The Emperor celebrated his conquests with games and magnificent triumphs, but his heart was dead in his breast; for Theodora had died in the year 548. No more could her bold spirit buoy him up and spur him on. Sunk in sadness and gloom, he trusted no one henceforth. Even Belisarius, the most loyal soldier of the Empire, fell under his master's suspicions and held no more posts of power. In the year 565, the aged Justinian died, thus ending the greatest reign in the history of the Eastern Empire.

THE BYZANTINE EMPIRE 115

Struggles with Lombards, Slavs, Avars, and Persians

For a hundred and fifty years after the reign of Justinian, the Empire slowly declined. Justinian's wars and buildings had overtaxed the people, and enemies pressed from three sides: in the East, the Persians; in the Balkan Peninsula, the A'vars and the Slavs; in Italy, the yellow-haired Lombards.

The Lombards, or Lan'go-bards, were fierce Germanic barbarians famous for the *long beards* which had given them their name. As they came down out of Germany fighting with rival tribes, Al'boin, King of the Lombards, killed Cu'ni-mund, King of the Gep'i-dae, and made a goblet of his skull. Likewise, he took to wife the dead King's daughter, Rosamund. Then turning ambitious eyes from the Danube to Italy, he led his hordes over the Alps, seizing on land in Italy, which is still called the plain of Lombardy. But in the midst of his wars, he was killed by his outraged queen.

"While he sat in merriment at a banquet in Verona, with the cup which he had made of the head of his father-in-law," reports Paul, the Lombard historian, "he ordered it given the Queen, and invited her to drink merrily with her father.

Celebrating the conquest of Italy, the boisterous King Al'boin forces Queen Rosamund to drink from a goblet made from her father's skull. Paul the Deacon (720-790 A.D.), who wrote *The History of the Lombards*, saw this goblet.

Gold mounting of a horse-collar with barbaric animal designs. Grave of a Lombard chieftain buried 600 A. D.

"Then Rosamund, hearing this, conceived in her heart a deep anguish. Straightway she felt herself burn to revenge the death of her father by the murder of her husband, and she presently formed a plot with Hel-mech′is, the King's squire. While Al′boin was sunk in his noon-day sleep, she ordered silence in the palace. Removing all other arms, she bound his sword fast to his bed, and let in Helmechis, the murderer. Alboin, suddenly roused, perceived the evil which threatened and reached his hand for his sword. This being tightly tied, he found he could not draw; yet did he seize a foot-stool and defend himself for a time. But unfortunately, alas! this most warlike and very brave man, being helpless against his enemy, was slain as if he had been a person of no account; and perished through the scheming of one little woman alone."

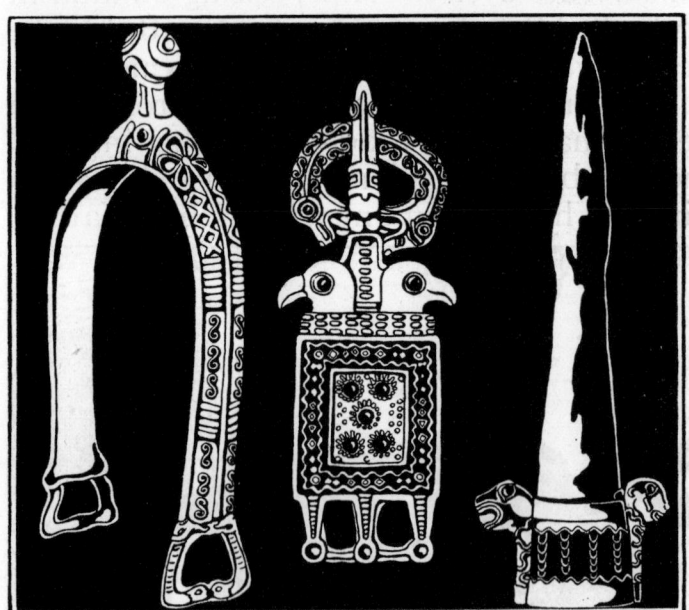

Other Lombard objects like those worn by the warriors of Alboin. Left, heavy gold spur, the knob engraved to represent eyes. Center, gold buckle with bird and animal designs, and a jeweled plate. Right, iron spear-head mounted to the wooden shaft by a band of red enamel and gold, carved into dragon heads like those from the Oseberg ship, and showing the Lombards as Nordic barbarians. (See p. 220.) All objects on pages 158 and 159 came from the same grave of a Lombard chieftain. Durlacher Brothers, London; exhibited at Burlington Fine Arts Club, London.

THE BYZANTINE EMPIRE

The death of Alboin, however, did not end the Lombard conquests. Soon the Byzantine Empire retained only one patch of land in Italy's heel and toe, and one broad belt that extended through Ravenna and Rome. Yellow-haired Lombard Kings, crowned with their famous Iron Crown, now ruled over most of Italy.

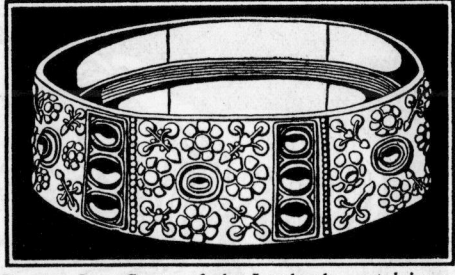

Famous Iron Crown of the Lombards, containing a circlet said to be a nail of the True Cross. (Monza.)

Meantime, Hun-like horsemen, the A'vars, threatened the Eastern Empire and Slavs roved down from Russia, into Greece and the Balkans. The Slavs belonged to the brown-haired, gray-eyed Alpine race which was known for its round bullet heads, and in their westward migration they had followed in the wake of the Germans. They were a pastoral people holding property in common, and they worshiped Sva'to-vit, god of light, and Trig'lath, a three-headed god. In vain did the Byzantine emperors try to stop these invaders. The Balkans soon fell to the Slavs.

Gold and enamel collar showing a Lombard chief and his warriors. The chief has the long beard which gave the Win'ni-li their name Lombard. According to legend, the Winnili once fought the Vandals, and Woden, besought by the Vandals, promised victory to those whom he saw first at dawn; but Frigga, Woden's wife, bade the Winnili women arrange their long hair like beards, and stand with their husbands in the east. Woden, greeting the sun, saw them first and cried: "Who are these *Long-Beards?*" thus giving to the Winnili both victory and their name.

Siberian ornament of a fight between a tiger and a fantastic animal. Probably Slavic. The style is heavy but powerful, and alive with movement. (Leningrad.)

"The year 581," wrote John of Eph'e-sus, "was famous for the invasion of the accursed people called Sla-vo'ni-ans, who overran Greece, and the country by Thes'-sa-lon'i-ca, and all Thrace, and captured the land and settled in it by force.

Slavs in the Balkan Peninsula! Lombards in Italy! And now new trouble arose. Chos-roes' II of Persia came sweeping through Asia Minor. Damascus and Jerusalem fell! The Persians slew 90,000 Christians! They took the wood of the "True Cross," acquired by Constantine's mother from Jerusalem to Persia, while the Persian King wrote insulting letters to Constantinople, taunting the Emperor there: "Do not deceive yourself with the vain hope in that Christ, who was not even able to save himself from the Jews!"

Christians were horrified! All from the least to the greatest, felt bound to make one supreme effort to beat back the Persian fire-worshipers and recover Palestine. The Emperor Her-a-cli'us vowed to take the field in person while the churches sent their treasures to pay the expenses of the war.

Siberian horsemen, probably Slavs, return from a victorious raid, each leading a captured horse. An enemy's head hangs from the leader's horse. (Leningrad.)

Here, in spirit, was the first of the crusades. Wrought up to a very high pitch of religious enthusiasm, the army marched out to save Christendom, to conquer the Holy Places and to bring back the "True Cross!"

In six successful campaigns, Heraclius saved the half-ruined Eastern Empire. He cleared Asia Minor of enemies, and

Persian gryphon relief from the statue of Chos-roes' II at Taki-i-bostan; a common textile design.

though Byzantium was besieged by 80,000 Avars and Slavs, he left the garrison there to save the capital-city, and remaining in the East continued to lay waste the land. At length the Persians, disgusted, threw their King into prison, and the new King they raised to the throne sued to the Emperor for peace, agreeing to return the "True Cross," with all the lands and captives taken in the war. Thus in 628 A.D., this first crusade came to an end. But a new power was just then arising in the East, a power which was destined to threaten the entire world of Christendom. In the very midst of his victories, Heraclius received a letter from an unknown Arabian prophet. The fellow styled himself Mo-ham'med, and called on all the kings of the earth to embrace his new religion, the great religion of Islam, of Allah, the one God.

Exquisite Persian tapestry of the 6th cent., showing a design of mounted archers and animals. (Cologne.)

IV
A New Power Arises in the East

Mohammed, the Camel-driver of Mecca
(570 A.D.—632 A.D.)

Arabia, vast, mysterious, enwrapped in silence and solitude, had slumbered through the ages, cut off from the rest of the world. The armies of the nations for many generations marched along her frontiers without disturbing her sleep. But a trump was about to sound. Arabia was to awake. All her scattered tribes, wandering the glittering sands, divided by hatreds and feuds, were about to find a leader. In the desert-city of Mecca, the orphan boy, Mo-ham'med, was tending his uncle's sheep; and the wide expanse of the desert, the free air which he breathed, the loneliness of the silences were breeding within him visions, energies, and powers.

His venerable old grandfather had been a wealthy man; but worldly goods were scarce in the household of his uncle, the worthy A'bu Ta'lib. By day Mohammed tended his sheep; by night in the caravansary he listened to camel-drivers who squatted around the fire, telling tales in the flickering shadows, tales of the Persians, the Christians, the Arabs, and the Jews. Mecca lay forty-five miles inland from the Red Sea, and her caravans journeyed from Persia northward into Syria. Many a time Mohammed watched long strings of camels file out the city-gate, their riders perched high among saddle-bags, and muffled to the eyes against the chill morning air.

A long string of pert, double-humped camels such as Mo-ham'med often saw. Persian tapestry, 10th cent. (Louvre.)

In the center of the city, above the flat-roofed, mudhouses that glistened white in the sun, rose the sacred Kaa'ba, or Cube, the holiest shrine of the nation, a curious, tall, square building, mysteriously draped in black. This Kaaba, tradition said, had been founded by the patriarch, Abraham; for as the Jews, through Isaac, called Abraham their father, so many Arabs said that they, too, were children of Abraham through Ishmael, that elder son whom Abraham sent to the desert in the days when Isaac was born. Mohammed's kindly grandfather, who had taken charge of the child when his fair young mother died, often spread a rug for the boy beneath the shadow of the Kaaba.

The Kaaba, center of worship at Mecca, draped with black cloth and containing idols, and the small, reddish-black stone from heaven, which the Arabians had worshiped for many generations. (Persian manuscript.)

And how strange were the thoughts of the child as he stared at that house of idols. In days long past, his grandfather had thought to sacrifice his best loved son, Ab-dul'lah, later Mohammed's father, to the gods who dwelt in the Kaaba; but the holy voice of the sanctuary had bidden him sacrifice a hundred camels instead! How nearly those gods of the Kaaba had claimed his father's life! Three hundred and sixty stone idols, one for each day in the year, stood solemnly ranged in the shrine around the great god Hob'al, carved of glistening red agate, the two stags of gold and silver, and the images of Abraham and Ishmael, his son.

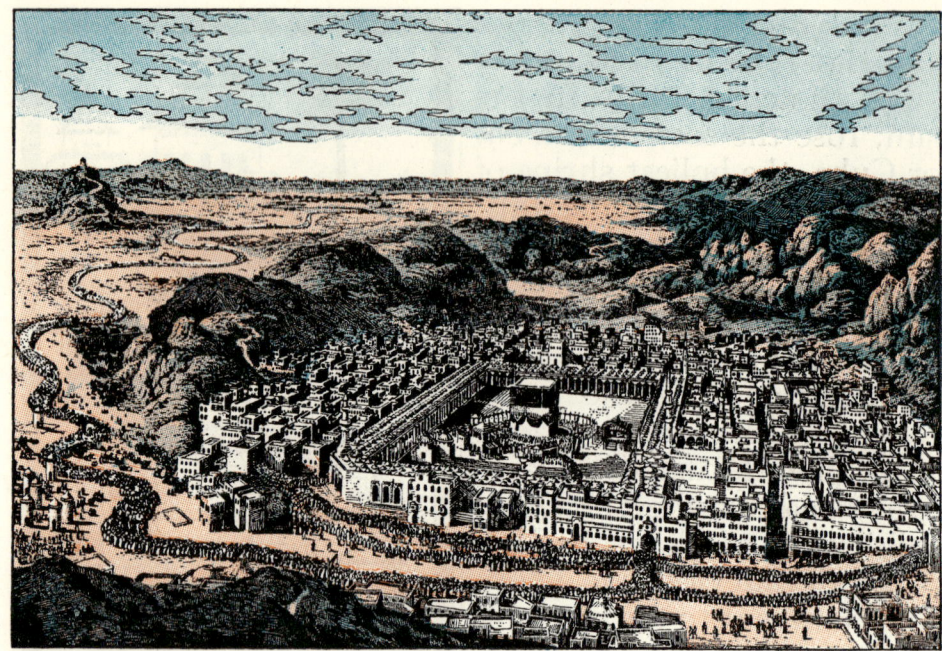

The annual pilgrimage to Mecca. So great is the throng, that worshipers gather in a long line far across the desert, and patiently await their turn to perform the prescribed rites, at the holy Kaaba. (Old Engraving.)

Here to the great square Kaaba, the tribes came year by year, to kiss the sacred black stone, which had fallen from heaven long ago in the primeval days of Adam, and to walk stripped naked, seven times around the temple itself. Four months of the year were sacred months to the Arabs; caravans might then travel without fear of thieving Bed′ou-ins, and hostile tribes camped peacefully side by side at the wells. These were the months of pilgrimage, when every man bent his steps towards Mecca to visit the shrine. Then Mecca awoke to new life. The wild desert tribes swarmed in. Trade and business flourished. Hides, and camels or horses, and bunches of golden dates were exchanged for cloth or weapons. At night there were drunken orgies, dancing girls, gaming, brawls. And when all business was ended, each sheik collected his tribe and vanished into the desert.

A NEW POWER

They were wild fellows, those Bedouins, vehement, fiery, impulsive, reckless of human life. Save in the sacred months, they swooped down on their swift horses and plundered the caravans. They did not think it wrong to rob, to plunder, to kill, and their women led miserable lives. They married as many as they chose, and divorced them when they chose, turned the poor things out when they were old and helpless, and often left them to starve. They did not like their girl babies, and buried many alive. Moreover, they worshiped the grossest gods,—a stone, a beast, a plant, a camel, a palm, a gazelle; and though they were proud and bold, they wasted their courage and strength on family or tribal feuds, forever at war with each other. The heart of Mohammed was sad. He was sensitive to human suffering. There was much in his world that was wrong, much he would like to set right.

He grew up a trustworthy youth, and when he was twenty years old, a wealthy kinswoman, Khadija, (Ka-dee'ja) a handsome and kindly widow, engaged him to ride with her caravans and direct the selling of her merchandise in the great world far away. Then a new life dawned for Mohammed,—travel, adventure, strange places, strange people, strange customs, strange faiths. Over and over again he heard Jew and Christian tell Bible tales, as he had when he was a boy in the caravansary of Mecca. He heard tales concerning one God till his mind was imbued with the thought,—not all those gods of the Kaaba, those solemn dead stone idols, but one God and one alone.

Young Mohammed reports to the widow Khadija, who, ten years his senior, soon becomes his wife.

In the world he saw in his travels three great religions held sway,—Judaism, Christianity, and the teachings of Zo'ro-as'ter. Pure they had all been once when their first great teachers taught them. Those simple, yellow-haired Nordics, the primitive Persian tribes, when they came down out of the north into the highlands of Persia, had held a pure and exalted faith in one beneficent God, A'hu-ra Maz'da, or Or'-muzd, Lord of Life and Truth, who was symbolized by light. Evil they had believed, was but the deceits of Ah'ri-man against whose lies men must fight until he was overcome. But oriental luxury, the stifling pleasure-seeking of Medes and Babylonians had degraded the pure Persian faith as taught by Zoroaster. Soon Ormuzd, the all-good, was swallowed up in A'shur, winged warrior with his bow; and the holy flames kindled by Zoroaster in the inner soul of man, the seeking for spiritual light, the wrestling with darkness and evil, were swallowed up by material flames, the Chaldean worship of fire, of the sun, the moon, and the stars.

To the mind of Mohammed the same thing had happened in Christianity. Jesus had taught a religion of love and trust in the goodness of God; but his followers were wrangling and quarreling, and persecuting each other. Moreover, Mohammed decided that Christians believed in three gods;* some said this Trinity was Father, Son, and Holy Ghost, some said it was God, Jesus, and Mary, but to the mind of Mohammed they had departed from one God. Abraham, Moses, Jesus, all had been great teachers but men had not listened to them. To Mohammed the ideal religion seemed to be Judaism, divested of ceremonial, plus Christianity divested of the doctrines over which men quarreled.

*In the Ko-ran', Sura V: verse 77, Mohammed says: "They surely are infidels who say: 'God is a third of three;' for there is no God but one God." In Sura IV, verse 169, he says: "The Messiah, son of Mary, is only an apostle of God. Believe, therefore, in God and his apostles, and say not: 'There is a Trinity.' Forbear!... God is only one God." See also Sura V: 116, 117 and Sura III: 73. In Sura II, verse 209, Mohammed says: "Mankind was but one people; and God sent prophets to announce glad tidings and to warn them, and He sent down with them the Book of Truth (the Bible), that it might decide the disputes of men, yet none disputed like those to whom the Book had been sent; for they were filled with jealousy of each other."

Mohammed's diplomacy. The Kaaba having been rebuilt, the chiefs contended for the honor of replacing the sacred stone. Mohammed had each carry a part of a cloak bearing it. (Jami 'al-Tawarikh MS., 1314, Edinburgh.)

He pondered much on these things, and from a shy, awkward lad, the young caravan-conductor slowly blossomed forth into a self-contained man. Soon Kha-di'ja noticed that his black hair was thick and curling, and his dark eyes could melt into dreams or flash with sudden fire. More and more she found herself looking forward eagerly to the youth's return from his journeys. What difference did it make that she was ten years his senior, and a widow with three children? Was she not still beautiful, and had she not plenty to offer a poor young camel-driver? She spoke to Mohammed gently when he came to her with reports, and she strove to break down the wall that rose between mistress and servant. But the young man was proud and reserved. She was his social superior, his mistress, his employer. He felt for her awe and respect. Then Khadija openly sent a slave to offer him her hand. Mohammed could scarcely believe that his lady had so condescended; but he gravely agreed to her offer, and the two were married and settled down in Khadija's spacious home.

And now for the first time in his life, the orphaned cameldriver was the master of a house, a splendid house, with a garden and a shady covered walk where he could promenade or sit to enjoy his leisure. Moreover, he and Khadija were very happy together. Mohammed loved his wife, and his marriage brought him that repose and freedom from daily toil which he needed for meditation. Three sons and four daughters were born, but the sons all died in infancy and Fa'ti-mah, the youngest daughter, became her father's pet. The Lady of Paradise, the Lady of Light he called her. And as he had no sons, he adopted his cousin A'li, son of A'bu Ta'lib, and he freed and likewise adopted Za'id, a prisoner of war, whom a relative had given to Khadija as a slave.

Thus for fifteen years Mohammed lived in Mecca, loved and respected by all. But the humdrum life of a merchant did not satisfy him. He must pierce the mysteries of life, of God, and of creation. He must find a way to correct the evils he saw about him,—the ignorant superstitions, the lawlessness and cruelty, the gambling, the drinking, and the terrible blood-feuds. Often he went to meditate in a cave on nearby Mt. Hira, a huge, barren rock that stood out solitary and shadowless, in the full white blazing glare of the pitiless desert sun. In the still hours of the night, in the calmness of early dawn, he was often alone in the cave, plunged in profoundest thought, deep in communion with that unseen yet all pervading Mind that speaks to the listening soul in every corner of the earth. Slowly heaven and earth seemed for him filled with visions. On a night of power and glory, when all nature seemed lifted up to the peace of the starlit heavens, a voice seemed to cry to Mohammed, surging like waves of the sea. Twice he struggled against it and did not answer its call. "Cry!" called the voice a third time, and an answer was wrung from Mohammed. "What shall I cry?" The answer came to him clearly: "Cry in the name of the Lord!"

The angel Gabriel appears to Mohammed. (Persian MS., 1314 A.D., Edinburgh University.) The inspiration of all great men has been, and is today, the perfectly natural experience of sincere and uplifted thought. Though it differs greatly in quantity, it is the same in quality with the least inspiration to good, beautiful or useful work, which fires the thought and ambition of the humblest man, woman or child. To many men, such experiences have doubtless been so vivid as to appear as objective visions.

When Mohammed came to himself, he hurried home to his wife. "O Khadija!" he cried. "I have become a soothsayer or one possessed or mad!" But Khadija calmly replied: "God will surely not let such a thing happen to thee; for thou speakest the truth, dost not return evil for evil, art of a good life and kind. What has befallen thee?"

Then Mohammed told how an angel had appeared that night unto him and Khadija straightway answered: "Thou wilt be a prophet unto this people." Thereupon she rose and sought out her blind old cousin who knew the Jewish and the Christian Scriptures. "Holy! Holy!" the blind man cried when he had heard her story: "Verily, this is the messenger who came aforetime to Moses! Mohammed will be a prophet!"

There followed for Mohammed three years of mental conflict; his soul was in a ferment. For a time no more visions came; Khadija alone consoled him. She kept alive his hope when no man believed in him, not even Mohammed himself.

Fragments of disjointed truth, based on Christianity and Judaism partly understood, burst from his fervent heart, pictures of heaven and hell, threats of a day of Judgment, denunciations of woe, and promises of delight for believers and the faithful, impassioned but earnest utterances, given forth in eloquent rhyme. Mohammed was now the poet, the dreamer, the visionary. He believed that he was fulfilling all that had been taught by Abraham, Moses, and Jesus.

"In the name of God, the Compassionate, the Merciful!" he cried. "By the noon-day brightness, by the night when she spreadeth her veil, by the star-bespangled heaven, by the day revealing his glory, believe that God is one! God is the hearing, the knowing, the pardoning, the rich, the powerful, the vast, the wise, the gracious! All in heaven and earth is God's. God is a sufficient protection!"*

His adopted sons, A'li and Za'id, next took up his faith, then A'bu Bak'r, the merchant, a prudent and vigorous man, and more and more other disciples. Slowly the dreamer and visionary became the warner and teacher. The poet became the missionary, urging no difficult doctrines, but giving an ignorant people definite, clear-cut commands:

"God is one God, Allah. There is no God but God. Men are the servants of God, the humble obedient servants. Islam means *obedience*, obedience to God, and Moslem means obedience, one who is obedient. Satan would tempt you to evil, but do not hearken to Satan. Do not drink wine, nor gamble; do not murder your children. Cease blood feuds, and deal kindly with orphans, dumb beasts and slaves. The great virtues are prayer and fasting, alms-giving, making pilgrimages, and obedience to the Ko-ran'.

*For Mohammed, the poet and dreamer, see early Suras of the Meccan period, Koran, translated by J. M. Rodwell.

A NEW POWER

Refuse to bow down to dumb idols! Obey God, Mohammed, His prophet, and the Koran, His book, and you will go to heaven; but if you disobey, you will surely go to hell."

Heaven and hell were both distinct and definite places. Hell was a place of fire, and heaven was a beautiful garden beneath whose shade rivers flow, a paradise with everything to delight the heart of an Arab, food, wines, and beautiful maidens, with bright eyes like hidden pearls.

> On that day shall they be thrust with thrusting into the fire of hell, . . .
> But mid gardens and delights shall they dwell who have feared God.
> Eat and drink with healthy enjoyment in recompense for your deeds.
> On couches ranged in rows shall they recline, and to the damsels with large dark eyes will we wed them.*

As followers thronged to Mohammed and forsook the idols of Mecca, the priests of the Kaaba protested. The traders, too, cried out. Mohammed's religion might destroy the thriving business of Mecca, if pilgrims no more came to visit the gods of the Kaaba. The prophet's own tribe, the Ko-reish', began to persecute him. His followers were thrown into prison, starved, or beaten with sticks, and exposed in the heat of the day to the burning sun of the desert. Some were even killed with excruciating torments. Mohammed himself was spared because men respected his uncle, but his heart was torn for his followers. For a moment he recanted and said it was no sin to worship the gods of Mecca. But immediately he repented and cried out that he had sinned. The Meccan gods were powerless. God alone was God.

Persecutions began anew. Mohammed and his followers were besieged in a narrow defile on the eastern outskirts of Mecca, and almost starved to death before a reconciliation was at last effected. And now both Khadija and Abu Talib died. No more would Mohammed's wife be by his side to encourage him. No more would his uncle protect him.

*See the Koran, Suras III and LVI. Definite conceptions of heaven and hell as places, came from Zoroaster.

The Moslem Paradise. A beautiful garden and the winged houris who attend good Moslems at death. The Houri Princess sits in a tree pavilion and a demon watches below. Heaven and Hell were not states of mind to Mohammed as they were to Jesus. To Jesus, Heaven, both here and hereafter, was the rich and expansive joy of goodness; Hell was the hideous mental suffering of sin; but to Mohammed, Heaven and Hell were real and definite places to which men went after death. Persian painting (1400 A.D. Sarre Collection, Berlin).

A dejected and broken man, he tried in vain to win converts on the oasis of Taif and was only given permission to return again to Mecca, on condition that he would not preach to the people of the town. Henceforth, he preached to strangers,—the traders and the pilgrims; but so eloquently did he speak that he gained certain converts from Yath'rib, a city which from of old had been a rival of Mecca. At last the elders of Yathrib invited him to come and take refuge in their town.

Mecca was in a ferment. His secret plans became known. Never could the men of Mecca let him establish himself on the path of their northbound caravans! They formed a plot to kill him. But no one family would bring on itself the danger of a blood-feud by committing the crime alone; so men from all families were chosen to strike him at the same time. All night they stood at his door, watching the man on his bed, but at dawn they found themselves tricked; the man on the bed was Ali.

A NEW POWER 131

Mohammed had fled through a window, and together with Abu Bakr, he had made his way to the desert. The men of Mecca were furious. A price was placed on his head. Horsemen scoured the desert and came so near his cave, that the heart of old Abu Bakr quaked with fear. "We are but two," he said, "against a multitude." But Mohammed straightway replied: "Nay, not two, but three; for Allah is with us!" For days Abu Bakr's daughter brought food to the cave. Then, procuring two camels, they made their way to Yath'-rib, whither they arrived in the year 622. With this flight, the *He-gi'ra*, the Moslem era began and Moslems still date all records from the time of the Hegira, as Christian records are dated from the year of the birth of Christ.

Once arrived in Yathrib, Mohammed began to preach and to win so many converts that the name of the city was changed from Yathrib to Me-di'na (the city of the prophet).

Mohammed preaches and his hearers listen in rapt attention, while Satan stands by helpless. (Persian miniature, Collection of Percy Sykes.) So sacred was Mohammed that his features were not painted, but covered with a white veil. Satan was as definite a person, and Hell as actual a place to Mohammed as were Heaven and the winged damsels called angels. So had they been to Zoroaster, and so they were to early Christians. (See Sura IV:42.)

"Prayer is better than sleep! Allah is great!" Thus a voice chanted every morning at sunrise. It was Bi'lal, Mohammed's gaunt, black, African servant, crying from the top of Mohammed's mosque and summoning the faithful to the first prayers of the day. They were not obliged to come to the mosque, unless the day was Friday. During the rest of the week, they might pray wherever they were, prostrating themselves before God five times in the twenty-four hours when Bilal cried from his tower; but on Fridays they came to the mosque; for Friday was the day when Mohammed arrived in Medina, and Friday was to the Moslems what the Sabbath was to the Jews, or Sunday to the Christians. The mosque was a great bare hall with neither benches nor pews. Here in the center of the room Mohammed preached from a pulpit around which his audience stood.

While Kha-di'ja had lived, Mohammed had married no other wives. He was fifty when she died, but now he made many marriages to bind his followers to him, to care for the widows of disciples who had lost their lives for Islam, and in hope of having a son. He married little Ay'e-sha, seven years old, the daughter of Abu Bakr; Sau'da, the fat and middle-aged widow, whose husband had died for Islam; Haf'sa, the daughter of Omar, fiery-tempered, whom none of his friends would wed. In all, he married twelve wives. The time was not yet ripe to do away with polygamy, the wedding of more than one wife; for Mohammed was giving his message to a semi-barbarous race. All he could do at present was to issue commands which might improve women's lives.

"Let women inherit property," he said; "and let a man marry no more than four wives. Do not divorce your wives easily. Try to make up quarrels and differences, but if you must divorce them, treat them with generosity." He did not order that women should live shut up in seclusion; but for their own protection, he counseled that they live in privacy.

A NEW POWER

"Men are superior to women," he wrote, "on account of the qualities with which God hath gifted the one above the other. Chide those for whose refractoriness ye have cause to fear. Remove them into chambers apart and beat them; but if they are obedient, seek not occasion against them." (Sura iv:38.)

And now he who had been first the visionary, the earnest seeker for truth, second, the admonisher and teacher, became at last the legislator, the warrior and the dictator, the founder of a new movement, using other weapons than the pen of the poet and scribe. The earnestness of those convictions which at Mecca had sustained him under all persecutions, stiffened at Medina into tyranny and violence. The men of Mecca had forced him to take up the sword in self-defense. He used it now as aggressor, persuading himself that all who refused to acknowledge Allah, and Mohammed as Allah's prophet, were worthy only to die. He began to incite his followers against their fellow-Arabs, and many were the skirmishes with caravans from Mecca.

At first Mohammed had hoped that Jews and Christians would unite under the faith of Islam; but he had long ago learned that Jews and Christians despised him. As his power increased in Arabia, he sent letters to the Emperor Her-a-cli'us and six other rulers of the East: "In the name of Allah, the Merciful. From the Apostle of Allah ... I summon thee with the appeal of Islam: become a Moslem and thou shalt be safe. God shall give thee thy reward twofold. And if ye decline, then bear witness that we are Moslems!"

The *Fatiha*, or Opening Sura of the Koran in Arabic.
Praise be to God, the Lord of creation,
The most merciful, the most compassionate!
Ruler of the day of Reckoning!
Thee we worship, and invoke for help.
Lead us in the straight path;
The path of those toward whom Thou hast been gracious;
Not of those against whom Thy wrath is kindled, or that walk in error.

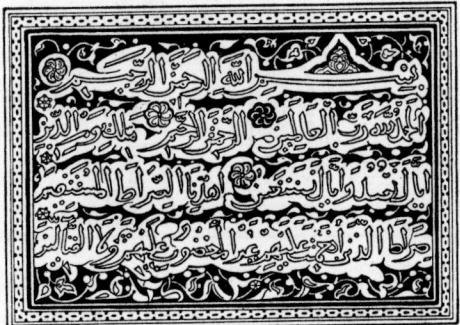

The ill-written scrawl caused much merriment in the palace of Her-a-cli′us and made a good story for the soldiers to repeat in the taverns of Constantinople. Chos-roes′, the King of Persia, tore his copy up in a fit of violent rage; the governor of Alexandria sent back a polite refusal, but added presents to soften his answer,—a slave-girl, a horse, a mule; while a powerful Arabian chief, according to common gossip, used his copy to patch a hole in a worn-out water-bottle!

Mohammed now commanded: "Slay the infidels!" Gone was the gentleness that had marked his preaching in former days. Gone was his old confidence in the power of abstract truth. At Mecca he had declared: "We hurl the truth against falsehood, and truth crashes into falsehood so that falsehood vanishes." But now in Medina he hurled armies instead of truth. "Let those then fight in the cause of God who barter this present life for that which is to come;" he cried, "for whoever fighteth on God's path, whether he be slain or conquer, God will in the end give him a great reward!" (Sura iv:76)

A castle surrenders to Mohammed. (Persian MS., Ca. 1314 A.D. Royal Asiatic Society.) Mohammed the Dreamer, has now become Mohammed the Warrior, and Islam a Gospel of the Sword. The Moslem commandment is not "Thou shalt not kill"; but "Thou shalt not kill a *believer*." To kill an infidel was a virtue. The weakest part of Mohammed's ethics was that a Moslem was obligated to do good only to another Moslem, and not to all men; but in general, the moral tone of Mohammed's teachings was high, and it was his followers who corrupted it.

At last, after eight years of warfare with caravans from Mecca, Mecca itself was taken, and Mohammed returned in state to the town that had driven him out. He announced that henceforth all good Moslems must make a pilgrimage to Mecca once in every year. Medina remained his capital, but Mecca became the religious center of all Mohammedanism, the very heart of Islam.

A federation of tribes still resisted Mohammed; but again he was victorious, and smashed the idol of the Bedouins. Thus he gradually brought the greater part of Arabia over to the faith of Islam. His teachings were clear and definite;

A caravan of Moslem pilgrims on their annual journey to Mecca, the religious center of Mohammedanism. (Persian manuscript. 1500 A.D. British Museum.)

simple warriors could understand them. He held up no perfect ideal as Jesus had done in Judea, but he offered improved beliefs to make men's lives much better. He taught that God is one with sincere and fervent faith; and in suppressing idolatries and the grossest of superstitions, in abolishing child-murder, drunkenness, and gambling, in reducing the number of wives men might have, in discouraging divorce, counseling kindness to animals, to women, and to slaves, he did much for his people, and gave the inspiration which in another century made these half-savage Arabs, world-leaders in culture and learning. When he died at the age of sixty-two, he had united the desert tribes, and become not only the undisputed religious head of a people but the actual ruler of the Arabs.

A Coptic woman. From a painted border in an Egyptian church probably built in the 6th century. The native Egyptians whom the Arabs conquered are still called Copts. They became Christians under Roman rule and maintained a very definite civilization. Today Arabs far out-number native Egyptians in Egypt, and present-day Egypt is thoroughly Arabic. The only actual descendants of the race who founded the Nile civilization are the Copts.

Mohammed was succeeded as head of the Moslem community by the first of the Caliphs,* A'bu Bak'r. Abu Bakr, ordered Mohammed's adopted son, Zaid, who had been the prophet's scribe, to collect all Mohammed's sayings which had never been gathered together during Mohammed's life. From every quarter of the desert, from date leaves, bits of skin, or shoulder blades of sheep, wherever men had written them, the words were collected and the Koran was made.

East, west, and north of Arabia were lands where infidels dwelled. There were souls to be won for Allah, riches for His servants, and Paradise with fair damsels as the last reward for all warriors! Hordes of fierce-eyed Bedouins polished their spears in the sand and groomed their fleet horses in rhythm to chantings from the Koran. And they made of Mohammed's teachings a gospel of the sword. Under the rule of Omar, the second of the Caliphs, the Arabs conquered Syria, Palestine, Assyria, Babylon, and Egypt. They swarmed into the lands of the Nile, far outnumbering the Copts, as the native Egyptians were called. Persia stoutly resisted, but Persia likewise fell before the fanatical fury of the invaders.

*The word "caliph" in Arabic means successor or vice-regent, and the caliphs were both kings and high priests.

A NEW POWER

The Moslems did not force their religion on these conquered peoples. They offered them the choice of paying a large money-tribute or accepting Mohammedanism. Syrian Christians readily accepted the faith of the Prophet; but the sturdy Persian fire-worshipers came more slowly and reluctantly into the Moslem fold. Omar succeeded in making the Arabs a nation of warriors, supported by the taxes collected from conquered peoples and under the following Caliphs the conquests of the Moslems went on uninterruptedly. Clear across Northern Africa swept their victorious hosts till they reached the Atlantic Ocean. There, their impulsive leader spurred his horse chest-deep in the surging, crested waves. "Almighty Lord," he cried; "but for this sea I would have gone into still remoter regions, spreading the glory of thy name and smiting thine enemies!"

But the sea did not check the Arabs. From the Pillars of Hercules, they looked with covetous eyes over fourteen miles of sea to where the Visigoths dwelt on the rocky coast of Spain.

Vis′i-goth′ic king and court. A manuscript illustration from Spain made during the reign of the Visigothic King, Chin′des-winth (642-652). Although representing Pharaoh in his palace, the architecture, costumes, arms, etc., are taken from familiar Visigothic objects. The Visigoths drew largely upon Byzantine civilization, and their succession of delicate arches raised on pillars was used by the Mohammedan conquerors in the Alhambra and elsewhere.

Roderick, the Last of the Visigoths

Bejeweled gold crown of the Visigothic King Rec-cens'winth (649-72). The King's name is formed by letters on chains. (Found at Toledo, Spain, now in the Cluny Museum. Paris.)

Long years in the pleasant land of Spain, with sunshine, slaves, and luxury, had weakened the once stout hearts of the savage Visigoths. Life was sweet under Spanish skies, and poison, bred of idleness, entered into their veins. Having no common enemy they fought with one another and when the Moslems drew near, many people in Spain wished they would cross the Straits. Celtic peasants on the farms had been ground down by taxes; native Iberians hated the Goths, and hundreds of Jewish merchants lived in fear of their lives; for the Christian rulers of Spain had ordered that every Jew should either be baptized or die, and naturally to the Jews, the Arabs appeared as deliverers.

While Tar'ik, the brave young officer who led the Moslem host, watched for the proper chance to cross the straits into Spain, the Gothic throne fell vacant. The old King, Wit'i-za, was slain and the nobles setting aside A'chi-la, his son, elected as ruler Don Roderick*, whose father had been the king till Witiza seized the throne. Achila fled to Africa, taking refuge with the Christian Count, Julian, ruler of the province of Ceu'ta, who hated young Roderick cordially, since common gossip said that Roderick had wooed and deserted the lovely young daughter of the Count.

*The title "Don" is an anachronism; it was not used until centuries later; but Roderick is always Don in the legends.

Forgetting aught but their hate, Julian and the fugitive Prince invited Tarik and his Moslems to enter Spain by their sides and overthrow King Roderick. Preparing a fleet of vessels, they crossed the narrow straits in 711 A. D. and landed under the shadow of the great Rock of Gebel Tarik.* The doomed Goths watching them come:

> Saw the dark blue waters flash before
> Their ominous way and whiten round their keels;
> Their swarthy myriads darkening o'er the sands;
> Their banners flaunting to the sun and breeze.
> Fair shone the sun upon their proud array:
> White turbans, glittering armor, shields engrailed
> With gold, and scimeters of Syrian steel.*

The sons of the Prophet had come! Islam was in Spain.

Now it chanced that Roderick himself was fighting far in the North. Ben'ci-us, his faithful cousin, hastily gathered an army and advanced to meet the invaders; but his army was slain to a man. Hurrying down from the North, Roderick rallied his Goths and advanced within sight of the foe.

Roderick marches to meet the invading Moslems. The Visigoths are yellow-haired, blue-eyed Nordics, although the army also contains some dark-haired Iberians of the Mediterranean race. This trace of Nordic stock is still seen occasionally in modern Spain, and it is not unusual to find a real Spaniard who is blonde and blue-eyed.

*Gibraltar is from Gebel Tarik, meaning *Rock of Tarik*. The poem quoted is Southey's *Roderick, last of the Goths*.

Visigothic warriors with large shields and visor-helmets. (Stone relief. Provincial Museum, Seville, Spain.)

High in the mountains near Ca'diz there lies a lovely lake and there, by a little river, the rival camps were set, one on either bank. But while the hosts waited for battle, treason was abroad. Two of King Roderick's leaders, who had once been friends of Witiza, secretly agreed to desert with all their followers when the day of battle should come. On the fourth day the battle was joined. Amidst cries of "*Al'lah Ak'bar!*" the Moslems charged on their foes, while with cries of "Roderick and Victory," the Goths rushed forward to meet them. Long the two armies fought. But when the Goths were hard pressed, the traitors changed sides in the battle. There were cries of "Treason! Treason!" On all sides confusion arose; and Roderick's army slowly melted into the hills!

Thus Spain was won for Islam. Some say that Roderick was slain; others say that he fled and was drowned while crossing a river, but the best-loved legend affirms that he never died at all, and that when the Christians of Spain are hard beset by their enemies, they need only call on Roderick, and lo! he appears in their midst!* They know him by his golden beard and his great horned, Gothic helmet and when his war-cry rings out, the foes of Spain always flee.

*A tomb discovered in the 9th cent. in Portugal, bears the inscription "Here lies Roderick, King of the Goths."

A NEW POWER

After this great victory, the conquest of Spain was easy. The Moslem chieftains parcelled out the land among themselves and established numerous strong kingdoms where their descendants built up a wonderful Moorish culture, which was to make Arabic Spain the center of civilization during all the Middle Ages.

The conquest of Spain, however, was not sufficient for the Arabs. Soon they scaled the snow-capped heights of the rugged Pyrenees, and were gazing down with envy over the pleasant meadows and fair lands of Gaul below. Hidden in those fertile valleys were monasteries filled with treasures, with gold and silver and jewels; and the eyes of the Moslems glittered as they thought of the plunder ahead.

Tarik was recalled to Arabia; but his captain, Ab'dur Rah'man, led the Moslems down through the rocky, difficult gorges into the rich lands of Gaul. The ruins of many a monastery smoked dismally in his wake, while saddle-bags grew heavy with the weight of jeweled crucifixes and ornaments of gold. It seemed as if nothing could stop the army of the Prophet. But at last, in the heart of Gaul, the Moslems came face to face with a strong Germanic race, the Franks.

Visigothic King in long robes renders justice on a throne before his castle. He is guarded by soldiers in knee boots, draped tunics, and characteristic egg-shaped Visigothic shields. Two Visigothic women in typical dress, one prostrate on the ground, make supplication before him. The scene, however, represents Solomon's judgment in Visigothic costume and settings. (A Visigothic chest with angular Germanic carving. Demotte Collection, Paris.)

V
The Franks
Clovis, Founder of the French Nation
(481 A.D.—511 A.D.)

The Franks had been among the last of the restless barbarian tribes to invade the old Roman Empire. For centuries they had lived as simple German tribesmen in their reed huts on the Rhine. Smooth-faced, save for huge moustaches, and with red or flaxen hair, they were hardy and huge of stature, wearing knee-breeches and tunics girded with a leather belt, from which hung battle-axes, poniards, and toilet articles, such as scissors, or wooden combs. Unlike most other barbarians, the Franks did not move bag and baggage all in a single migration, to the distant lands of the South. Instead, as the power of the Western Empire gradually grew weaker, they drifted across into Gaul in numerous little bands, which would at times combine for mutual protection. The original Celtic-speaking Nordics, who had mingled with brown-haired Alpines and black-haired Mediterraneans, in the broad fertile lands of Gaul, had long since lost their vigor by contact with Rome. They accepted the Franks as masters, and agreed to pay them tribute in order to live in peace in their fine Gallo-Roman cities. But the Visigoths in Southern Gaul, the Burgundians in the east, and the Saxons in the northwest, did not so readily yield.

A delightfully awkward, Frankish warrior with scissors for cutting his hair, a huge sword, and a soldier's round flask. The decorative band over the figure's head ends in characteristically Frankish serpent-heads. (Frankish grave-stone.)

Yellow-haired barbarian Franks, from the western half of the Rhine, mix with dark-haired Gallo-Romans in the fine Roman cities of Gaul. The yellow-haired Celts who settled in Gaul had become intermixed with original black-haired Mediterraneans, brown-haired Alpines, and Romans; but the Franks were pure blonde Nordics.

Now the grandson of that Mer'o-veus who harried Attila's rear in the days of the great retreat, was the young Frankish chieftain, Clo'vis. Tall, straight, blue-eyed, and fair-skinned, he wore two long plaits of hair which hung down over his shoulders; for long hair among the Franks denoted nobility, and one of the titles they gave their chief, was always "the *long-haired* King." There were four "long-haired kings" in Gaul, when Clovis became chief of the Mer'o-vin'gi-an Franks; but all four kingdoms occupied only a small stretch of land which lay between the Rhine, the river Somme, and the sea. Calling for help on these other "long-haired kings" and kinsmen, Clovis determined to make the Franks the masters of all of Gaul; and attacking the lone Roman province which reached from the Somme to the Loire, he conquered the Gallo-Romans at the Battle of Sois-sons'.

The Franks Become Orthodox Christians

Worshipers of Thor and Woden, the Franks in these new-conquered lands, first came in contact with God as the Christians understood him, a God who desired humility and mercy, instead of bloodshed. Laughing at this God in scorn, they shook their battle-axes in salute to their bloody Thor, and fell like wolves on the spoils of monasteries and churches. But it chanced at this time that in Burgundy there dwelt a beautiful Christian princess who was called by the name of Clo-til'da. Her uncle, Gun'do-bald, had killed her father and mother in order to seize the throne, and he would have killed Clotilda, had she not fled for her life. When Clovis heard of her beauty, he sent messengers to Gundobald, demanding Clotilda's hand. Gundobald dared not refuse; he had no wish to bring the Franks like ravening wolves on his land. So Clotilda was sent to Soissons, and Clovis found her so gentle, that he loved her with all his heart.

Burgundian plaque showing Jesus entering Jerusalem; made soon after they became Christians. (5th cent.)

Most of Clotilda's kinsfolk had been converted by A'ri-an missionaries, but Clotilda was an Orthodox Christian; and from the first she determined to lead her husband, Clovis, away from his heathen gods. When a son was born to Clotilda, her husband rejoiced so exceedingly that he let the child be baptized. But the baby fell sick and died, and in his angry sorrow, Clovis turned on his wife. "You took our son and caused him to be baptized a Christian," he cried; "and behold he is dead! My gods are angry with me, and yours are not able to help us!" And he rushed off to further fighting to give his spirit relief. But when a second son was born, Clovis again in his joy, allowed the babe to be baptized, and Clotilda's heart was glad. But before many weeks had passed, little Chlo'do-mer too, fell sick, and seemed about to die. And now, like a mad thing, Clovis called down curses on his wife's God.

King Clovis with the long hair of royalty. (Statue on his tomb, at St. Genevieve.)

But Clotilda calmed her husband and besought him to be patient. As she prayed, the babe recovered, and in his great relief, Clovis began to think more kindly of her God.

When he was next at war with the stubborn Al'e-man'ni, and facing certain defeat, he remembered Clotilda's God. Having called in vain on his own gods, he determined to try her God and bargain for aid. "If thou wilt grant me victory over these foes," he cried, "I will believe in Thee, and will be baptized in Thy name; for I have called on my gods, but they are far from helping me."* Lo, while the King thus prayed, the tide of battle turned. The Al′e-man′ni lost heart and fled before the Franks; and Clovis decided that God must be more powerful than Thor!

Great was the joy of the Queen when Clovis returned and told her of his promise to her God, and many were the preparations for the baptism of the King. On Christmas Day of the year 496 A.D., Franks and Gauls gathered in thousands at the Christian church in Rheims. White hangings, tapestried canopies, and a hundred gleaming candles lent splendor to the scene, while incense sweetened the air, and the chanting of monks rose and fell. It was a setting well calculated to inspire tremendous awe in the hearts of the simple Franks. Behind the candle-bearers, and the sacred symbol of the cross, Clovis himself, clad in white, and followed by three thousand warriors, likewise clad in white, approached the old Bishop Re-mi′, who forthwith baptized the King and all his men.

Clovis is baptized by St. Remi and a bishop, while Queen Clotilda looks on. (Ivory diptych, Rigollot, Amiens.)
*History of the Franks, by Bishop Gregory of Tours (538-594) who knew personally of many of the events he related.

Following their leader's example, most of the Franks became Christians. Then their fortunes began to prosper. The bishops of Gaul supported them, and gave to their campaigns against Arian Burgundians, and Arian Visigoths, the sanction of crusades. Many Orthodox Gallo-Romans living in these heretic kingdoms, regarded Clovis as a God-sent deliverer. Thus, backed by Orthodox Christians, Clovis subdued the Burgundians and would have conquered all Gaul, had he not feared the power of Theodoric, the great Ostrogothic King who ruled in Italy.

So great had Clovis now made himself that the Emperor An-as-ta′ti-us in far away Constantinople did him the empty honor of creating him a consul, and sending him a diadem and the purple consular robes. Then Clovis took up his residence in a wooden palace which he built at Lu-te′ti-a on the Seine, a group of little mudhuts lying on an island in the river, and forming the rude beginnings of the mighty city of Paris.

Frankish king armed with the ancient *scramasax*, or sword-knife, although wearing a later costume of robe and crown. (9th cent. MS.)

But the robe of a Christian convert did not change the heart of Clovis. He was still both savage and cruel. Having conquered all his foes, he turned on his kinsmen and friends. Often had he been aided in war by his Mer′o-vin′-gi-an relatives, the long-haired kings of the Franks; but now he sent to Clo′der-ic, son of Siegbert the Lame, King of the Rhineland Franks, suggesting that Siegbert had grown so old that Cloderic ought to succeed him. Cloderic promptly slew his own father, and offered rich treasures to Clovis.

But the envoys of Clovis stabbed the young King; and Clovis, coming with an army, made himself King in his stead. Next, Clovis seized on Car'ar-ic, King of the Northern Franks, shut him and his son up in a monastery and afterward ordered them slain, pretending that they had not aided him in his war with the Gallo-Romans.

The third kinsman, the King of Cam-brai', being hated by his own people, was hauled before Clovis bound. Clovis indignantly cried: "Why have you disgraced your race? You were better dead than a prisoner!" And raising his battle-axe, the first Christian King of Frankland smote the helpless prisoner, so that he fell down dead. Then he cried out: "Alas! I am now left without a kinsman!"

"The Lord cast his enemies under his power," wrote Bishop Gregory, "because he walked with a right heart before Him, and did that which was pleasing in his sight!"

According to Frankish custom, the kingdom of Clovis at his death was divided among all his sons, and so developed into four separate Frankish states. In addition to the city of Paris, Au-stra'-si-a rose in the east with a wholly Frankish people; Neus'tri-a in the west, with Gallo-Roman inhabitants, and Burgundy along the river Rhone.

Gallo-Romans in Neus'tri-a rode in a modified Roman pleasure chariot, called the *carruca*. The vigorous Frankish conquerors, however, spurned such luxurious transportation and continued to ride only horses. (9th century MS., Brussels.)

THE FRANKS

Left and right, Frankish buckles; center, ring of Chil'der-ic, father of Clovis, with his long hair in two braids.

Mayors of the Palace, and "Do-Nothing" Kings

For nearly two hundred years, Merovingian kings ruled the three Frankish kingdoms, but they were unworthy descendants of their powerful forefather, Clovis. Giving themselves up to luxury, many died very young, leaving only infant sons to succeed them on the throne; yet such was the reverence still felt for the line of the great Meroveus, that the Franks put up with their useless kings, while real control slowly shifted to the important Mayors of the Palace.

"For many years," wrote a great Frankish writer,* "the house of the Merovings was destitute of vigor, and had nothing illustrious about it, save the empty name of King. For the rulers of their palace possessed both the wealth and the power of the kingdom, bearing the name of Mayor, and directing all matters of state. There was nothing for the King to do save to sit on the throne like the effigy of a ruler, hearing foreign envoys harangue him, and answering with words put into his mouth, while pretending to speak for himself. His royal name was profitless, and his allowance of revenue was at the discretion of the mayor; nor was there anything he could really call his own, save one royal manor of moderate value. There he kept his family, and his little band of servants. When he had to travel, he rode in a covered carriage drawn by oxen and driven by a rustic retainer."

*E'gin-hard, secretary to Charlemagne, writing about a hundred years after the events here chronicled.

Front and side views of the gold-bronze folding throne of Dag'o-bert, made by St. E'loi. (Bibliothèque Nationale.)

Men laughed at these weak Merovingians, and called them the "Do-Nothing-Kings." The only descendant of Clovis who showed any real vigor, was "Good-King Dagobert," who ruled all three Frankish kingdoms in 629 A.D. Dagobert waged successful wars, encouraged learning and art, revised the Frankish laws, and riding through his towns on horseback, he administered cases of justice. Nevertheless, his rule over all three Frankish kingdoms was not in the least secure. In Neus'tri-a, he was "assisted" by a most self-assertive Mayor, the powerful Pip'pin of Landen, and by his famous treasurer, St. E-lig'i-us, or E'loi. Indeed, Dagobert is chiefly remembered today as the foolish, ridiculous hero of an old French nursery rhyme, in which he is generally ordered about by Eloi, the great saint.

A coin of King Dagobert. An old French nursery rhyme runs:

King Dagobert once wore
His breeches hindside before.
Said Eloi, the friar:
"Oh, my King, and sire,
Those fine clothes on you
Are all wrong side to!"
The King said: "You don't say?
Then I'll turn them the other way!"

THE FRANKS

Charles Martel, and the Battle of Tours
(714 A.D.—741 A.D.)

Charles Martel was the great-grandson of Pip'pin of Land-en. His father, another Pippin, had been Mayor of both Au-stra'si-a and Neus'tri-a; but the family really belonged to Austrasia, and was much more in sympathy with their old Teutonic ancestry than with the newer, half-Gallic ideas of Neustria. Charles was not the son of his father's wife, and when the father died in 714, this wife, Plec'tru-dis, cast young Charles into prison, and tried to make her own grandsons Mayors of Neustria and Austrasia. But Charles escaped from prison and called on the Austrasian Franks to rally round his standard. Under his leadership they beat the army of his step-mother; and Charles became Mayor of the Palace for a reunited Frank-land, placing on the throne a little Merovingian prince who was only seven years old. He then subdued the Saxons, the Bavarians, and the Al'e-man'-ni. He put down powerful revolts in Provence and A'qui-taine, earning in all these wars the name Martel, or "Hammer" from his persistent striking against all resistance. He even forced the Frisians into some sort of submission, though he was never able to turn them into Christians.

Frankish scribe with staff and script. He is surrounded by an entirely new kind of arch,—the horse-shoe arch used later by the Arabs in the Alhambra, and other Spanish buildings. Miniature in the *Laws of the Barbarians*. (Library, Monastery of St. Gall, 731 A.D.)

True, Radbod, Duke of the Frisians, had once been persuaded by Charles to submit to Christian baptism; but as Radbod approached the font, he turned to the bishop and said: "Where are my ancestors now?" "In hell," replied the bishop; "in hell with all unbelievers!" Backing away from the water, and snatching a weapon from someone, Radbod then fiercely cried: "I had rather feast with my forefathers in the great halls of Woden, than live in Heaven with those fasting little Christians!" And he marched off in a huff!

Charles Martel and his little king lived in rustic simplicity in various rural palaces which were scattered throughout the realm, while cities were abandoned to solitude and decay. Charles was the strongest ruler in Europe; he issued decrees in his own name, summoned the national assembly each year, and appointed as bishops and abbots, warriors who kept their own armor and would not wear clerical dress. The Church supported him staunchly; the army idolized him; and it was well for Christendom that Charles had grown so strong, for just at this time the Moslems entered Gaul.

For some years the Duke of Aquitaine had kept the Moslems in check; but in 732 A.D., they defeated the Duke and advanced on Tours. This danger united all Franks in one determined effort. The Duke of Aquitaine fled to Charles; and on the plains near Tours, the "Hammer of the Franks" met the vast Arab host.

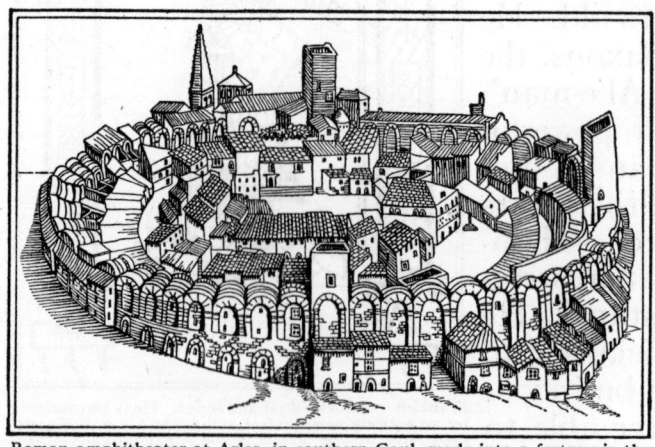

Roman amphitheater at Arles, in southern Gaul, made into a fortress in the eighth century, when the Mohammedans swept down to sack and ravish.

For seven days the two armies stood facing one another, the Arabs beating their drums and clashing their harsh, strident cymbals, working up their emotions into feverish enthusiasm, while the Franks grimly waited in silence. In the misty dawn of the eighth day, the Arabs attacked on their horses. With whirling scimitars, trumpet-blasts, the din of drum and cymbal, and harsh cries of *Al'lah Ak'bar!* the desert tribes charged home! But it was as if they had charged against a wall of ice. The Frankish infantry locked their shields and laughed at the showers of spears. With their terrible battle-axes they hewed down both horse and rider at a single mighty blow. Wave after wave of the Arabs surged against that iron wall, to fall back in plunging disorder. All day the battle raged. Not until darkness fell did the Arabs retire to their camp, leaving heaps of their choicest warriors dead or wounded on the field. The Franks then loosened their helmets, and rested in their places, keeping their hands on their swords. But the night passed by in silence. When morning broke still and gray, the Frankish host stretched their cramped limbs and peered through the morning mist, but they saw no sign of the foe. Only the dead lay in heaps on the plain, and there came from the Arab camp no morning call to prayer, no trumpet call to arms.

Fearing some trick, the Franks marched warily in battle array to see what had occurred. They found in the Arab camp only the wounded and dead. Charles the Hammer, relentless, terrible, had conquered the Moslem host! Europe was saved for Christianity, and the Moslems retired into Spain, never again to make any real attempt to conquer Gaul. The Franks described the battle as "The Victory of Tours," but the Moslems called it "The Pavement of Martyrs," and their songs tell how in the hush of a quiet summer evening, ghostly voices can still be heard over those fatal meadows near Tours, calling the faithful to prayer.

Pippin the Short, First of the Carolingians
(741 A.D.—768 A.D.)

The Frankish king surrounded by his court of military chieftains, dictates the laws which shall govern his kingdom. (14th cent. MS.)

Charles Martel, for all his power, had never declared himself King; but his son and heir, Pippin the Short, deciding that the time was ripe to assume the title of King, sent to ask advice of the Pope. Now it chanced that just at this time the Lombards were marching on Rome, intending to conquer all Italy. The Pope, in his hour of danger, had asked help of Constantinople; but there was now great bitterness between Constantinople and Rome, and no help whatever was sent. The Pope bought the Lombards off; but he knew he had purchased safety only for a little time, and was looking about him anxiously in search of a new protector, when Pippin's envoys reached Rome. Beholding these tall, powerful Franks, the Pope felt that here was a nation who could fight even Lombard warriors! He, therefore, answered Pippin that he who had the most power, should be the King of the land. This was enough for the powerful, ambitious Mayor of the Palace. He promptly cut off the long hair and beard of the "Good-for-Nothing" King, and shut him up in a monastery; and when the Pope shortly afterward came to pay a visit to Frankland, Pippin received him in state.

THE FRANKS

As the Pope and his escort descended the Alps they were met by a band of sturdy, yellow-haired Frankish nobles, at whose head rode young Karl, the eldest son of Pippin, a boy only twelve years old. The Pope was delighted with Karl who asked innumerable questions. The boy could not read nor write, for there were no schools in Frankland; but when the Pope talked of books which told tales of heroes and marvels, Karl's gray eyes widened with interest, and he determined that some day he would not only learn to read, but help others to do the same.

During the months that followed, Pippin and the Pope talked earnestly together. Pippin promised to fight the Lombards, while the Pope crowned Pippin, King of the Franks, and anointed Karl his successor. Until this time kings had crowned themselves, or been raised on the shields of their people; but now for the first time, the Pope went back to the customs of Bible days when kings were anointed by the high priest, and regarded as the chosen of God. Thus the Mayors of the Palace became the Kings of Frankland, receiving their title from the Pope, and Pippin drove the Lombards out of Rome and Ravenna. In the powerful Kings of the Franks, the Popes had found a champion far stronger than the Eastern Emperor in Constantinople.

Gold-bronze chalice bearing a dedicatory inscription of Charlemagne, 788 A.D. The design is pure Germanic, with fantastic interwoven forms. (See page 96.)

Charlemagne
(768 A.D.—814 A.D.)

When in the fullness of time, young Karl succeeded to the throne, he was the idol of the Franks. Tall and broad of shoulder, gray-eyed and fair-haired, he was the ancient type of the true Germanic warrior. No man in the land was a mightier hunter or wrestler, a stronger or swifter swimmer, and he loved the simple dress of his own Germanic people. "He wore next his skin a linen shirt and breeches," wrote E'gin-hard, his secretary, "and above these a tunic fringed with silk, while hose fastened by bands covered his lower limbs. He protected his shoulders and chest in winter, by a close-fitting coat of otter or marten skins, and flung over all a blue cloak. And he always had a sword girt about him, usually one with a gold and silver hilt and belt."

Now when Karl ascended the throne, the counts who ruled the counties into which the land was divided for convenience in government, all swore allegiance to him save the count of Aquitaine. So Karl was obliged to go and fight the rebellious count; but he put him to rout completely, and cleverly won the hearts of his Aquitanian subjects by giving them as King his own little son, Prince Louis, who had been born in Aquitaine. Proudly the Aquitanians bore the small boy to their capital, to become a true man of Aquitaine. King Solomon himself could have thought of no wiser way to win rebellious subjects!

Bronze statue believed to be Charlemagne the Warrior, on horseback. It was cast during Carolingian times.

THE FRANKS

With his own land thus at peace, Karl turned against the Lombards, those turbulent, light-haired warriors who once again threatened the Pope; for Karl believed that the Church was civilizing the world and must carry on its work unhindered. With a host of mail-clad warriors, he swept down in full force on the rich green plains of Lombardy with their rows of tall, straight poplars. The Lombards had thought Pippin terrible; but the reputation of Karl and the sight of his mighty army struck terror into their hearts before even a blow was struck. The Lombard King, Des-i-de'ri-us, watched from the walls of Pa'-vi-a for the coming of the Franks; and beside him stood one, Ot'ker, who knew the young Frankish King well, having visited at his court.

Lombard women like those who watched with dread the approach of Charlemagne's host. (S. Maria in Valle, Cividale; 8th century.) Byzantine influence was strong throughout Italy, and they wore Byzantine costumes with elaborately decorated tunics. The story of Charlemagne's advance is condensed from the MS., of a monk of St. Gall, who related events exactly as he had heard his father tell them. (See incident on page 203.)

"And when the advance guard appeared, which was stronger than the armies of Darius or Julius Caesar, Desiderius said to Otker, his companion: 'Is Karl with this mighty army?' And Otker answered: 'Not yet!' One by one, the Frankish companies took up position in the field before the ancient Italian city. The noise of their horses' hoofs was like the rumblings of thunder.

Lombard woman's portrait head with high coiffure.

As each passed, Desiderius, turning to Otker said: 'Surely Karl is here!' But Otker answered, full of dread: 'When you see a harvest of steel waving in the fields, and the rivers dashing steel-black waves against the city-walls, you may know that Karl is here!' Then they saw Karl, the man of steel, his arms covered with plates of steel, his iron breast and broad shoulders protected by harness of steel. His left hand carried aloft the iron lance. His shield was all of steel, and his horse was iron in color and spirit. Steel filled the fields and roads! The rays of the sun were reflected from gleaming steel. The people, paralyzed with fear, did homage to bristling steel. 'Alas the steel! Alas the steel!' resounded their wild cries. The mighty walls trembled before the steel. Then Otker said to Desiderius: 'There you have Karl!' And he fell to the ground like one dead.''

Gold book-cover of Queen The-od'e-lin'da, from Monza.

So was the story of Karl's approach told by the Monk of St. Gall, whose father told him the tale. After an eight months' siege, the city of Pa-via fell and the spirit of the Lombards was broken. Desiderius ended his days in a monastery; and all the great Lombard chiefs submitted at once to Karl, nor did they ever rebel again against him, or his friend the Pope.

As a sign that the Lombard kingdom had come to an end at last, Karl left one of his sons to rule in Lombardy and assumed for himself the "Iron Crown," a narrow gold circlet containing a nail from the true Cross, which had been the pride of the Lombards.

Lombard gold cross from the grave of Duke Gu-sulf'.

Now only the Saxons remained to trouble the peace of Karl's realm with their frequent plundering raids. This stubborn race in their salt-marshes along the cold shores of the Baltic, were still persistently heathen. They worshiped trees and fountains, and believed in were-wolves and fairies; and their gods were O'din, the one-eyed, and Thor of the blazing hammer. Karl dreamed of civilizing his troublesome Saxon neighbors by adding their lands to his own, but the Saxons fought fiercely and savagely to keep their independence. They would not yield to the steadily growing power of the Franks.

The-od'e-lin'da donates the Treasure of Monza to the Church of San Gio-van'ni. (Cathedral of Monza, 595 A.D.)

The tree-idol, Ir'min-sul, the Saxon god of justice, holding a pair of scales. He was still worshiped long after the people had become Christians. (Woodcut, from the *Annales Circuli Westphaliae*, 1656.)

Karl destroyed their tree-idol, Ir'min-sul, carved in the likeness of a man; he forced many to be baptized, and he set up monasteries filled with brave missionary monks; but as soon as he left the land the monasteries went up in flames, the monks were massacred, and the Christ-child gave way once more to Thor, the God of Battles, who kept a seat and a drinking horn in the lofty halls of Val-hal'la, for all who died in battle. In the end Karl was obliged to transplant thousands of Saxons to other parts of Frankland, where they slowly grew civilized.

Under Karl, Christianity became as certainly as Islam a "Gospel of the Sword," and because of his fame as a warrior, men first hailed him as "Car'o-lus Mag'nus," Karl the Great, or Charlemagne.

But of all Charlemagne's campaigns, that against the Moslems of Spain, as told in the *Song of Roland*, has been best known through the ages. To the Mayfield, or annual gathering of Franks, there came three rebellious Moslems, who besought the aid of Charlemagne against their lord of Cor'do-va; and Charlemagne, thinking thus to add Spain to his kingdom, agreed to march south very soon. The Moslems promised to meet him with large and loyal armies, and to open up to him the gates of their various towns. But once in Spain, Charlemagne found that only the small towns surrendered; no Saracen army came to his aid, and the larger cities defied him. He had to turn north again, and as he repassed the Pyrenees, his baggage train with its guard, among whom was young Count Roland, was set upon by robbers and destroyed. From these simple events, there grew up a mass of ballads which changed the story entirely.

Attack of a city by warriors in chain-armor like the Frankish army of Charlemagne. (9th cent. MS., St. Gall.)

The Minstrels' Song of Roland

For seven long years had Charlemagne fought the good fight in Spain. All the land had he conquered from the highlands to the sea. Before the might of his arms, castle and keep went down; no city could withstand him save only Sar'a-gos'sa, the strong-walled mountain town. In Saragossa, Mar'sile, the helpless Saracen chief, bewailed his miserable lot, till crafty counselors came and argued in his ear, "Send gifts to Charlemagne! Send lions, bears, and steeds! Send silver and rich gold! Say that thou seekest peace, and promise at St. Mi'chael's feast to visit the Great King, and then to be baptized. Thereat he will depart, and we will break our oath, rise up, and win back Spain!"

Marsile rejoiced to hear such words of trickery. He sent ambassadors with gifts to Cordova, and these found Charlemagne within a blossoming orchard's shade, there seated on a golden throne, with flowing beard and robes.

Charlemagne receives the oath of fidelity at the yearly assembly of nobles. (14th cent. MS., Library of Arsenal.)

Around him stood his peers to watch the martial games at the great spring gathering of fifty thousand Frankish warriors. Unto him the Saracens most humbly offered peace. Then up spake bold young Roland, sister's son to Charlemagne, the bravest and best-loved of all the King's knights. "Marsile hath tricked us once. Why trust his promises again?"

But Ga'ne-lon', step-father to that splendid youth, stood by, dark-browed and evil, jealous hatred gnawing at his heart. "Rash fool!" he cried. "Thou arguest for war because thou prizest thine own glory more than all the lives of these, thy fellows here!" Whereat the King cried out: "Enough! We will accept the offer of Marsile!"

Then Roland and his comrade Oliver, pressed forward eagerly, beseeching that to them, the King should give the dangerous task of bearing back his answer to the Saracen chief, safe within Saragossa, that strong-walled mountain town beside the swift-flowing waters of the Ebro.

Ga′ne-lon′ the traitor, plans to betray Roland, when the hero requests the dangerous task of guarding the rear.

But Charlemagne refused their rash request and bade them name some other in their stead. Quoth Roland: "Ganelon was anxious for the peace! Why not send Ganelon?"

With inward fury Ganelon now heard these words, and inwardly vowed vengeance on the youth; for well he knew the expedition to Marsile would be so dangerous, that he who went might nevermore return. But Charlemagne, in his imperial dignity, delivered unto Ganelon his glove, as emblem of the office he bestowed, entrusting to his care the message to Marsile. Both rage and fear made Ganelon unsteady as he took the glove, so that he let it fall. Then great dismay fell over all. "That bodeth little good," men said. "While Roland lives, will fighting never cease!" cried Ganelon to those two Saracens who journeyed by his side.

"But we could rid thee of him! Only see that he commands the rear-guard when thy great King Charlemagne departs at length from Spain!" the Saracens replied.

And so they planned to slay young Roland, and the chief, Marsile, gave Ganelon rich gifts and sent him safely home. And Ganelon delivered unto Charlemagne the keys of Saragossa, reporting that the infidels submitted to his will. Then Charlemagne believed his task was done; gratefully he thanked God and made all ready to depart for home.

"Who asks to lead my rear guard?" cried the King.

"Ah, who so brave as Roland?" Ganelon replied.

But Charlemagne made answer with some heat, "Nay! Roland shall remain with me!" Then Roland did himself so earnestly entreat to be entrusted with the dangerous post, that Charlemagne at last, though most reluctantly, gave his consent. Yet on the night before he left, his rest was troubled with strange dreams, through which the face of Ganelon passed ominous and dark. Foreboding ill, he bade young Roland sad farewell.

> Now Roland the Count, hath ascended to the top of a barrow green
> Arrayed in the mail of his hauberk—better hath no man seen!
> Laced on his head is his helmet; right well it becometh a knight!
> No weapon forged may cleave it, how starkly soe'er one smite.
> To his side is Durendal girded, the golden-hilted sword!
> A shield from his neck is hanging that hath never failed its lord.
> A spear on high hath he lifted with fluttering pennon white;
> Low as his wrist are swinging the golden fringes bright;
> In his armor arrayed he seemeth a passing goodly knight . . .

With 20,000 brave men, with Oliver, his friend, dearer than any brother, with Turpin, the doughty Archbishop, who thought it no shame to tuck up his robes and strike a blow for Christ, Roland now waved farewell to the vanguard filing past in the narrow gorges of the rocky vale below. "Farewell till we meet in France!" he cried.

With the traitor Ganelon, in their midst, the vanguard marched toward home; but a nameless sense of evil haunted the souls of all, and their hearts were back with Roland with the rear-guard on the treacherous soil of Spain.

Frankish warriors preceded by a soldier carrying a standard in the form of a fish. (9th cent. MS., St. Gall.)

> High were the peaks and the valleys deep,
> The mountains wondrous dark and steep;
> Sadly the Franks through the passes wound;
> Fully fifteen leagues did their tread resound.
> To their own great land they were drawing nigh,
> And they look on the fields of Gascony.
> They think of their homes and manors there,
> Their gentle spouses and damsels fair.
> Is none but for pity the tear lets fall,
> But the anguish of Karl is beyond them all.
> His sister's son at the gates of Spain
> Smites on his heart, and he weeps amain.

Early the following morning, the rear-guard gaily advanced, young Roland and his friend Oliver riding blithely side by side. In joyous converse they passed out of the glistening sunlight into the darkness and gloom of the Pass of Ron′ces-val′les. Then suddenly Oliver reined in his horse, and shaded his face with his hand. "Behold!" he cried, and his voice was hoarse; "the work of the traitor Ganelon!"

> To a high knoll Oliver spurreth; to the right he looked therefrom;
> Up the long green valley, he seeth the Saracens come . . .
> Helmets begemmed are flashing, shields blaze against the sun,
> The mail-coats glint through the surcoats with broidery overdone;
> Surges on surges of war-waves!—their numbers baffle the sight!
> Yea, Oliver's spirit is 'wildered, that he may not count them aright.
> Down from the crest of the barrow, full swiftly hath he spurred;
> He hath come to the Frankish heroes, bearing an evil word.

"Now shall we have grim battle," Roland cried to his men. And his warriors answered boldly: "A curse on him who flees!" But Oliver, seeing the enemy outnumber them five to one, begged Roland to blow on Ol'i-phant, the horn that the King himself bade him sound in case of need.

> "Sound Oliphant, Roland my comrade, and straightway shall Charlemagne hear;
> He is threading the mountain gorges! Still, O still is he near."
> "Now God forbid," cried Roland, "that for any heathen born
> It shall ever be said that Roland hath stooped to sound his horn!
> Shall I be on the lips of my kinsmen, a byword, a shame and a scorn?"

Thrice Oliver besought Roland to wind one good blast on his horn, and thrice Roland answered: "Nay!" Then good Archbishop Turpin bade the Franks kneel in prayer and prepare their hearts for the battle.

> Now waxeth the battle wondrous, and its travail passing sore;
> Well Oliver and Roland the burden of that day bore;
> The Archbishop too, he fighteth, and a thousand sword-strokes ring;
> There are the twelve Peers smiting, unflinching, unfaltering.

Marsile himself fought with Roland; but Roland smote him so sore that he was borne from the battle, wounded unto death. Each man in that small Frankish host did wondrous deeds that day. Yet one by one, did they fall.

Amidst a great heap of slain, Roland urged a last handful to stand to their posts till the death. And the Saracens, fearing that handful, attacked them but from a distance. Mortally wounded thus, Oliver called to Roland, and Roland, although half-blinded, fought his way to his side. Then each laid his head to the other, and so did Oliver die.

The death of bold Roland. The horn which he blows is copied from one called an Oliphant horn in the Louvre.

Left alone of all that staunch and valorous Frankish host, did Roland and Archbishop Turpin at last fight shoulder to shoulder; till Turpin, too, sank to the ground. Then Roland, laying his friend on the grass and slowly unlacing his helmet, blew one long mournful blast on Oliphant, his horn.

All nature shuddered with terror; for over the sunny fields of France there broke a hideous storm. Across the heavens the thunder rolled, the livid lightning flashed, and earth was shaken with grief. Then far away Charlemagne heard the sound of Roland's horn. "Our Roland is in danger!"

"Nay! nay!" quoth Ganelon, "belike he is but hunting."

Again that mournful call came wailing far away.

"Never would he call like that unless in direst peril!"

"Nay! nay! he but chases a hare!"

Yet still a third time came that blast, so long now and despairing that none might mistake its meaning.

"Roland is in extremity!" Charlemagne cried in anguish; and he bade his men turn about and let all the trumpets blare that Roland might know he was coming, coming with all the thunder-beat of thousands of marching men!

At sound of Charlemagne's trumpets the Saracens fled from the field, yet fleeing, they flung back missiles till Roland was nigh to death. Then slowly, with mighty effort, he collected from mountain and valley the bodies of his twelve peers and dragged them to Archbishop Turpin's feet, that they might receive one last blessing. While laying Oliver there, Roland swooned for grief, and Turpin, seizing his horn, painfully raised himself to fetch his friend some water from the brook that ran nearby. But in his act of mercy, Turpin, too, fell dead, and Roland came to his senses to find himself alone. Grasping his good sword Du'ren-dal' and Oliphant, his horn, he toiled to the top of a hill that he might look off to Spain, and die with his face toward the foe. Then lifting his sword, he tried with all his strength to break it, but the steel showed never a dent. So he laid Durendal beneath him with Oliphant, his horn, that even in death he might guard them; and there on the height, he died, committing his soul to God.

Charlemagne reached the valley. Deathly stillness reigned over all. He called on his peers by name. Not one there was to answer. And on the height, with his face toward Spain, they found the hero Roland. Great was the grief of all. Charlemagne hotly gave chase to the fleeing Saracen host, and defeated them in a great battle; then bearing the body of Roland, he sadly returned to France. Laden with chains, dark Ganelon was condemned to death as a traitor; but wherever men loved brave deeds, they sang of Roland the hero, who stood to his post till the death.

Charlemagne Becomes Emperor of the West

Charlemagne now ruled all the land between the Atlantic Ocean and the Adriatic Sea, and from the borders of Denmark to the river E′bro, in Spain; but the greatest moment of his life came on Christmas Day in the year 800 A.D., when he was visiting Rome. The great church of St. Peter was crowded to the doors. The air was full of incense; a thousand candles sent light and shade playing among the pillars; and over the kneeling multitude there hung a solemn hush. Charlemagne was on that day to be crowned by the Pope, not as King, but as Emperor! The Pope had no real right to crown anyone as emperor, since the Emperor in Constantinople was still called Emperor of the Romans; but at this time the Eastern ruler was a cruel and wicked woman who had blinded her own son in order to seize the throne. No one wanted such an empress. Moreover, she was too busy fighting the troublesome Moslems to interfere in Rome; so Charlemagne was acclaimed with enthusiastic shouts as the first Emperor of the West since the days of the fall of Rome, more than two hundred years before.

Crown (Treasury at Vienna), sandals, and robe (Abbey of St. Denis) of Charlemagne worn when he was crowned Emperor of the Roman Empire, by Pope Leo III, who thus brought to life, the neglected Western Roman Empire.

Ivory chessman. Gift of Ha-roun'-al-Ra-schid' to the Emperor Charlemagne. (Cabinet des Médailles, Paris.)

Byzantine fabric with an elephant design, from the tomb of Charlemagne. (Staatliche Museum, Berlin.)

And now only the Byzantine emperor and the brilliant Ha-roun'-al-Ra-schid', Caliph of Bagdad, ruler of Islam, and hero of the opulent *Arabian Nights*, could rival Charlemagne. From "Bagdad's shrines of fretted gold with high-walled gardens, green and old," Haroun sent gifts to Charlemagne; rare perfumes, spices and silks, ivory chess-men and books, and that beast so strange to the Franks, a royal elephant. Haroun permitted Christians to visit unmolested the holy places in Palestine, and Charlemagne let Moslem fleets put into his seaports to trade the luxuries of the ancient East. The Arabs in those days were far more cultured than the Franks. Haroun had fine universities in Egypt, in Spain, and Bagdad; but Charlemagne, when he came to the throne, had not one good school in his kingdom. Remembering his boyish interest in books awakened by the Pope so many years before, he sent to monasteries in Italy, Spain, and England, engaging scholars to come and establish schools in Frankland.

Thus Charlemagne acquired the services of the Lombard, Paul the Deacon, and the learned Englishman, Al'cuin, who started a school at the palace. There, every day, Alcuin taught the children of Charlemagne; and sometimes the Emperor himself with the Queen and members of the court, would come and take part in the lessons, though Charlemagne never learned to make his letters very well. The royal family sat on a platform in the center of the hall, while among the rushes that strewed the floor, other students sat on benches. They studied reading and writing, nature-study, grammar, and history. Other monastery schools were now established in Frankland by Alcuin and his fellow-teachers, and in these sheltered places of learning children were taught free of charge, and grown-up monks learned how to copy manuscripts neatly and properly.

Jewel-encrusted bookcover, with carved ivory center plaque, which belonged to Charlemagne. (Cabinet des Médailles, Paris.)

Elaborate initial, containing figures of men and animals. Such drawings were called "illuminations." Alcuin's Bible. (Brit. Mus.)

Dedicatory sculpture from the shrine of Charlemagne at Aachen, showing the Emperor with a model of the building.

A Royal Progress

In winter the royal family lived at Aa′chen or Aix′-la-Chapelle′, where Charlemagne built a fine chapel; but during the summer months the court moved constantly from one royal estate to another in different parts of the country.

A colorful sight it was when the Emperor took to the road. First came gaily dressed heralds to clear the way with their trumpets; for roads in Frankland were narrow, and it would never do for the King to find the road blocked by a farm-wagon laden with produce, or a wandering flock of sheep. Next came mounted soldiers, keeping a lookout for robbers; and then came the Emperor himself, surrounded by his body-guard. As companion, he might have one of his sons, or Alcuin, or possibly a chance-met merchant, thus learning how to help his traders by hearing of their difficulties.

THE FRANKS

The merchant would gossip freely about nobles who charged such heavy tolls at their bridges that a man was well nigh ruined; while others refused to repair bridges so rotten that a heavily laden pack horse was in danger of falling through! And the Emperor would listen gravely and later warn these nobles to change their ways at once.

Not far behind the Emperor, came the Queen in her litter, carried between two horses, or riding on a white mule. With her rode the royal children, a crowd of ladies-in-waiting, and still more attendants and soldiers. The party swept up the road with such a glitter of lances, such a jingle of bells, clatter of hoofs, and flutter of gay-colored cloaks, that peasants working in the fields stared open-mouthed at the sight. Trailing behind the procession, came servants with wagons of clothing, blankets, and household goods.

Each day the party sent word ahead that they would stay overnight at some convenient monastery. Then what a to-do there was preparing for so many people, monastery servants putting up beds, cooks killing dozens of chickens or roasting huge joints of meat, while the abbot flew about like a swallow, inwardly hoping that Charlemagne and his hungry court would not honor him more than one night.

Peasants like those who stared at Charlemagne and his court. They are barefooted, or have their legs bound with leather thongs. (Illuminations from a work written in Salzburg, 818 A. D., now in National Museum, Vienna.)

Charlemagne's villas were certainly no marvels of luxury. An ordinary residence consisted of "a royal house built of stone, in the very best manner, having three rooms. There were seventeen other houses built of wood within the courtyard. There was one stable, one kitchen, one mill, one granary, three barns."* Inside the house there were "coverings for one bed, one table-cloth, one towel, two brass kettles, two drinking cups, one frying pan, one lamp, two hatchets, one knife, and two spades edged with iron."

Round about the courtyard there was a hedge or wall, inclosing the usual garden gay with flowers and fruit. Here Charlemagne and his family could take their meals on fine days, and here the Queen spent much time spinning and weaving with her ladies, or watching the antics of the peacocks strutting about in the sun. Sometimes school was held in the garden, and little Pepin and Louis with their crowd of brothers and sisters listened to their lessons there.

In the evenings, all the court gathered in the garden; the older knights talked to the Emperor, or played checkers, while the younger ones wrestled, matched swords, or listened to some strolling minstrel, who sang ballads to Charlemagne, using the crude Frankish tongue.

On one estate the court would stay until it had eaten up all the pigs and game, the vegetables, fruit and grain, that the peasants had paid as rent. Then they packed up and moved on. But, wherever the Emperor stayed, he visited the neighboring villages, held court, and administered justice. The Franks, like all German tribes, had their own peculiar methods of settling their disputes. If a man was accused of murder and could not prove himself innocent, Charlemagne would order him to pay so much *man-money* or *wergild* to his accuser. Murdering a Frank was expensive; killing a slave or a foreigner was cheaper.

*Condensed from Charlemagne's *Capitularies*, the laws which the Emperor made to suit the needs of his people.

Charlemagne and his court are entertained by a wandering minstrel in the garden of a royal villa. The brick building huddled among wooden out-buildings is purely Frankish in its gaily colored brick, and masonry laid in definite patterns. With this Charlemagne has combined what most struck his barbarian tastes in the classic architecture of Rome, the florid Corinthian pillar. As yet no sign has appeared of the turreted castles that characterize the Middle Ages. This hall copied from one of the buildings actually erected by Charlemagne, still standing at Lorch.

One of the most expensive men in the village to kill, was by law, the village smith, since without his skill at the forge, the village would be quite helpless. If a man cut off another man's nose, he had to pay twenty shillings; if an eyebrow, two shillings; if a thumb or forefinger, ten shillings, because the injured man would be of no more use as a soldier.

A silver Frankish sword of Carolingian times, engraved with animals, and a fully-armed warrior with lance, sword, and wolf-helmet. (Berlin.)

To anyone accused of committing some crime that could not be proved in court, Charlemagne offered a chance of proving his innocence. He might challenge his accuser to a fight, or choose the "ordeal by water," wherein he plunged his hand into boiling water, and if it came out unhurt thereby was accounted innocent! Or he might choose the "ordeal by fire," and prove his innocence in walking blindfold among red-hot plow-shares, or carrying a red-hot bar for ten yards without being burned!

On his own estates, Charlemagne could administer the laws himself; but in other parts of the empire, his counts had to do it for him. These counts sometimes mistreated the peasants; so Charlemagne chose trusted men called *Missi Regis*, or "King's messengers" who went out in pairs, one bishop and one nobleman, to act as a check on them.

Realizing that months of fighting and yearly meetings at the Mayfield caused the peasants much suffering, Charlemagne for the first time, allowed poor men to club together and send one armed man in their place to the army. He also allowed local landholders to lead their own tenants into battle.

For more than forty years Charlemagne gave of his best to the people whom he loved. It is true that he was a warrior and often unduly aggressive; but he lived in a fighting age, and the real desire of his heart was to govern justly and kindly. From one end of the world to the other, men knew him as Karl the Great, Karl, the lover of learning.

VI
The Medieval Church
The Rise of the Papacy

Decorating the banquet-hall of the Pope's palace in Rome, was a picture made of brilliantly colored bits of stone, like the mosaics in Sancta Sophia. In this picture Jesus was shown bestowing the keys of heaven on one of the first popes of Rome, and giving to the Emperor Constantine, a banner and a cross. This was meant to signify that the Pope and the Emperor were the chosen servants of God, and therefore, all people on earth must obey them.

Gradually the followers of Jesus had come to believe in a *catholic* or *universal* Church, which included all true believers wherever they might be. To this one universal Church all must belong who hoped to be saved. "Whoever separates himself from the Church," wrote St. Cyprian, in the third century, "is separated from the promises of the Church. He is an alien, he is profane, he is an enemy. He can no longer have God for his Father, who has not the Church for his mother." Thus it was early established in the Church, that belief, rather than daily living in accordance with the precepts of Jesus, was the key to eternal life. The Apostle Paul had said: "Behold *now* is the accepted time; behold, *now* is the day of salvation," and Jesus had said: "The Kingdom of God is *within you*"; but to Christians of that day it was not the *now* that mattered. They did not realize that men might now begin to divest themselves of evil, and now and forever find the kingdom of heaven in their own hearts where Jesus had said it was; but felt that all this life was a mere preparation for a future life, where correct belief could usher them into a glorious but concrete Heaven, or save them from a flaming and hideous Hell.

Almost as soon as Christianity had become a recognized religion, a sharp distinction was made between the officers of the Church who were called the *clergy*, and the people, or *laity*. The government of the Church and the teaching of its members fell to the clergy, and within a short time a Church organization developed, modeled after the old Roman governmental organization. In each city there was a *bishop*, and at the head of the country communities, there was a *priest*, who took his title from the elders or *presbyters* mentioned in the New Testament. Bishops in the most important towns, having more influence in Church affairs, came to be called *archbishops*, and were given the power to summon the bishops of their district to councils; while the archbishops of the five largest cities received the title of *patriarch*. There were four patriarchs in the eastern half of the Empire, at Antioch, Jerusalem, Alexandria, and Constantinople; but only one in the western half, at Rome.

Pontifical robe of Pope Leo III, who crowned Charlemagne, Roman Emperor.

The Roman Church, however, was supposed to have been founded by the immediate followers of Jesus, those energetic disciples, Peter and Paul.

The Bible mentions Paul's presence in Rome; and there had long been a tradition that Peter had been the first Bishop of Rome. In a passage in the New Testament, it is recorded that Jesus said: "And I say unto thee, that thou art Peter, and upon this rock will I build my Church; and the gates of hell shall not prevail against it. And I will give unto thee the keys of the kingdom of heaven." This was understood to mean that Jesus had made Peter the head of his Church, and the followers of Peter his successors on earth. Therefore, the Roman Church came to be looked upon as the "Mother Church," and its patriarch as head of the Church in the West; and the Emperor, Val-en-tin′i-an III, commanded that bishops throughout the West should receive as law all that the Bishop of Rome approved. Six years later a Council at Chalcedon declared that Constantinople should have the same power in church government; but this was never accepted in the Western, or Latin Church, which was gradually separating from the Eastern, or Greek Church.

Jesus gives the keys of heaven to the Pope. (10th cent. Mosaic, Rome.)

Bishops of carved ivory used as chessmen. They wear low mitres, carry the crosier of office, and are seated in low chairs. The rear view shows the hair below the mitre and the carved chair back. (12th cent. British Museum.)

All bishops, and even priests, were at this time called popes. The name *pope* was taken from the Latin word *papa*, meaning *father*; and not until the time of Gregory VII, who died in 1085, was it definitely stated that the title Pope should be applied only to the Bishop of Rome.

When O'do-a'cer put an end to the Roman Emperors in the West, and the Ostrogoths, Visigoths, and Lombards created disorder and tumult in the ancient Western Empire, only the Pope remained stable. Other rulers, other races, came and went in Italy; but through all these changes of fortune, the popes retained their power. Thus the people gradually came to look on the Pope as their natural leader, and even the barbarians, except for the A'ri-an Goths, began to think of the Pope as the spiritual head of all the people on earth. The man who did most to make the Western Church a mighty organization, and the Pope at Rome the most powerful leader in all of Europe, was Pope Gregory I.

Pope Gregory the Great
(590 A.D.—604 A.D.)

Gregory was the son of a rich Roman nobleman. His mother was a saintly woman who brought up her son to be an earnest and zealous Christian. His father taught him the duties of citizenship, and while still a young man, he was elected Prefect of the city. But wealth and political power could never satisfy Gregory. In spite of entreaties from friends, he put off his robes of office, gave his property to charity, and turned his father's palace into a monastery. Here he himself lived as a monk until the Pope sent him as his representative to the Imperial Court at Constantinople. And now for six years he studied the strength and the weakness of imperial government; but he greatly disliked the luxury and worldliness of Constantinople, and the haughty disdain for far-off, barbarian Italy.

Pope Gregory the Great. The Holy Spirit, represented by the dove, whispers in the Pope's ear, words of counsel and wisdom, which he writes in his instructions to the Church. Gregory wears the beard of the Franks, and has his hand raised in blessing. (Early 11th cent., book-cover of silver metal. Munich.)

Returning again to Rome, he continued his old monastic life till the Pope died of the plague, and Gregory was chosen to succeed to the papal throne. Hearing of his election, Gregory fled from the city, for he had no wish to take up again the burden of public life; but he was brought back and crowned. Thus forced into office, Gregory took up his work with all his heart and soul. He dismissed the scented courtiers, who had surrounded his predecessors, and governed his household like a monastery. The Christian clergy, he believed, should set their flocks an example of clean and honest lives. "The conduct of a prelate," he wrote, "should surpass the conduct of the people, as a shepherd's life does that of his flock." His own days were filled with good works. While other popes spent the papal revenues in building or adorning churches, Gregory used his riches to lighten the lot of the poor, and to send out missionaries.

Pope Gregory sending missionaries to convert England. A 10th cent. MS. attributed to St. Dunstan of Canterbury, a cathedral founded under Gregory the Great.

In Constantinople he had seen how uninterested in the West the Byzantine emperors were, and he decided that the Church must take the place of the Empire. He therefore encouraged the bishops of Gaul and Germany to visit Rome, and so wisely did he talk and act, that not only his own bishops, but the rulers of Western Europe accepted his leadership in all things.

THE MEDIEVAL CHURCH

Aiming always to make the Church beautiful, Gregory brought from Byzantium to Rome the sonorous Gregorian chants, the first really fine church music. Christian church music had had its beginning in Byzantium, and just as Christian church architecture expressed itself in arches and domes, rising to a central point and falling again, so the early Byzantine chants swelled upwards to a climax, and then sank in rhythmic cadence. Instead of being made to fit poetry

A page of church music with Latin words and a picture of a bishop dedicating a church. After years of singing only from memory, men learned to write music down, and they first used square notes with no indication of time and pitch of the scale. (Metz Pontifical, 1302-16, Private Library of Sir T. Brooke, Bart.)

as in the hymns of the Greeks, Christian music followed a prose rhythm, considering only the natural accent of the sentence. Church music consisted of the music of the Mass, called the *Missal*, and the chants of the Hours of Office, called the *Breviary*. Gregory thus made the service of Mass a dignified, sonorous ceremony taking a full three hours.

Bishop's throne, or ivory *cathedra*, called the chair of Maximian (Bishop 546-556) exquisitely carved with Biblical scenes and representations of the apostles, and decorated with intertwined leaves, among which appear stags. (Ravenna.)

In spite of his earnestness and humility, Gregory persecuted heretics with all his power and strength. An Arian was to him a worse enemy than any infidel. So while his heart yearned to bring the blessings of Christianity to barbarian tribes, he did his best to drive the Arian Christians out of Italy, Spain, and Gaul.

The Venerable Bede reports that Gregory, when yet but a humble deacon in his own monastery, became greatly interested in the heathen Angles of England. Northern England had had some missionaries from monasteries in Ireland, but since Roman culture had vanished, the island had become heathen. "It is reported," wrote Bede, "that some merchants just arrived at Rome on a certain day, exposed many things for sale in the market-place; and abundance of people resorted thither to buy. Gregory himself went with the rest, and among other things, some boys were set for sale, their bodies white, their countenances beautiful, and their hair very fine. Having perceived them, Gregory asked from what country they were, and was told from the island of Britain. Again he inquired whether those islanders were Christians or were still pagans, and was informed that they were pagans.

"Then fetching a deep sigh from the bottom of his heart, 'Alas, what pity,' said he, 'that the author of darkness is possessed of men of such fair countenances; and that being remarkable for such graceful aspects, their minds should be void of inward grace.' He therefore, again asked what was the name of that nation, and was answered that they were called Angles. 'Right,' said he, 'for they look like angels, and it becomes such to be co-heirs with the angels...' "*

He then besought the Pope to send him to convert the English; but the Pope was compelled to refuse his request; the Church needed him at home, and it was not possible at that time for such an important Churchman to be spared from Rome. Not until he himself became pope could he take any further steps to Christianize the Angles. Then he sent his friend Augustine to carry out the work he had longed to do himself. Fearing the "fierce, barbarous and unbelieving nation to whose very language they were strangers," Augustine and his comrades turned back from their first expedition; but strengthened by Gregory, they set off once again and landed on the island of Than'et, lying in the mouth of the Thames. From there they sent Frankish interpreters to King Ethelbert of Kent, saying that they came from the holy Pope in Rome and had "brought a joyful message, which most undoubtedly assured to all that took advantage of it, everlasting joys in heaven, and a kingdom that would never end."

St. Augustine's throne in Canterbury Cathedral, a massive carved stone chair. (From a photograph.)

*Bede's *Ecclesiastical History*. Bede (672-735 A.D.) was an English monk who wrote a history of the English.

The Venerable Bede writing in the monastery of Jarrow concerning the conversion of England to Christianity. (MS. British Museum.) Quotation on this page is from Bede's *Ecclesiastical History of the English Nation* (672-735 A.D.)

"The King, having heard this, ordered them to stay in that island where they had landed, and that they should be furnished with all necessaries, till he should consider what to do with them. For he had before heard of the Christian religion, having a Christian wife of the royal family of the Franks, called Bertha. Her, he had received from her parents upon condition that she should be permitted to practice her religion with the Bishop Luid'hard, who was sent with her to preserve her faith. Some days later the King came into the island, and sitting in the open air, ordered Augustine and his companions to be brought into his presence, thus taking care that they should not come to him in any house, for, according to an ancient superstition, if they practiced any magical arts, they might impose on him indoors. But they came furnished with divine, if not with magic virtue, bearing a silver cross for their banner, and the image of our Lord and Saviour painted on a board. Singing the litany, they offered up their prayers to the Lord for the eternal salvation both of themselves and of those to whom they were come. When Augustine had sat down, pursuant to the King's commands, and preached to him and his attendants the word of life, the King answered thus: 'Your words and promises are very fair, but as they are new to us, and of uncertain import,

I cannot approve of them so far as to forsake that which I have so long followed with the whole English nation. But, because you are desirous to impart to us those things which you believe to be true and most beneficial, we will not molest you, but give you favorable entertainment, and take care to supply you with your necessary sustenance; nor do we forbid you to preach and gain as many as you can to your religion.' Accordingly he permitted them to reside in the city of Canterbury, and did not refuse them liberty to preach."

In time, "won over by the simplicity of their innocent life and the sweetness of their heavenly doctrine," many Angles and Saxons believed, until finally the King himself was baptized, and Christianity was established in England.

Thus Gregory made his influence felt throughout all western Europe, and though none of his immediate successors was nearly so great as he, they claimed the same homage. And when later popes found their military protector in the Frankish Emperor, they soon separated entirely from the Greek Church in the East.

St. Augustine sent by Pope Gregory as missionary to England. In the little squares, Jesus raises Lazarus, enters Jerusalem in triumph, is taken prisoner, and bears his cross. (An ancient illuminated MS. in the Library at Cambridge).

The Monks of the West: Benedict
(About 480 a.d.—543 a.d.)

The men whom Gregory sent out as missionaries were monks. Pilgrims to the East had brought back to the West the custom of leaving the world to live apart as monks, and the ideals of these men were everywhere the same; to escape from a world of vanity and sin, and to devote this life to prayer, and discipline of the body in order to become worthy of a place in heaven after death. There were not many hermits in western Europe, for the climate was too cold, and the people of the West did not take kindly to meditation in solitude; but a monastery offered shelter and food, as well as a sure path to heaven, so the number of monasteries grew apace. At first there was no definite rule for the behavior of monks and nuns, and they wandered at will from place to place; but just as St. Basil saw the need for a definite monastic rule in the East, so St. Benedict saw the need in the West.

Benedict of Nursia, like Gregory after him, was the son of noble parents and was educated in Rome. But, also like Gregory, he hated the things he saw in city life, and determined to forego all thoughts of an earthly career. One night he fled from Rome, and made his way to a cave in the lonely Sabine Hills, some thirty miles away. It was a desolate place. The silence around was unbroken save by the wail of the wind, or the cry of some wild beast.

For three years Benedict lived alone, thinking only of God, and of his own sinful state. Only one person knew of his existence there. A monk from a neighboring monastery occasionally brought him food, which Benedict drew up on a rope to his inaccessible cave. Seeing no one, speaking to no one, dressed in a coarse hair shirt, he prayed and meditated all through the hours of the day; and at night, to chasten his body, he rolled in a bed of thistles.

But in spite of his secrecy, the fame of his holiness spread abroad, and other young men came to dwell as hermits in neighboring caves. They urged Benedict to be their leader, and deeming it the will of God that he should aid his fellow-mortals, Benedict agreed. He established a monastery in the Sabine Hills, where he governed these men as abbot. Soon he had founded twelve other monasteries around his own, and such a good name for godliness did Benedict's monasteries gain, that patrician fathers in Rome began to send their sons to be taught in the Sabine Hills. But an envious priest forced Benedict out of the neighborhood; so he went further south and established the monastery of Mon′te Cas-si′no where he drew up his famous Rule.

According to Benedict's Rule, monks must obey their abbot, cut themselves off from all worldly pleasures, renounce their wealth, and give themselves up to labor and prayer. They could not own property—not even the smallest trifle. They could not walk abroad. If sent away, they could not eat without the abbot's permission. They could not receive letters from home, and were sent to bed very early. Once in the order, they were never allowed to withdraw; and any violation of the rules, entailed private admonition, whipping, or expulsion. Soon Benedict's Rule was adopted by other monasteries, and became general throughout Christian Europe.

St. Benedict of Nursia, founder of monasticism in the West, who gave a Rule for guidance and discipline, greatly praised by Pope Gregory and adopted throughout all Europe. (MS. illumination, British Museum.)

The Clergy

Now the monks were not priests. They could not hear confession, nor perform the Mass. Monks stood halfway between the laity and the clergy, who came in closest contact with the people. Many of the clergy did much in these very troublous times to bring the half-civilized people of Europe to a little higher level. Priests must understand the meaning of the Lord's Prayer and the Creed in the way that St. Augustine and the other great saints had explained it, and they must not put in any ideas of their own. They must know the services by heart, and be able to sing them without mistake. In the great cathedral churches there were many priests. The *dean* was in charge of the cathedral; he arranged the services and took the bishop's place during his absence. The *precenter* was responsible for the music. He trained the boys in the cathedral school to sing the chants, often playing the organ himself; and he watched the boys like an eagle to see that they did not play by moulding hot candlewax! The *sacristan* rang the bell, and locked the church doors at night.

Boys singing in a choir of elaborate, fantastically carved wooden stalls under an ornate wooden canopy. (Stalls from MS. called Henry VI's Psalter.)

Celebration of Mass in an oratory. On the table are the bread and wine, over which the priest is swinging his censer. Behind are communicants awaiting the Holy Eucharist. (9th cent. MS. Private Collection Firmin-Didot.)

There were five services a day in the great cathedrals, and nine on Sundays; so the bishops chose certain priests to live near the cathedral and take turns in conducting the Mass. Thus when the bell rang for service, the good people of the town would see two or three of these *canons* walking sedately across the green toward the cathedral door.

In addition to the city clergy, all the land in Christendom was divided up into parishes, which usually consisted of a village, and the farms in the neighboring fields. The village was nothing more than a straggle of thatched wooden hovels nestling under a hill, but it boasted two stone buildings. One was the mill to which everyone brought his corn to be ground. The other was the parish church. The mill belonged to the lord of the village, whose big house was visible through the trees half of a mile away, but the church belonged to the villagers. Square and solid it stood, its stone walls many feet thick, its tower where the bell hung, a look-out in times of danger. The church was big enough to hold all the people of the village, for no space was taken up by seats.

The people stood or knelt on the rush-strewn floor through the long hours of the service, and only the lazy ones leaned against the pillars or walls. To one side of the church was the church-yard, fenced off so that cows and sheep might not trample on the graves, and close by was a two-roomed house, which served as a second home to everyone in the parish, for here lived the village priest.

The village priest did not pretend to be a clever man, but he knew more than his neighbors, because he could read and write if people did not hurry him too much. He could decline a Latin noun, conjugate a Latin verb, and knew many Psalms by heart. But best of all he knew the hearts of his people, for he had grown up among them, and was a peasant like themselves. Therefore, they trusted him and came to him with their sins and difficulties, certain that he would help them. When a man lied to his neighbor, or struck him in anger, or did anything else of which he was ashamed, he was not happy until he had confessed his sin to the priest, and been forgiven. Then as a sign of repentance, the priest would order him to say so many prayers each day; or to visit the shrine of some saint, or to fast,—but not too severely, because no man could plough all day if he did not eat a little, and the priest was a kindly man. He loved his little flock.

In every little hamlet and village the priest was the leader of the people. He christened, married, and buried them. He served them in the church on Sundays and holidays. In his sermons and in his daily life, he comforted the heart-sore and wretched, and taught all by word and example to hold fast to right living. He also taught the children in the shade of the little church porch. Here he told them stories of the saints, and taught them to recite the Lord's Prayer, and the Creed. Having no books he could not teach them to read, but most of them learned to add and subtract by cutting notches on bits of wood.

The priest tried to look after his people's bodies as well as their souls, and the old women of the village told him all he did not know about the use of herbs. Mugwort, they said, was good against poison, fevers, and witches. Figs were good for broken bones, and the juice of aloes stopped hair from falling out. A sudden pain, which was caused by the arrows of mischievous elves, could be cured by holding a shield of branches over the patient and singing an old heathen chant containing the words: "Flee witch to the hilltop!" But by ending the chant with the words "so be it, Lord," the heathen spell was turned into a Christian one!

Demons attacking St. Guthlac. Medieval Christians, more pagan than Christian, actually thought such real devils tormented men and they are often pictured in manuscript illuminations. (12th century Harley Roll, British Museum.)

The country people were slow to forget the old ideas that had flourished in the reed huts beyond the Rhine, before the Franks moved into Gaul, and before Clovis was baptized. As he walked in the woodland, the priest would sometimes come upon a man stooping over something in the path, and singing softly to himself. Then the priest would see him light three candles, and drop the wax three times on one particular spot of ground; and he would know that the man had lost some cattle and was using the old trick to discover the thief by bewitching a hoof track! Such sights made the priest feel sad; a good Christian would have placed the three candles before the saint's shrine in the church, and then in a proper way, the cattle would have been returned.

The simple, kindly village priest who brought the only teaching of higher things, to his flock of toil-worn peasants.

But in most things the people obeyed their priest; for to them he stood for the majesty of Rome. Each man set aside a tenth of his goods each year for the Church, and at harvest time one sack of corn from each farmer found its way to the priest's spare room, or into his barn. Each woman brought the first basket of berries she gathered, a fat spring chicken, a dozen eggs, a honeycomb, or a round yellow cheese. One third of these good things had to go to the bishop of the diocese, and another third to the lord of the village, but the rest belonged to the priest. To the simple village folk their priest with his shabby cassock, and work-worn hands, was a figure dearly beloved. He made them feel that in spite of poverty, toil, and hard knocks, they were men with immortal souls no less than the lord in his castle. He taught them that fighting and eating were not the only joys to be had. He taught them that they must love their neighbor, and not try to get the better of him all the time. He taught them all they knew of gentleness, forbearance, and Christian courtesy.

THE MEDIEVAL CHURCH

A Little Monk of St. Gall, a Benedictine Monastery

Not long after Charlemagne's time, a little kinsman of the Emperor called Not'ker, the Stammerer, was growing up to manhood in the monastery of St. Gall. The monastery was perched in a valley amongst the foothills of the Alps. The dark pines stood sentinel around it, and the hills rose range on range, until on the far horizon, the white peaks of the Alps wreathed themselves in clouds. In front, steep gorges descended, and far down below, Lake Constance sparkled like a jewel. Sometimes when spring was come, the boy hearkened to the voices of the waterfalls that spoke to him from the hill-sides, and yearned to leap like them down to the valley below; for he was but twelve years old. Nevertheless, in general, he was happy to think that he belonged to the brotherhood and would some day become a monk.

Notker looks down upon the monastery of St. Gall in its high valley among the towering Alps. (Monastery reconstructed from a plan of St. Gall. The story is from the Chronicles of St. Gall in *Monumenta Germaniae*.)

A mother in the presence of a bishop and an abbot, offers her child to the service of the Church. (13th century MS. Brussels.) Serfs and nobles had equal opportunities. Incidents quoted from the *Life of St. Stephen of Obazine.*

Notker slept in his clothes, with ten other boys in his dormitory, and his day began at midnight, when the boys tumbled out of bed for the first service in the chapel. When the time had come to get up, the master who slept with the boys, would "rise very softly and just touch each of the children gently with a rod, that he might awake them from sleep." But if any boy lingered in bed, let him beware of that rod! By the light of one candle, the boys arranged their long black robes, and drew their cowls over their heads. Then stifling their yawns, they marched silently two by two into the chapel. And woe to the boy who "raised his eyes but a little in church, or smiled but faintly, or slumbered but lightly, or negligently let fall the book which he held, or made any needless sound, or chanted too fast, or out of tune," for "he received forthwith either a rod on his head, or an open hand on his cheek so loud that the sound of the blow rang in all men's ears."

After the service the boys returned to the dormitory and slept until sunrise; then up again and to work. Some helped the gardener, who raised the vegetables and fruits for the monastery. Some went to the kitchen itself to help prepare the morning meal. Others went into the fields and led the horses for the monks who ploughed the land for the grain.

The boys breakfasted in their own refectory. When all had taken their places at the long wooden tables, the master said grace, and they sat down to their plates of steaming barley porridge. Table manners were enforced with the ever-ready rod at the master's side. Said Hugh of St. Victor in his *Rules of Novices*: "Let nothing be done with uproar or tumult, but keep all thy limbs disciplined with modesty and tranquillity; not as some do, who are no sooner set down than they show the intemperance of their souls by the unquiet agitation and confusion of their limbs."

To prevent unseemly chatter, one of the older boys read aloud from a suitable book. After breakfast came lessons, all in Latin, because that was the language of the Church, and of all books in the West. Notker and his comrades, like the boys in Charlemagne's school, studied reading, writing, and music. They read the Scriptures, and the writings of the Christian church-fathers, like St. Augustine and St. Basil; but from Aristotle, Pliny, and other old pagan writers, they learned about many strange creatures. The unknown places of earth they were told, were inhabited by fire-breathing dragons, by sea-monsters, like the Kraken, which dragged down even the largest ships, and most wonderful of all, the Phoenix, that golden bird which lived for a hundred years and then burned itself to ashes! All these tales were accepted as actual facts.

Medieval schoolboys learned that very real fire-breathing dragons inhabited unexplored places (13th cent.).

The monastery cloister surrounding the inner garden, where the monks delighted to walk and talk, or meditate.

After the midday meal, everyone in the monastery was supposed to rest for a time. In winter the dormitory was almost the only warm place, for it had hot air under the floor; but in summer, Notker liked to sit in a shady corner of the cloister. The boys' chapel, dormitory, and school rooms, like the main buildings of the monastery, were built in the form of a hollow square enclosing a little garden, which was gay with grass and flowers, and had in the center a fish pool. A covered walk ran all around the square, and this was called the *cloister*. Here Notker would sit with a book, looking up now and then to watch the flight of a butterfly, or listen to the song of a bird. But all too soon the chapel bell rang, and the afternoon's work began.

THE MEDIEVAL CHURCH

There were at the monastery of St. Gall, many excellent craftsmen, skilled in the working of precious metals, in the carving of ivory and wood, and in the fashioning of musical instruments. When a man became a monk, he was allowed to carry on his trade in the monastery workshops provided he did it humbly and not to his own vain-glory. Indeed, a monastery was the only place where a craftsman could work in peace in these days of trouble and fighting. Notker learned how to make, and play a harp, a lute, and a queer sort of violin with only one string. On other days he spent many happy hours with chisel and hammer, and a bit of stone in the sculptor's workshop, or in watching the figures on an ivory book-cover take shape under the clever fingers of the master carver. Sometimes he secured permission from the abbot to go to the big *scriptorium*, where the copying of manuscripts was done; and Sintram, the master copyist, would let him write a sentence or two from a precious volume of Vergil. Then he looked over Sintram's shoulder, and watched him design a larger capital letter filling it in with rich reds and blues and precious bits of thin, heated gold leaf.

Monk copying a manuscript in a *scriptorium*. For centuries the monasteries were the only guardians of learning in Europe. Here, too, were kept the only records of historical events, until the rise of nations. (15th cent. MS. Paris.)

Abbot of St. Gall wearing over his shoulders the priestly stole, a long narrow band of elaborately embroidered silk which hung down on each side almost touching the ground. (9th cent. MS.)

Before leaving, he would run upstairs and peep into the high-arched library where the benches were crowded with studious brothers. There was always silence in the library. If a monk wished to change his book, he waited until he caught the eye of the librarian. Then, if he wanted a book by a Christian author, he made motions as if he were turning over the leaves of a volume; but if he wanted one by a pagan author, like Vergil, Herodotus, or Pliny, he scratched his ear as a dog does, "because," said St. Benedict's Rule, "unbelievers may well be compared to that animal." In spite of pretended contempt, however, the earnest brothers read and copied their non-Christian books with care.

On special occasions Notker was sent with a message from his own inner school, where boys were trained to be monks, to the outer school of the monastery, whither came neighborhood boys, who would go back into the world as soon as their school days were done. Through the unglazed windows, he saw the sons of serfs sitting by noblemen's sons, for the good monks made no distinctions and learning was free for all.

Then Notker would go up the hill, and, sitting under the pine trees, look down on the monastery, watching the last rays of sunshine touch the tower of the church, while the monastery buildings nestled in satisfied peace beneath its protecting shade. And there came floating up to Notker all the familiar sounds—the chanting of the monks, the chatter of tongues in the garden, the lowing of cows in cowsheds, and the merry clang of the blacksmith.

THE MEDIEVAL CHURCH

After supper and the final service, the boys went to bed very early. The dormitory must be silent, and therefore the beds of the smaller boys were placed between those of the older ones; and some time during the day, the master went around and examined all their beds to see if any boy had hidden in his blanket a favorite pen, or a piece of bread, or perhaps a home-made fish-hook; for St. Benedict's Rule strictly said: "No monk shall possess anything of his own — books, paper, pens, or anything else, for monks are not to own even their own bodies." For this reason the monks' robes had no pockets, and their beds were their only hiding places. If the master found anyone breaking this rule, he whipped the culprit soundly.

Thanks to the gifts of friends, and possessions surrendered by monks on joining the brotherhood, the monastery was rich and owned all the land for miles around. Much of this land was rented out in small sections to peasant workers, who came up every month to bring their rents of cheeses, or wine, or yearling calves to the steward. If, as an Irish monk said, the three sweetest sounds of increase were the lowing of a cow in milk, the din of a smithy, and the swish of a plough, nowhere in the western world was there sweeter increase than under the wide shadow of the monastery wall.

Serfs or peasants, such as those who worked for the monks on the broad estates of the monastery of St. Gall, doing everything by hand. The monks were the first to teach better methods of agriculture. (10th cent. MS. Gotha.)

When the monasteries were the only hospitals and charitable institutions, monks fed the poor and destitute.

Other visitors came every day when the monastery bell rang for the midday meal. These were the beggars. They clustered around the porter's lodge in their rags, and stretched out greedy hands to the almoner, the brother who doled out alms. Notker sometimes watched them almost snatch the loaves out of the almoner's basket. Aged folk, cripples, and lepers, found comfort and assistance at the monastery gate. Moreover, scores of strangers claimed hospitality of St. Gall. Almost every night as the sun went down, there came a knocking at the outer gate, and whether the benighted traveler was a brother-monk or a pilgrim, a nobleman or a peddler, the door-keeper opened to all. The pilgrims and peddlers were lodged in rough wooden houses between the workshops and the farm-buildings, but they ate heartily enough of the excellent fish and mutton which the guest-master provided, and their sleep was not a bit less sound because the unglazed windows looked out on the pigsties. Moreover, they were not obliged to pay a penny for their lodging. But, if they showed signs of lingering without cause, the stalwart monastery servants promptly put them out, for the abbot would not encourage vagabonds.

During his youth, Notker saw more of the richer people who were lodged in the new stone guest-house next to the abbot's chambers. Such visitors ate at the abbot's table, and were made free of the whole monastery. Often they were led away to see the fine new baths in the hospital next door. St. Gall was proud of its hospital, its doctors, its garden of herbs, and its cloister, where the sick could convalesce in the air.

An abbot on horseback with a hat over his hood, giving his benediction to the salute of some passing traveler on the little-traveled road. It was seldom, however, that an abbot left his monastery. (St. Alban's Book, Brit. Mus.)

Many a fever-stricken Italian, many an injured hunter, or battered victim of robbers, owed his life to the care he received in the monastery of St. Gall.

In the room where the old monks sat in the sun, there was one very aged blind man, who had served in Charlemagne's army; and Notker often supported him as he crept to the chapel and back. Knowing that little Notker was born of Charlemagne's line, the old man told him long tales concerning his famous ancestor, stories which Notker remembered and in later days wrote down.

Story-time in the monastery was during the long winter months when light failed at mid-afternoon, deep snow shut out the world, and the brothers gathered for warmth in the great calefactory. In this room, as in the boys' dormitory, hot air was forced through the floor, and was comforting to sandaled feet after the cold flagstones on which the monks walked in the church. Soon shaven heads appeared, as winter hoods were pushed back; limbs relaxed and tongues were loosened. Candles and pine-torches set the shadows dancing and tales of holy marvels began to go round.

An old Frankish monk spoke up to tell a tale of St. Gall. He said that one evening while St. Gall was praying at the foot of a rustic cross, a bear came down from the mountain, and began to eat the berries which the saint had gathered for supper. Seeing the thief thus busy, St. Gall rebuked him for eating that which he had not himself gathered, and bade him earn his supper by bringing wood for a fire. The bear, with downcast eyes, went lumbering off to the forest, but returned in a very short time with a goodly supply of dried branches, which he laid at St. Gall's feet. The saint then forgave him his sin, yet warned him to keep to the mountain tops, and avoid being tempted again.

A brother who had traveled in England next told about St. Guth'lac, the hermit of Croyland Isle, in the great fens of North Cambridge. "A horde of hideous demons," he said, "beset St. Guthlac's monastery and seizing on the good abbot, tumbling him through the air over the gates of Hell, holding him upside down, and in most unseemly fashion, maliciously showing his legs. But St. Guthlac reached earth in safety where he found St. Bartholomew waiting to put a scourge in his hand. Then he seized the Prince of the Devils, gripped him by the neck and gave him so sore a scourging that the devils fled in haste."

Devils tumble St. Guthlac through the air, showing his legs in unseemly fashion, while the friendly St. Bartholomew hands Guthlac a scourge. (12th cent. Roll of St. Guthlac, British Museum.) (See also the companion illustration and note on page 193.)

THE MEDIEVAL CHURCH

Not to be outdone, an English monk told of St. Cuthbert who wandered in England and Scotland, teaching the lonely shepherds. "On a certain day," he said, "St. Cuthbert was going forth from the monastery to preach with one attendant only, and when they became tired with walking, Cuthbert said to his follower: 'Where shall we stop to take refreshment?' 'I was thinking myself on the same subject,' said the boy; 'for we have brought no provisions with us.' The man of God replied: 'My son, learn to have faith, and trust in God who will never suffer to perish with hunger, those who trust in Him.'

An eagle supplies St. Cuthbert with a fish for his dinner. (MS. British Museum.) Incidents from the *Life and Miracles of St. Cuthbert* are condensed from Bede's *Ecclesiastical History* which contains many stories of this nature.

Then looking up and seeing an eagle flying in the air, he said: 'It is possible for God to feed us even by means of that eagle.' As they were thus discoursing, they came near a river, and behold, the eagle was standing on its bank. 'Look,' said the man of God, 'there is our handmaid, the eagle. Run and see what provision God hath sent us, and come again and tell me!' The boy ran and took from the eagle a good-sized fish, which she had caught. But the man of God reproved him: 'Why have you not given part to God's handmaid, the eagle? Cut the fish in two pieces and give her one, as her service well deserves!' He did as he was bidden, and carried the other part with him on his journey. When time for eating came, they turned aside to a village and made an excellent repast, while Cuthbert preached the word of God, and blessed Him for His mercies."

St. Cuthbert sets sail in a small boat for the land of the Picts where he at once establishes the Christian Church. (MS., British Museum.)

The murmur of applause which greeted this story, encouraged the stranger to tell of a certain young monk, who though treated by monastery surgeons, had nearly lost the sight of an eye. One day by fortunate chance, he took some of St. Cuthbert's hairs from a relic box in the monastery and clapped them to his eye. Some hours later he found his eye whole, as though never troubled with a swelling.

So the stories went. Outside was a world in arms, where only the fittest survived, where a man might be king today, and tomorrow only a beggar; but inside the cloister was peace with interesting, beautiful work. Here all men were equal, and served their fellowmen. Some of the monks and clergy earned a bad name for laziness, greed, and bad behavior, but in general the early clergy were good, and if the Church had not kept alive an interest in art and learning, if it had not cherished all that it knew of Christian ideals of conduct, Western Europe might have gone back into darkest barbarism during these unsettled times, when out of the greatest confusion, new nations were slowly emerging with a civilization containing both Germanic and Roman ideas.

VII
The Viking Adventurers
(800 A.D.—1010 A.D.)

The Break-Up of Charlemagne's Empire

After Charlemagne's death, his great Empire fell to pieces. The names given to his descendants proclaimed what weaklings they were,—Louis the Pious, Charles the Bald, Charles the Simple, Charles the Fat. Louis the Pious had neither power nor ability. Moreover, to make himself safe on the throne, he blinded his young nephew so cruelly that he died. Having gained his Empire by treachery, Louis lived among traitors all the rest of his days; his own three sons took up arms to wrest the Empire from him, and when he died, a bitter old man, they fought with one another to secure more power.

Charles the Bald, descendant of Charlemagne and ruler of the so-called Roman Empire, guarded by angels and attended by two captains and two princesses. See front cover. (MS. illumination, 870 A.D., State Library, Munich.)

Lothair, the eldest son, received the title of Emperor, and the other two sons, Charles and Lewis each received a kingdom; but when Lothair tried to take these kingdoms from his brothers, Lewis and Charles met at Strassburg and took an oath of alliance before their assembled armies.

"*Pro Deo amur*," said Lewis the German, using the South Frankish tongue, that his brother's French soldiers might understand, "*ab Ludher nul plaid numquam prindrai, qui meon vol cist meon fradre Karle in damno sit.*"

"*In Godes minna,*" said Charles the Bald, repeating the same oath in the language of North Frankland for Lewis's German soldiers; "*mit Ludheren in nohheiniu thing ne gegango, the minan willon imo ce scadhen werhen.*"

In English both oaths are the same: "Out of love for God," the two said, "with Lothair I will not willingly enter into any agreement which may injure this my brother."

These Strassburg oaths are important as the earliest remaining examples of the French and German tongues. The French is half-way between Latin and modern French, and was spoken by the people in that district which was formerly the Roman province of Gaul. The German is almost pure Teutonic without any mixture of Latin. So different had the languages of these two peoples become, that though both were descended from German tribes, the pure-blooded Germans east of the Rhine could no longer understand the Celtic-Roman Germans dwelling west of the River.

In the following year, 843 A.D., all three sons of Louis the Pious made a treaty at Verdun. Charles the Bald took the greater part of what is now France and Belgium; Lewis the German took most of the lands beyond the Rhine; and Lothair took Italy with the title of Emperor, and a long narrow stretch of land called Lo-tha-rin'gia, or Lorraine, which having no natural boundaries, was to be henceforth, forever, a bone of contention claimed by both Germans and French.

As yet there were no separate nations, for the inhabitants of all three kingdoms continued to call themselves Franks; but the lands thus roughly marked out, were never united again, and the divisions made by the Treaty of Verdun marked the beginning of the nations of modern Europe. After many centuries the district west of the Rhine

Charlemagne's Empire as divided by the Treaty of Ver'dun', 843 A.D. The kingdom of Charles became modern France; the kingdom of Louis became Germany; and the kingdom of Lothaire broke up into the little nations of Holland, Belgium, and Switzerland, in the south forming part of Italy.

became France, and the district east became Germany. From the middle land of Lo-tha-rin'gia came the little nations of Holland, Belgium, Switzerland, and the ever-contested Al-sace'-Lor-raine'. Meantime, the three Frankish kingdoms continued to fight with each other, while outside enemies preyed on their unprotected lands.

On the west were the strange, secret men of Brittany, Gauls who had never been properly conquered by either the Romans or the Franks. Rallying under their chiefs, they raided the Frankish farms, burning crops and stealing cattle. Nor would these Breton chiefs pay homage to anyone; they laughed at the Frankish troops, led them into ambush, then melted away and hid among the bleak Breton hills.

Mag'yars in wide breeches and fur shoes, enter Hungary under their chief, Ar'pad. Their Queen rides in an ox-cart (900 A.D.). From a panorama in Budapest, painted after scholarly research under the direction of Arpad Feszty.

From the east came small dark horsemen, bold and lordly of bearing, neighbors of the Turks and the Tartars. These were the warlike Mag'yars, who swarmed down out of Asia, and crossing the Carpathian Mountains under their leader, Ar'pad, descended into the ancient Roman province of Pan-no'ni-a, where the Huns had once had their stronghold, and where A'vars, Sla-vo'ni-ans and Gothic tribes had lived. Casting covetous eyes over the fertile green plains, they drove the Slavonian people from their mud huts and earthen fortresses, and settled down in Hungary in the year 895.

On the south, the Saracens from Spain and Northern Africa sacked coast-towns in Italy and the cities in southern Gaul. They wrested Sicily from Constantinople. They conquered Corsica, Sardinia, and most of Southern Italy. The waters of the Mediterranean swarmed with their pirate ships. They devastated the country about Rome, and even sacked St. Peter's, which was then outside the city walls.

VIKING ADVENTURERS

But from the north there came the most terrible foe of all. Too often as the morning mists rose from the river meadows along the valley of the Seine, a city watchman, looking from his tower, spied the high-curved beaks of ships with dragons on their prows, creeping up the river; he saw the gleam of winged helmets, and heard the splash of oars. With a groan he seized his horn and blew a hoarse blast that sent the townsfolk tumbling from their beds, crying: "The Norsemen! The Norsemen!"

Then women snatched up their children and took refuge in the church, while men caught up their weapons and ran to defend the miserable wooden walls of the town. But though they sold their lives dearly, that night the sky would be red with flames and many a weeping mother would turn her head from the deck of the Norsemen's dragon-ship for a last look at the home she was certain she would never see again.

A Viking dragon-ship leads in an attack on the defenseless hamlets of Europe. Since these lusty, northern barbarians eagerly welcomed death as the summons to Val-hal'la, the Christians of Europe were no match for them.

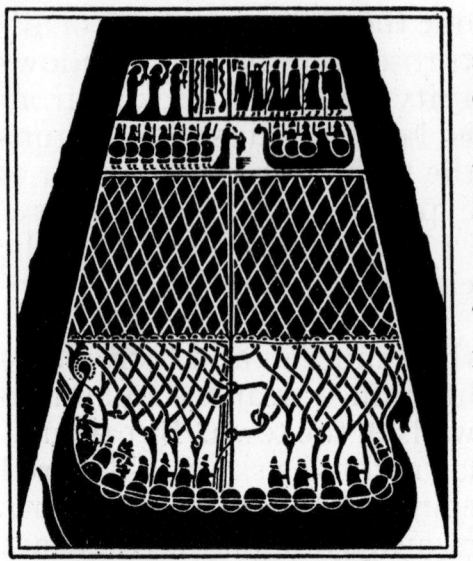

Ancient Viking ships and warriors on the Sten-kyr'ka stone from Gottland. (Bugge, *Norges Historie*.)

An old French chronicler sitting in the cloistered alcove of a monastery, wrote in his sheep-skin copy-book: "In the year 841, the Danish pirates from the shores of the North made a raid into the country of Rouen, with fire and sword. They pillaged the city in their fury, and slew and took captive the people." And the very next year he wrote again: "A fleet of Northmen came suddenly at break of day, capturing and killing men and women, leaving only the buildings, that have been saved by a ransom of silver."

All Christendom suffered from the fierce attacks of these Norsemen. They pillaged alike the shores of France, England, Scotland, Ireland, Spain, and Italy, even venturing as far as Greece. So terrible did they seem that for years a special prayer was said in the churches on Sunday: "From the fury of the Northmen, good Lord deliver us!"

From the creeks or *Viks* of Norway, from whence came the name *Vikings;* from the rivers of Denmark and Sweden, these red-haired pirates came, swooping down on the land. While other Teutonic tribes had entered the old Roman Empire in the fifth and sixth centuries, these sons of the Sea, the Gray Mother, had remained in their northern homes, worshiping the old gods and wringing a scanty subsistence from the cold, barren land of their fathers; but now they boldly began to answer the beckoning call of the Sea. "They are glad when they have hopes of battle," says an old saga, "they leap up in hot haste and ply the oars, snapping the oar-thongs."

VIKING ADVENTURERS

Long and graceful were the Viking ships with a dragon's head at the prow, a dragon's tail at the stern, and rows of bright round shields decorating the sides. Sails were of red and white, or brilliantly striped with blue, often finely embroidered and sometimes lined with fur. *Deer of the Surf*, *Raven of the Waves*, *Horse of the Sea*, the ships were lovingly called, and out in the foam with careless glee the adventurers boldly rowed, a hundred, perhaps, in a boat.

Norsemen settled in France, in the district still called for them Normandy. Colonies were founded in England, Scotland, Ireland, and the islands of the Orkneys and Shetlands. Viking rovers from Sweden went to colonize Russia. They explored the misty seas of the distant North Atlantic, discovered and colonized Greenland, visited Labrador, Newfoundland, Nova Scotia and New England; and since their religion painted a paradise of feasting and fighting to be gained only by death in battle, all warriors sought conflict; and action and adventure were to them the breath of life.

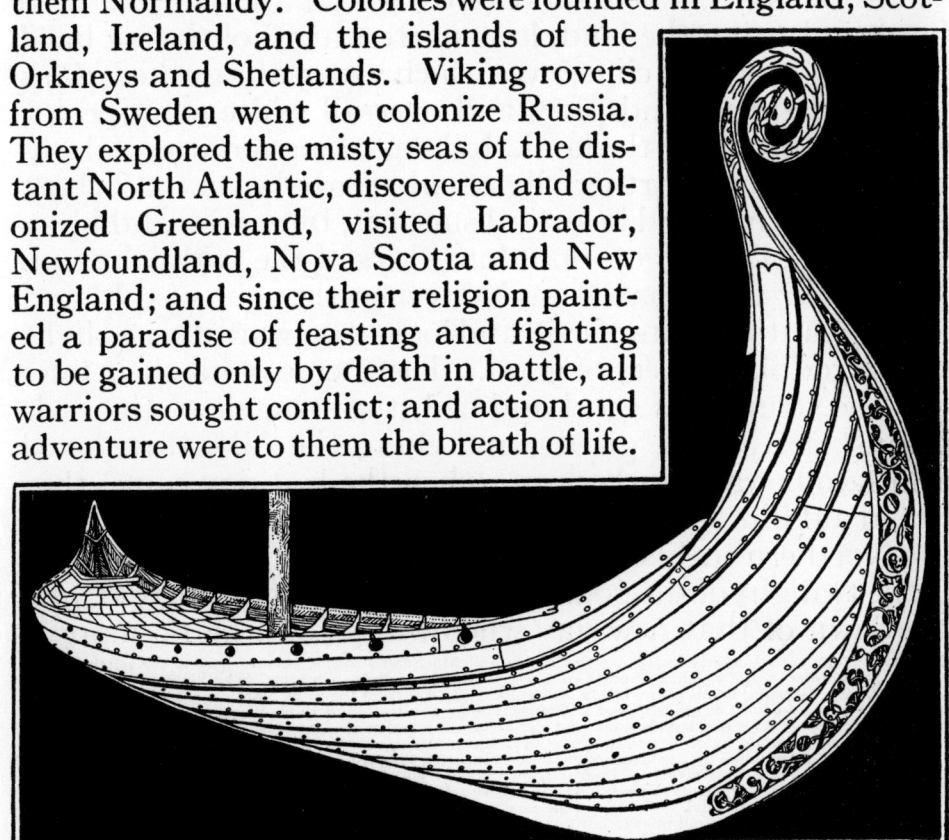

Viking ship found at Ose'berg near Os'lo, Norway (800-850 A.D.). In a wooden tent behind the mast of this ship were buried a Viking Queen, her handwoman and numerous belongings. The entire ship was then enclosed in an earthen mound topped with stones. (See pages 217, 220, 221 for carved wooden articles buried in the ship).

Grand and tragic was their faith like the land from which they had come, full of the struggle those barren shores had forced upon her sons, yet gleaming with beautiful fancies as lovely as their summer, and filled with a strange, deep yearning for ultimate goodness and joy. In their homes in Northern Europe during the long, snow-swept winters the sun never rose from the sea; and the endless slow monotony of day after day of darkness was only relieved on clear, frosty nights when the flare of the northern lights played weirdly across the sky. Their shores were grand and rugged, deep fjords indenting the land, long narrow arms of the sea lined with tall, frowning cliffs, over which waterfalls gushed; dark forests of spruce and pine; and over all white snow-peaks, solemnly guarding the land. Icebergs, long months of darkness, the flash of northern lights, alternated with three short months of vivid and beautiful summer, blue skies and bluer seas, sweet rich vegetation, long days of the midnight sun. No wonder then that these Norsemen thought of cold and ice as gigantic spirits of evil, and looked on warmth and light as the godlike powers of good. The theme of all their tales was the struggle of good and evil, the struggle of the gods against destructive giants; and Odin, the All-father, loved courageous warriors because, when the last day came, they would aid him in fighting evil. In hall-houses of the North, the Northern scalds or poets sang old, old tales of the gods, of the twilight of the gods, of the tragic end of the world, and the dawn of that new day when evil should be no more.

Norse mythology is particularly important to English and American readers, because it was the religion of our own heathen ancestors, and touches us more closely than Greek or Roman myths. Whether our ancestors were English, French, German, Danish, Swedish or Norwegian, all came from the same Nordic stock and believed these same myths of the gods. The graceful and idyllic mythology of Greece and Rome bloomed beneath sunny skies; but Norse mythology grew in a land of snow and ice. Hence, it was distinguished not only by vivid fancies but by tragedy and a grim humor found in no other race and continuing to color Northern thought even to our own day. Norsemen driven from home by the tyranny of Harald Harfagir, sought refuge on the desolate, volcanic island of Iceland in 874 A.D., and there preserved their religion and poetry unchanged; while other Teutonic nations gradually became affected by Roman and Byzantine Christianity. It is from the collection of these records known as the *Elder Edda,* and made in Iceland by Saemund the Learned, the most precious relic remaining of ancient Northern literature, that we know these old tales of our fathers. They are also to be found in the *Heimskringla,* or *Sagas of the Kings of Norway,* written in the 13th century by Snor'ri Stur'lu-son, an Icelander. The Norsemen were not finally converted to Christianity until about 1030 A.D., when they were forcibly Christianized by their King, St. Olaf, who broke the wooden statues of the gods and destroyed their shrines. Most of the Norse gods were then declared to be demons or witches, and such tales about them as the missionaries could not eradicate, were transferred to various saints; but even in recent times belief in fairies and trolls has lingered in the hearts of the peasants of the Northland.

The beginning: Ni′fl-heim, land of mist; Mus′pells-heim′, land of fire; and Y′mer taking shape in Gin′nun-ga-gap′.

Norse Tales of Creation and the Gods

In the beginning, the morn of time, there was in the center of space a dark and yawning gulf, Gin′nun-ga-gap′, the abyss, north of which lay Ni′fl-heim, the land of mist and darkness, and south of which lay Mus′pells-heim′, the blood-red land of fire, where Sur′tr, the great flame-giant guarded the frontier. Now streams from a spring in Niflheim gushed over into the cleft and froze in the cold of the gap, rolling down as blocks of ice with a mighty roar like thunder; but sparks from Muspellsheim, fell on this ice and sent up great clouds of steam which changed in their turn into hoar-frost.

Born of this action of heat and cold, there came to life mid the ice blocks the huge ice-giant, Y′mer, who groped about in the mist and the gloom in search of something to eat. Discovering a giant cow, he straightway consumed her milk, while the cow, likewise searching for food, licked the salt from an ice block and so brought to light the hair of a god imprisoned in the ice. As the cow continued to lick, Bu'ri stood forth from the ice. From Buri, the gods were descended; but from Y'mer the frost-giants sprang. Odin, Vi'li, and Ve, the grandsons of this Buri, slew the gigantic Ymer, and in the flood of his blood all his descendants perished, save for a single couple who made their escape in a boat and settled in Yot'un-heim' to produce a new race of giants.

Odin, Vili, and Ve next started to form the world. They rolled the body of Ymer into the yawning gulf; of his flesh they made Mid'gard, the earth, hedging it with his eyebrows. His blood became the sea, his bones the giant hills, his jagged teeth the cliffs, his curly hair the trees, and his great skull made the sky, which was upheld by four dwarfs, *Nordi*, *Sudri*, *Austri*, and *Westri*, from whom the four points of the compass were called *North*, *South*, *East*, and *West*. To light the world the gods made stars from the sparks of Mus'pells-heim'; but of two more brilliant sparks they formed the Sun and Moon, which they placed in golden chariots driven by Mani and Sol. But alas, gods had mated with giants, good had been mixed with evil; and so they made themselves imperfect; and as only the perfect endures unto eternal life, the gods would some day be destroyed. So, Mani and Sol were pursued in their course by two fierce and hungry wolves, which would overtake and devour them in the Twilight of the Gods

A Norse idea of the sun, and the wolves with yawning jaws which seek to devour Sun and Moon. (Belt buckle, National Museum, Copenhagen.) With Mani, the Moon, in his chariot, rode two children, Hiuki and Bill, snatched by Mani from a cruel father who made them carry water all night. Our English ancestors called these children *Jack* and *Jill*, and said they could see them with their pail clearly outlined against the moon.

Trolls, the typical Norse goblins. (Norse carving from the Oseberg ship, 800-850 A.D.) Trolls were grotesque little creatures often having long noses, while dwarfs were little men. Dwarfs could go instantaneously wherever they wished to be, and each had a tiny red cap which made him invisible. They envied man's taller stature, and often tried to improve their race by stealing unbaptised children and leaving the human mother their own little wizened offspring. Such dwarf-babies were known as *changelings*, and when a human mother found a changeling in her baby's cradle, she could only recover her own child by brewing beer in egg-shells, or by holding the dwarf-child's feet to the flames, so its parents, hearing its cries, would hasten to claim their own and return the stolen child. But in general the dwarfs were kindly. They kneaded bread, ground flour, performed countless household tasks and harvested grain for the farmers; but if they were ill-treated they straightway forsook the house and never came back again. After the introduction of Christianity, a Northern ferryman insisted that he had been hired to ply his boat over the river many times during the night and that at every trip his vessel was so loaded down that it nearly sank; yet he could not see a single passenger. When his night's work was over, he received a rich reward, and heard a voice explaining that he had carried all the dwarfs over the river, as they were leaving the country forever to punish the people for their unbelief! (Guerber's *Myths of Northern Lands* is an interesting popular account.)

Having made Sun and Moon, the gods now made Nott, or Night, and gave her a coal-black chariot and the coal-black steed, Hrim-faxi, from whose mane fell hoar-frost and dew to refresh the earth at night; and Night wedding Dawn, brought forth Day, a young and resplendent god, who drove a radiant white steed shedding light from its glorious mane.

While the gods were thus engaged, a host of maggot-like creatures was breeding in Ymer's flesh. Crawling in and out, they attracted the notice of the gods, who summoned them to their presence, and divided them into two groups. Some were ugly little fellows with large heads, green eyes, and short legs; and these were banished to the underground whence they could never come forth as long as it was day. They were called *dwarfs, trolls, gnomes, brownies,* or *goblins*; and they spent all their time in the depths of the earth, collecting gold, silver, and jewels, which they stowed in secret caves, or fashioning marvelous metal-work, for they were clever smiths.

The useful, good and beautiful among the little creatures that breeded in Ymer's flesh were called by the gods, *elves*, or *fairies;* and they dwelt in the realm of Alf'heim, half-way between heaven and earth. So tiny were these elves, that they could flit about unseen to care for the flowers, birds, and butterflies; and they slipped down on the moonbeams to dance upon the earth. Holding one another by the hand, they danced around in circles, thereby making fairy rings where their little feet had trod. Honey and milk were often left for the fairies.

Having so far ordered the universe, Odin, Vili, and Ve, walking along the seashore, perceived two blocks of wood carved in a human form, and calling these to life, the three gods thus made the first man and woman who peopled Midgard, the earth.

The gods themselves dwelt in As'gard, high above the earth, living in golden palaces in a golden age of happiness, which was long undisturbed by evil. Over Odin's hall towered the giant tree of life, Ygg'-dra-sil, having one root in Ni'fl-heim, one root on the earth and one in Asgard itself, near the Ur'der fountain, where those three weird sisters, the Norns, wove their web of fate. From the topmost bough of Yggdrasil, a falcon watched heaven and earth; but far down in Niflheim, the horrible dragon, Nid'hug, gnawed at the root of the tree, knowing well that its death would be the final signal for the downfall of the gods. Connecting heaven and earth rose Bif'rost, the bridge of the rainbow, and Heim'dall, who guarded this bridge, had so keen a sense of hearing, that he could hear the grass grow.

Odin or Woden, chief of Norse gods, represented the all-pervading spirit of the universe.

Odin or Woden, the All-father, was chief of the gods in Asgard, and *Wodensday*, or *Wednesday*, was held sacred to him. In his eagle-helmet and sky-blue cloak, he sat on his mighty throne, overlooking the world, while two ravens perched on his shoulders and two wolves crouched at his feet; but when he rambled on earth, he wore a broad-brimmed hat to conceal his loss of an eye, for he had given one eye to purchase a draught of wisdom from the giant Mi'mir's Spring. By Odin sat Frig'ga, his Queen, twirling her jeweled distaff to weave webs of bright-colored clouds. Frigga was goddess of the atmosphere, and when the snow flakes fell, people said she was shaking her feather-bed; when it rained, she was doing her washing, and the white clouds were her linen in the sky.

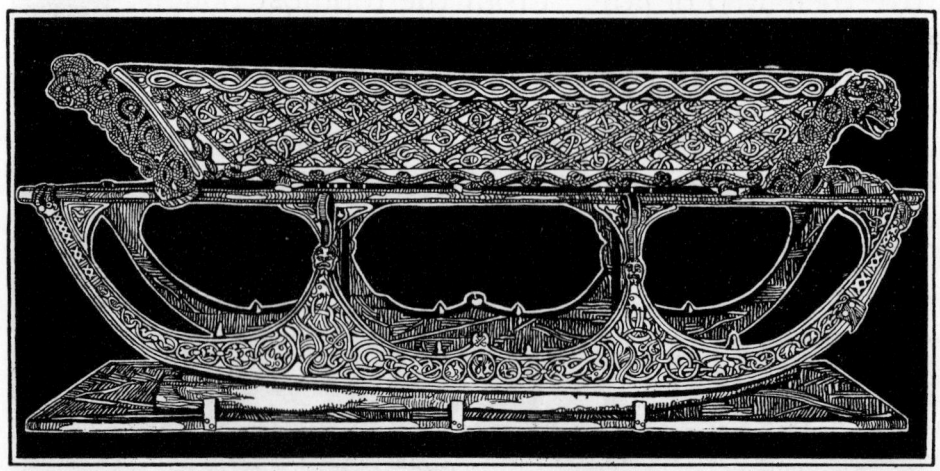

A beautifully carved Viking sledge buried in the Ose'berg mound, to bear the Viking Queen on the snowy parts of her journey to the Underworld. Buried with the Queen were three other sledges, a wagon, beds, tent-poles, etc.

Odin's palace, Val-hal'la, the Hall of the Chosen Slain, stood in a marvelous grove whose leaves were of shining gold. It had five hundred and forty doors, each so exceedingly wide that eight hundred marching warriors could enter it abreast. Its walls were of glittering spears; its roof of golden shields; and unto this glorious spot, Odin welcomed all warriors who lost their lives in battle; while those who died in their beds must go to the gloomy Underworld, the dark, pale realms of Hel, forbidding goddess of death. Riding horses, or driving in wagons burned on funeral ships or pyres, these unfortunate ghosts came at last to Helgate, where the fierce blood-stained Hel-hound, Garm, continually kept strict guard.

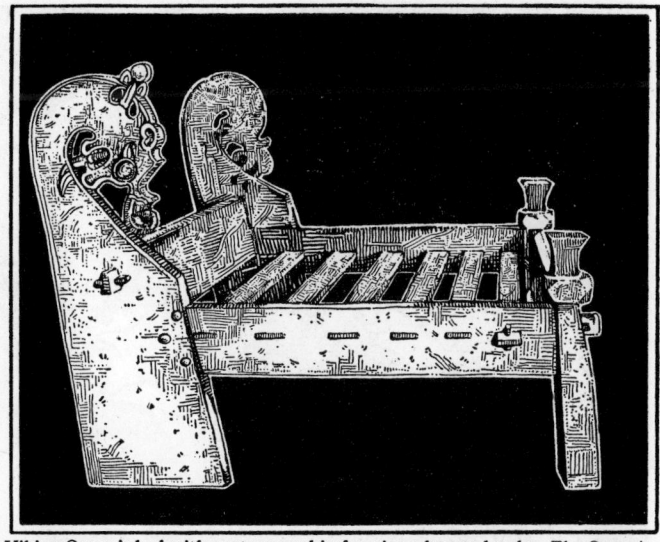

Viking Queen's bed with posts carved in ferocious dragon-heads. The Queen's body lay on this bed which had down quilts, pillows, and rugs. (Oseberg Ship.)

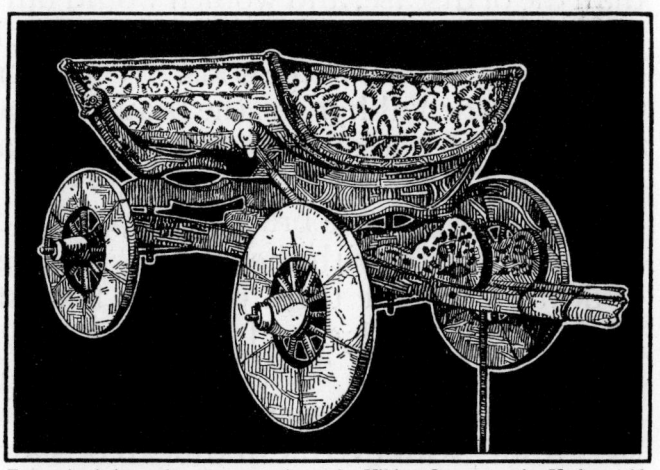

Four-wheeled wooden wagon to bear the Viking Queen to the Underworld. (Oseberg Ship.) Grotesque beings appear among the carvings. (See pp. 212, 217.)

A beautiful Val-kyr'ie or Battle-Maiden, with flying hair, seeks in a battlefield for heroes worthy of Val-hal'la.

No wonder that to reach Val-hal'la and escape Hel's colorless kingdom, a Northern warrior would kill himself rather than die of disease, and women would fall on a sword or leap from a precipice, that their souls might join those they loved in the bright home of the gods. Whenever a battle occurred, Odin sent the Val-kyr'ies, the beautiful Battle-Maidens, who rode through the air with flying hair, clad in blood-red armor and carrying glittering spears. These maidens chose the heroes who were brave enough to aid the gods in their last great battle with the giants. They gave them the kiss of death and bore them on their fleet steeds over Bifrost, the Rainbow Bridge, and up into Valhalla where Odin himself received them. There the heroes drained great horns of mead and ate of the sacred boar, which though daily butchered, always came to life in time to be slain and cooked again before the following meal. Having thus eaten and drunk, the heroes amused themselves by fighting with one another, but the terrible wounds which they dealt, all healed instantaneously as soon as the dinner horn sounded! Then bearing each other no grudge, they rode gaily back to Valhalla, to feast in Odin's presence, attended now by the Valkyries, while the scalds sang of war and adventure. Such beliefs made a fierce race of warriors who flung themselves into battle, fearlessly facing death as the Kiss of the Battle-Maidens and the welcome to glorious hall of Valhalla.

The chosen slain from earth's battlefields fight and feast in a heaven of glory, at the shining hall of Valhalla.

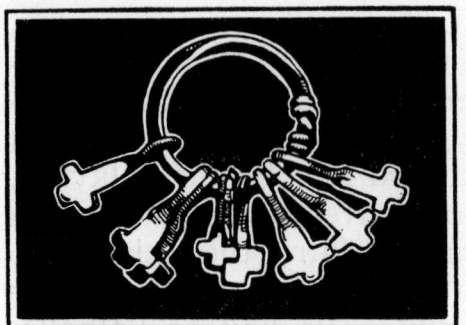

Hammers of Thor strung on a chain. (Indviken.) Northmen made the sign of Thor's hammer to ward off evil and secure blessings, as they later made the sign of the Cross, being little changed in their hearts through their conversion to the religious ideas of Christianity.

Thor was the eldest son of Odin and Frig'ga, and *Thorsday*, or Thursday, was sacred to him. As a child Thor was so strong that soon after birth, he amazed the assembled gods by playfully throwing about ten loads of heavy bearskins. Thor was god of the peasant-folk, and he dwelt in a wonderful palace, where he welcomed peasants after death, as their masters were welcomed in Valhalla. Thor was also god of the thunder, and he wielded a magic hammer from which flashed the lightning. So sacred was this hammer that Northern people made the sign of the hammer as they later made the sign of the Cross to ward off evil and secure blessings. The same sign was made over a newly-born babe, when water was poured on its head and a name was given to it. As this huge hammer of the thunder-bolts was usually red hot, Thor wore an iron gauntlet which enabled him to grasp it firmly, and the hammer had the magic power of returning always to his hand whenever he hurled it from him.

Tall, well-formed, and muscular, with bristling red hair and beard, Thor rode in a brazen chariot drawn by two swift goats, whose hoofs struck sparks from the sky; and the rumble of his chariot made the roll and roar of the thunder.

But in spite of his hammer of the thunder-bolts, Thor was never considered as the injurious god of the storm; he was the good god of Spring, thunder-storms that broke the cold force of the winter; and he hurled his weapon only against the cruel frost-giants. As these giants nipped tender buds with their blasts and hindered the growth of flowers, Thor once made up his mind to go to Yot'un-heim and slay them.

Accompanied by the god, Lo'ki, and Thi-al'fi, a young attendant, Thor tramped through the giant-world till he found himself at night-fall in a bleak land full of mist. Looking about for some shelter, the three perceived a strange house with one side entirely open. Finding the house deserted, they flung themselves down wearily, and went to sleep on the floor. Soon a fearful noise awoke them and they felt the earth trembling and rocking as if from a mighty earthquake. Afraid lest the wide main roof of the house should fall in, they fled to a little wing, where they slept for the rest of the night; but at dawn, as they left the house, they saw not far away the enormous form of a giant lying asleep on the ground and perceived that the terrible earthquake had been produced by his snores, while what they had thought was a house, was only the giant's mitten, the huge thumb being the wing into which they had crept for safety. Thor dealt the great creature a blow with his powerful magic hammer, but the monster only murmured that a leaf had fallen on his face. Two more terrific blows he mistook for a bit of bark or a twig, which he tried to brush from his face. At last he really awoke and learning that Thor and his comrades were bound for the castle of the Giant-King, he guided them for a day's journey.

The gods found Ut'gard-Lo'ki's castle built of glittering ice with icicles as pillars, but when they approached the throne the huge King said with contempt:

"Such puny fellows you are! What can such tiny weaklings do against us?"

"I can beat any giant at eating!" Loki boastingly cried.

So the King had a great trough of meat brought in. At one end he placed the god Loki, and at the other his cook. Loki gobbled as fast as he could and soon reached the middle of the trough; but he found that whereas he had picked the bones clean, his opponent had eaten both bones and trough!

Thor's great strength avails him nothing against the magic trickery of the giants, and he cannot even lift their cat.

Scornfully, Ut'gard-Lo'ki said it was very plain to be seen that these little boasters from Asgard, could not do much at eating. Whereupon, Thor was so nettled that he vowed he could empty the biggest drinking vessel in the house! A horn was accordingly brought; good drinkers, Utgard-Loki said, emptied it at one draught, weaker fellows at two, and very small drinkers at three. Thor drank till he thought he would burst, and still the liquid came up almost to the rim of the horn. A second and third attempt accomplished nothing more. Next, Thi-al'fi ran a race and was defeated by a young giant; while Thor, being challenged to show his strength by lifting the giant's cat, found himself able only to raise one paw from the floor. At last the Giant-King called in his old nurse Elli, as the only opponent worthy of wrestling with such a weakling, but Thor found himself thrown and defeated by an old woman! The gods were all forced to admit that they were beaten by the giants!

The next morning, Utgard-Loki escorted his guests to the borders of his land, where before saying farewell, he confessed that he had won his victories not by superior power, but by tricking his guests with magic. He himself was Skry'mir, the giant in whose mitten they had slept, and he had interposed a mountain between his head and Thor's blows which alone had saved him from death. Loki's opponent in eating was Logi, Wild Fire, which can devour anything; Thi-al'fi had run a race with Hugi, or Thought, than which none can run more swiftly; Thor's drinking horn was connected with the sea where his draughts had produced a great ebb; the cat was the Midgard snake which encircled the world and which Thor had nearly pulled out of the sea; and the old nurse Elli, was Old Age, against which none can wrestle. Having finished these explanations and warned the gods never to return, Utgard-Loki vanished. Thor angrily brandished his hammer to destroy the giant's castle; but such a mist enveloped it that it could not now be seen, and Thor was obliged to go home without having accomplished his purpose of wiping out the race of giants.*

Loki, Thor's companion, was the god of mischief and evil. When first he appeared in Asgard he seemed extremely pleasing and became a comrade of the gods, but slowly he revealed the evil that was in him, and he became the counterpart of the medieval Satan, the deceiver, and Prince of Lies. Through him evil entered Heaven, and all his offspring were evil. He was the father of three monsters, Hel, the hideous goddess of death; the terrible Midgard snake whose writhings made the tempests; and Fen'ris, the monstrous wolf, who would devour Odin himself in the last days of the gods.

*As Thursday was named for Thor, so all but one of the English days of the week received from the Anglo-Saxons the names of Germanic gods. Sunday is the Sun's day; Monday, the Moon's day; Tuesday, Ti'u's day (see page 236 for Tiu); Wednesday, Woden's day; Thursday, Thor's day; and Friday, Freya's day. Only Saturday recalls Roman connection with the German barbarians, since Saturday is Saturn's day. How the French language in these early days had separated from that of the purely Germanic tribes and become much more Romanized, is traceable in the modern French days of the week, which practically all have Latin names. Lundi is Luna's day, Luna being the Latin for Moon; Mardi is Mars-day, Mars being the Latin equivalent of Tiu, the Norse god of war; Mercredi is Mercury's day, Jeudi is Jove's day. Vendredi is Venus' day, Venus being Freya, goddess of Love.

Loki once wrought great mischief among the gods in Asgard. It chanced that the lovely I'du-na, goddess of immortal youth, had wedded the gentle Bra'gi, god of poetry and song, and before this beautiful pair the trees ever budded and bloomed, and earth was covered with flowers. Iduna had a magic casket in which she kept certain apples which conferred immortal youth on all who partook of them. The gods themselves warded off old age by eating daily of Iduna's apples, and dwarfs and giants all longed to obtain this wonderful fruit. One day, Odin, Hoe'nir, and Loki, having made an excursion to earth, were trying to roast an ox, but since the meat remained raw in spite of the roaring flames, they knew there was magic at work. An eagle on a nearby tree agreed to remove the spell if the gods would agree to give him all the food he could eat. The gods at once consented; the eagle fanned the flames with his wings and soon the meat was cooked. But when the bird seized in repayment, three quarters of the ox, Loki angrily struck him. Then to Loki's dismay, his stick stuck fast to his hands and to the eagle's back, and the bird flew off dragging Loki wildly through the air. It now appeared that the eagle was Thi'as-si, the fierce storm-giant; and he would not let Loki go till he promised to lure Iduna from her home in Asgard so that he, Thiassi, could obtain her precious fruit.

A few days later, when Bragi had gone away on a journey, Loki told Iduna that he had seen nearby some apples just like hers. Taking a crystal dish filled with her own magic fruit to compare with those Loki described, Iduna set out in the company of the mischievous Prince of Lies. But no sooner had they left Asgard, than Loki deserted Iduna; Thiassi swept down from the north, caught her up in his talons and bore her swiftly away to his barren and desolate home.

Bragi, god of poetry, was borne to Asgard in a ship; and at Yuletide men drank his health in cups shaped like a ship. Then the head of the family would solemnly pledge to do some great deed of valor during the coming year. All the guests made similar vows and as they had by this time usually drunk very freely, they began to outdo each other in declaring their big intentions. This custom in honor of Bragi gave rise to the English verb *to brag*.

There in the cold land of storms, Iduna, the lovely and youthful, pined and grew pale and sad, while all earth out of sympathy likewise grew pale and sad. Yet Iduna would not give Thi'as-si one bite of her magic fruit. Time passed, and the gods in Asgard, having no magic apples, began to grow old and infirm, while Bragi vainly sought his Iduna everywhere. Then Odin, suspecting Loki, ordered him to go and bring Iduna back.

Wearing the guise of a falcon, Loki flew to Iduna's chamber, and changing her into a swallow, he bore her off in his claws. But Thiassi discovered his loss, and set off in swift pursuit. Anxiously looking out from the walls of the Heavenly City, the gods, bent and gray with age, suddenly saw Loki coming with the Storm Giant close in his wake. Making enormous efforts, Loki cleared the wall and sank exhausted in Asgard, while the gods fired great piles of fuel to singe Thiassi's wings and blind him with smoke. Thus he fell stunned in their midst, and they fell before him and slew him. Iduna returned to Asgard, youth returned to the gods, and the warmth and bloom of life-renewing spring returned to the barren sorrowing earth.

But to the dismay of the gods there appeared one day in Asgard, Thiassi's daughter, Ska'di, come to demand satisfaction for the murder of her father. Skadi was goddess of winter. Clad in silvery armor, short white hunting dress, white fur leggings and showshoes, she carried a glittering spear that shone like a dazzling icicle and there followed her one of those strong, white, wolf-like Eskimo dogs.

To appease this young powerful giantess, the dwellers in Asgard said she might wed any of the gods, provided she chose her husband only by his feet.

Norse conception of Odin with huge head and tiny body, riding his magic steed. Below is his sacred bird. (Gold medallion. British Museum.)

Thus the gods stood in a circle all covered except for their feet, while Ska′di made her selection. Choosing the best formed pair of feet, which she thought must belong to Balder the Beautiful, god of light, Skadi found to her great chagrin that she had selected Ni′örd, god of the summer-seas, of harbors and fishermen; and Niörd bore her off to his palace, which stood beside the sea. There, Niörd loved to watch the seagulls, or the gentle gambols of seals; but the sound of the waves, and the shriek of the gulls, so disturbed Skadi, that she implored her husband to take her back to Thrym′heim. Niörd agreed to her pleadings; but he found the thunder of avalanches, and the cracking of ice in Thrymheim unbearable. So they came to an agreement. Niörd spent nine nights out of every twelve in Thrymheim, and Skadi spent the remaining three nights in Niörd's palace by the sea; but on earth this time appeared as the nine long months of winter and the three short months of summer.

Ska′di, goddess of Winter, spends the three months of summer with her husband, Ni′örd, beside the peaceful sea.

Frey, god of sunshine, on his golden boar whose bristles symbolize the sunbeams, and Freya, his sister, in her chariot drawn by cats. As goddess of love, Freya entertained lovers and married pairs in her palace after death. Cats, as symbols of purring affection were sacred to her as doves were sacred to Venus; but when Christian missionaries said that Freya was not a goddess, but a demon, the Northern people said she was leader of the witches who held their hag-like revels on a barren mountain-top on the horrid Val'pur-gis-night, and hence to this very day a witch is always shown as being accompanied by a cat. These ancient Norse gods by no means lost their reality in the Norseman's mind before the coming of Christianity. They merely became very real devils, or certain saints.

Frey was the son of Niörd and Skadi. He was god of sunshine and warm summer-showers, and he ruled the kingdom of Alf'heim where all the light-elves lived. With his sword of the sunbeams he fought the ice-giants, and he rode in his ship of the Clouds, that wonderful magic vessel which could be drawn out so large as to hold all the gods and their steeds, or folded up so small as to be thrust out of sight. Frey also rode on a golden boar, whose bristles gleamed like the sun's rays, or in a golden chariot from which he lavishly scattered fruits and flowers over the earth. Freya, the goddess of love and increase, to whom the day Friday was sacred, was the golden-haired sister of Frey, and she rode through the air in a chariot drawn by softly purring cats.

The Fall of St. Olaf. St. Olaf, who was King Olaf II, Haroldsson of Norway (1015-30), had been converted to Christianity, and with the aid of priests and bishops from England, he made a vigorous attempt to convert all the Northmen. He met with strenuous opposition, however, especially from the local chieftains, to whom their lusty, blustering gods of battle, not less than their gods in the sun-chariot (see p. 30), and moon-chariot, exerted a strong appeal. St. Olaf fled from Norway before Canute, and upon his return was slain in battle.

The Yule month was sacred to Frey and Thor, and began on the longest night of the year, when the days would henceforth grow longer, thus heralding with feasting the longed-for return of the sun. The word *Yule* meant *wheel;* for the sun was supposed to resemble a wheel revolving across the sky. All Northern races considered Yule the greatest feast of the year. In honor of Frey, they ate boar's flesh, and the boar's head was brought with ceremony into the banquet-hall, while the Yule log was burned on the hearth. So popular was this feast that the famous King Olaf of Norway, when making his people Christians, transferred most Yuletide customs to the observance of Christmas Day.

Now beside the gods of Asgard, there were also gods of the ocean, cruel and destructive powers; for the Norsemen suffered much from the sea, and knew little of the smiling waters that made the Greek sea-gods kind. Ae'gir, old man of the Ocean, with claw-like fingers clutching to drag things down in the waters, dwelt in a coral palace in the cool, green depths of the sea. He and his terrible wife, Ran, the goddess of shipwrecks, had nine capricious daughters, the snowy-armed, wave-maidens. In their shimmering blue-green veils, these damsels were often gentle, and played around the ships of the Vikings; but when the Wind was abroad, they chased each other frantically, shrieking with boisterous noise, tearing their hair and veils, and flinging themselves on the rocks.

But while all the gods and sea-powers dwelt in friendly fashion, assembling often together, one god dwelt alone. This was the silent Vi'dar, god of primeval forests and of the eternal, deathless, primitive force of life. Vidar was destined to survive the death of the other gods and rule the new heavens and earth. Pondering on the future, on eternity, and infinity, he dwelt now in a palace far away in deep woodlands, where reigned eternal silence and the solitude he loved.

The Twilight of the Gods at last drew on apace. Evil had come to Asgard with Loki, the Mischief-maker, and the end of the world was at hand. Odin and Frigga had twin sons, Ho'dur, god of darkness, somber, silent and blind, and Bal'der, god of light, beautiful, pure and radiant. All the earth loved Balder, and he lived with his innocent wife, Nan'na, the fresh, young Blossom, in a shining palace so pure that nothing unclean could enter it. But one day, Frigga learned from certain of the giants, that Balder was in danger. Sending out her messengers, she made all living creatures, metals, plants, and stones, swear never to injure Balder. The oath was readily taken; for everything loved the radiant god and basked in the light of his smile. Only the mistletoe on the oak at the gate of Val-hal'la seemed so puny and weak, that no one thought of asking an oath from such a tiny thing.

Discovering now that nothing on earth could harm their beloved Balder, the gods on the playground of Asgard, where they usually cast golden disks, invented a merry new pastime. They stood Balder up before them and cast all manner of missiles at the radiant, glowing god, laughing to see every one glance aside and refuse to touch him. But Loki, was jealous of Balder, and disguised as an old woman, he went to where Frigga sat spinning, leading her on to boast that everything on earth had vowed not to harm Balder, save the weak, little mistletoe, too small to be feared.

The death of Balder. Wicked Loki induces the blind Ho'dur to shoot the deadly mistletoe shaft at the shining god.

Loki then, by magic fashioned the mistletoe into a tough, strong shaft, and seeking the blind god Hodur, where he sadly stood by a tree, unable to share in the sport, he induced him to try a shot, and guided the blind god's aim. But instead of the shout of laughter which Hodur expected to hear, there rose a cry of terror, for Balder the Beautiful fell, slain by his brother's blow. Sadly mourned heaven and earth, and sadly mourned the gods. They built a great funeral pyre on Ringhorn, Balder's ship, and there they laid Balder's body with that of Nanna, his wife, who had died of grief on his pyre. High rose the leaping flames, as the gods sadly watched the vessel disappear in the west.

Then Frigga and Odin sent Hermod, the messenger of the gods, to beg the goddess of death, to give Balder back again. But Hel said she would only consent if all things on earth wept for Balder. So the gods sent heralds out to beg all things to weep, and every living thing wept, till the messengers came to the giantess Coal, lurking in her dark cave, and she, being Loki in disguise, refused to weep for Balder. Hel, therefore, kept her prey till Rag'na-rok' should come.

The gods banished Loki from heaven, but he roamed about the earth and tempted men to evil; so Thor set out and caught him, though he turned himself into a salmon and hid in a cataract. Then the gods bound Loki in a cave, and fastened a serpent above him to drop its poison on his face; and had not his faithful wife, Si'gyn, caught the drops in a cup, he would have suffered at all times the tortures which he endured when she left him to empty the cup.

The last days would now soon come! Balder, the light of the world, was hid in the depths of Hel, and evil was rife on the earth. The wolves who pursued the Sun and Moon would soon overtake their fleeing prey, and Nid'hug, the dragon of the underworld, would gnaw through the roots of Ygg'dra-sil, the heavenly tree of life. Then the dark red bird of Ni'fl-heim would loudly crow its warning, and Heimdall, guarding the Rainbow Bridge, would blow a loud blast on his horn. Gods and heroes would sally forth and gallop over the Rainbow Bridge to the field of the final battle. The terrible Midgard snake would wriggle out of the deep and hasten to join the fray. Out of the north on a frozen ship the fierce frost-giants would come, and up through a crevice Hel would creep, followed by bloodless spectres, the terrible dragon, Nidhug, and the hideous Hel-hound, Garm. The skies would be rent asunder and the great flame giant Sur'tr, bearing his flaming sword, would appear with all his sons. Loki would burst his bonds and leading the forces of evil would advance to the Rainbow Bridge, attempting to enter Asgard; but the glorious arch would sink and fall in the depths with a crash.

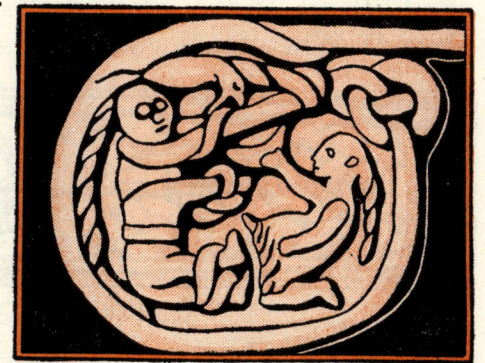

Loki and Si'gyn. (From Gosforth Cross.) Faithful Sigyn holds the cup which catches the serpent's poison.

Odin or Vi'dar with his shoe made from the bits thrown away by cobblers, braces his foot in the jaw of the terrible, devouring Fenris-wolf.

Riding Sleip'nir, his eight-footed steed, Odin would stop by the drooping, half-dead tree of life, to say farewell to the Norns, whose web of fate would lie in pieces at their feet. Then the hosts would clash in the last terrific battle. Surtr, consuming fire, would slay the sun-god, Frey. Ti'u the terrible god of war, fighting Garm, the Hel-hound, and Heimdall fighting Loki, would kill each other in battle. Thor with horrible effort would slay the Midgard snake; but be drowned in the flood of its blood, and the Fenris-wolf would swallow Odin in its jaws. Then Vidar would brace his shoe, made from all the bits thrown away by northern cobblers, in the lower jaw of the wolf; and seizing his upper jaw, would tear the creature asunder. All evil would be destroyed; the earth would be burned with fire and sink down into the sea; but out of the ruins would rise a new heaven and a new earth, purified by fire and water, repeopled as of old, but with a race wholly good; and over this new universe Vidar, the eternal, should eternally reign. Such gods as survived would find the golden disks with which the gods had played. Then they would perceive that the highest palace in heaven had never been consumed; and there they would find all the virtuous and the good. So evil would be destroyed and good triumphant reign.

Heimdall with his horn blows the loud blast which warns the gods when the terrible Midgard snake appears. (From the Gosforth Cross.) Since the Norsemen of Iceland were not converted to Christianity till the eleventh century, but came in contact with it in their Viking raids six centuries before, it is possible that some vague knowledge of Christianity colored their picture of a new heaven and new earth in which dwelleth righteousness without any idea of evil.

VIII
Life in the Feudal Age
(About 900 to About 1300)

Lords and Vassals

Vikings, Slavs, and Saracens harassing Western Europe! Nobles defying each other and fighting like snarling jackals to snap up the scattered fragments of Charlemagne's ruined Empire! Fire and sword, famine and pestilence throughout all Western Europe, and above all, that cry for help: "From the fury of the Northmen, good Lord deliver us!"

Where, in these troublous times, could a plain man find protection? As yet in Europe there were no nations, no royal armies or navies, no organized law, no police force to protect the weak and to punish the wrong-doer. Might was the only right, and woe to the man who was poorer or weaker than his neighbor; for if Viking and Saracen left him in peace, his own neighbor came and destroyed him!

There was only one solution to the problem. A man must buy the help of someone stronger than himself. So, throughout Europe, peasant farmers and small landowners went to the nearest noble and said: "If you will protect our lives, we will give you our land and you shall be our lord." This was the process called *commendation*.

Peasants driving a harvest wagon uphill. Such poor men had to purchase protection from Vikings and other invading tribes, or from thieving neighbors by *commending* themselves and their lands to the nobles; thus giving up land and liberty and binding themselves to their lords as *serfs*. (From Luttrell Psalter, 1340 A.D.)

Serfs, little better than slaves, bound never to leave the land, plough the fields for their masters. (Luttrell Psalter.)

Now, since land in those days meant wealth and power, nobles were only too glad to make such bargains with their poorer neighbors. Therefore, they said to the peasants: "I will promise to protect you from harm. I will accept your land in payment, but you must work on the land as you have always done, and give me most of the proceeds. Moreover, you must promise never to leave the land; and I will be your lord and you shall be my man." This process of commendation went on until all the land was owned by the nobles and worked by peasants who, though not slaves, were absolutely bound to their lord, and to the soil. They were no longer free men but were henceforth called *villeins* or *serfs*.

Nobles and ladies, too proud to work with their hands, play garden ball. (Fresco, Castle of Runkelstein, 14th cent.)

THE FEUDAL AGE

The main difference between a noble and a serf was that the serf worked with his hands and the noble did not. But some nobles were very poor, owning a few meager acres, while others had vast estates; so the poor nobles, like the serfs, bound themselves to great lords, giving service as fighting men in return for protection. They became *vassals* of their overlord, and held their estates as fiefs from him.

The Latin word for fief was *feudum*, and gradually the whole order of society changed into what was called the *feudal system*. At the head of the state was the King, to whom theoretically all land belonged; below the King were the great dukes and counts, whose vast estates were in themselves little kingdoms; and below the dukes were barons and knights. The feudal noble was always undisputed lord within his lands. He collected taxes and tolls, administered justice, and led the people in battle, dwelling in a castle on some high hill, where the people from the village below could find refuge.

An elaborate turreted castle of the later Middle Ages, surrounded by a wall and moat. Beneath its walls, peasants harrow and seed the land. Such castles developed from the crude wooden towers erected about 900 A.D., as protection against raids; in the 15th century after the invention of gun-powder, castles ceased to be built. (Miniature, about 1416. From Musée Condé, Chantilly.)

Boys robbed cherry-trees, and owners threatened punishment even in feudal days. (Luttrell Psalter, 1340.)

The earliest feudal castle was one great tower or donjon made of wood and surrounded by a wall and a moat, which was crossed by a wooden drawbridge. Later, this tower was made of stone and then other towers were added, until the nobles were living in the elaborate, turreted castles of the later Middle Ages.

The sons of a feudal noble were little troubled with learning, but they must be well trained in arms. They must learn to sit firmly in the saddle and to handle sword, lance, and shield. Moreover, they must learn to bear themselves gracefully and to serve noble guests at table; for waiting on people of higher rank was a privilege, and even a duke was proud to serve a king.

Sir Goeffrey Luttrell's family with two visiting clergymen dine in the great room of the castle. A noble youth receives the dishes from the cook at left, and waits upon the table. (Luttrell Psalter, about 1340 A.D. British Museum.)

THE FEUDAL AGE

The summers passed gaily enough in the castle, with the nobles going a-hunting or a-hawking with falcons trained to catch little birds and bring them back to their masters; but in winter the castle was dreary, and exceedingly cold and damp. The family spent most of their time in the one main dwelling-hall where a huge fire burned on the hearth in the center of the room, sending up clouds of smoke to blacken the ceiling with soot and escape imperfectly through a hole in the roof above. Narrow, unglazed slits formed the uncomfortable windows, and the stone walls were covered with skins, with the heads of boars and deer, or with the embroidered tapestries made by the castle women. In this one room the family lived, sleeping in curtained recesses, and eating their meals at a table on a platform at one end. The attendants of the household seated themselves at meal-time at tables lower down in the body of the hall; with hunting knives and fingers they made short work of the steaming joints of venison or wild boar which formed the bulk of the meal, while each person heaped up the bones and scraps before him. Silver cups of wine graced the high table; but the lesser household quaffed their cider or ale from huge leather flagons or wooden bowls.

Noble and lady falconing. The lady wears the glove which is the perch. (14th cent. MS.)

Falcons dart after birds, and one returns with his prey to his noble master. (14th cent. MS.)

There was little to do in winter but eat and drink, and watch the snow drift in through the unglazed windows, but when spring came again, the nobleman opened his castle and held his feudal court; for one of his chief duties was to see justice done among his vassals, since he was the only judge to whom one could make an appeal in an age when there were no national courts, no royal judges or laws.

The feudal court of justice was usually held in the great hall of the castle or before the castle gate, and here the nobleman sat in his high-backed chair of state, surrounded by his vassals. When each complainant had said his say, the nobleman and his vassals deliberated on the case. If they came to some decision, the noble gave judgment at once; but often it was hard to see which of two contestants was really in the right, and then the noble judge ordered the matter settled by means of the time-honored ordeal, the appeal to the judgment of God.

Lord of a manor dispenses justice to peasants at the manor gate. (Tapestry.)

There were many ways of appealing to the judgment of God. Women, ecclesiastics, and men of very low rank might be made to face the ordeal by fire, boiling water, or hot iron; but men of higher and equal rank made use of the ordeal by battle.

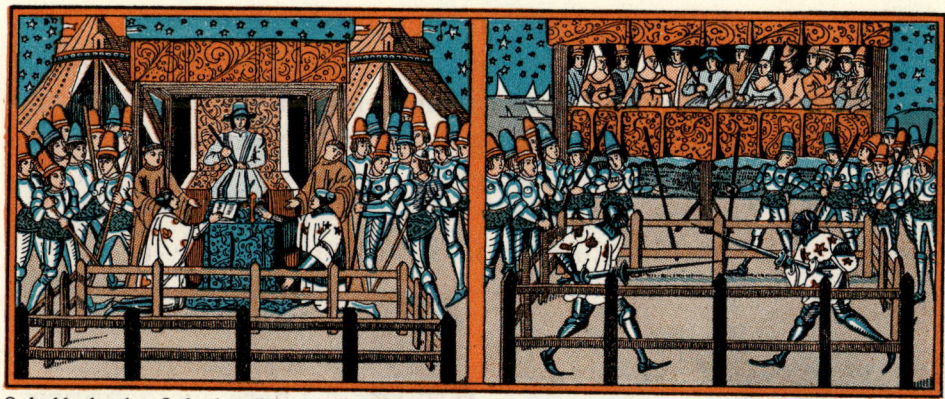

Ordeal by battle. Left, the religious preliminary. Before the lord who presides, each noble kneels, places his hand on the Bible and the cross, and takes oath that his cause is just. Right, the two nobles determine by battle which has sworn the true oath. (MS. 15th cent.) So firmly did people believe in the absolute certainty of true judgment by ordeal, that they often went to the most ridiculous lengths. A man named, Anselm, once stole many valuables from the cathedral of which he was treasurer; his accomplice having betrayed him, he challenged the accomplice to ordeal by battle despite his guilt, and came out victorious. Encouraged thereby he set up as an expert burglar and stole a golden dove containing hair of the Virgin Mary. The bewildered populace knew not how to determine who had taken the sacred relic, when a worthy priest proposed that a baby be taken from each parish and thrown into the pond according to the ordeal by water. The babies that sank would determine the innocent parishes. Each family in the guilty parish must then throw a baby in the pond. When the guilt had thus been fastened on a certain house, all its inmates were to be flung in the pond, thereby at last discovering the thief. (See McCabe's *Abelarde*).

In view of their overlord and his court, they fought until one was dead or had yielded to the other. Then the loser was accounted guilty; his estates were forfeited and his name dishonored; for God would have given victory only to the righteous, and from the judgment of God there was no appeal.

To this feudal court of justice likewise came new vassals to do homage for their fiefs, for when a vassal died his lands went back to his overlord; and a grown son must visit the overlord and receive the lands again directly from his liege. The new vassal must kneel before his lord, bareheaded and unarmed. He must place his joined hands between the lord's hands in token of submission, and promise to serve his lord against all other men. Then the lord must raise up, kiss him on the mouth as a sign that his homage was accepted, and finally present him with some symbol, a glove, a lance, or a twig; for no medieval bargain was ever considered complete without some such tangible symbol. That done. the new vassal rode home, the legal lord of his fief.

A Town Fair in Feudal Days

The country boasted few towns in the days of the feudal system; most people lived in castles or in little villages; but what towns there were belonged, like the villages, to the nobles and could be sold or given away just as the noble chose. Towns were only large villages with walls or fortifications; but whether large or small, those towns where bishops resided were distinguished by being called *cities*.

There were houses everywhere in a town even on the town-walls. Streets were narrow and crooked with buildings all jumbled together, each story projecting somewhat beyond the one below until the upper stories almost met above the streets. The best rooms of a merchant were in the rear of his house and opened on a pretty garden, while the front of the house formed the shop where interesting wares were displayed, and where a picturesque sign before the door indicated the owner's trade.

Medieval houses still standing in York, England. The upper stories of the houses project out over the crooked street making it dark and gloomy. The counters of the shops are placed directly on the street.

Car-cas-sonne', a great medieval fortified city of the French kings, existing today exactly as it was in the 11th and 13th centuries. It dates from the days of the Visigoths, and is built upon the ruins of Roman ramparts. (Photograph.)

Such towns had their yearly fairs to which merchants took articles which were not produced on most fiefs. One bright summer's day a caravan of worthy Flemish merchants crossed the flat fields of Flanders, journeying from Bruges to the Fair of Troyes, in France. Each merchant in short cloak and flat, round hat, rode beside his own pack-train and kept an eye on the well-stuffed bales, balanced panier-fashion on either flank of his mule. Travel was very slow, at the snail's pace of a pack-train, and there were constant stoppages. A knight with armed followers clattered by, and the merchants and their servants hastily drew themselves and their mules to the left of the roadway out of reach of possible sword-thrusts*; presently a portly abbot ambled past, riding a sleek-white mule, and the travelers doffed their hats to the worthy man as he acknowledged their homage and raised his hand in blessing to these intrepid Flemish merchants.

*When swords were used for defense, the rule of the road was "Keep to the left," thus placing passers on one's right, as it is easier to strike to the right with a sword. Many European countries still pass to the left; but America was colonized by musket-bearing people. Muskets must be at the right shoulder for firing, and naturally point left, so, to keep passers on the left, men pass to the right. America has forgotten the reason, but still passes to the right.

Merchants and peddlers bound for the fair. (Medieval MS.) Travel, even for short distances, was exceedingly difficult during the Middle Ages; roads were mud-holes and bridges scarce. When the young priest Ben′e-zet′ succeeded in building the famous Bridge of A′vig-non′ in 1177, it was so great an event that all the city rejoiced and the old French nursery song, "*On the bridge of Avignon, there they dance, there they sing,*" still celebrates the achievement.

All too often a farm wagon, stuck in a sink-hole, blocked up all the road; for the nobles through whose land the public highway passed, never kept the road in repair, though they gained rich revenues by collecting tolls at every ford or bridge, exacting a coin or two for each person, mule, and bale of goods which crossed their rickety bridge.

The Flemish merchants planned each day to reach some resting place before the sun should set, since robbers infested the road, and it was by no means safe to travel after dark. Now and then they spent the night in the guest-house of a monastery; but as a rule they put up at some inn; for inns were growing more numerous as the years passed.

Some of these inns were mere hovels standing at the crossroads. Here the travelers ate their own food and slept wrapped in their own cloaks, lying on benches in the one room which the poor little house contained. But in larger towns like Soissons, sounds of noise and revelry proclaimed an inn with a public-room, where travelers ate and drank around a trestle-table, sitting on wooden benches or long-legged wooden stools. Here the tired Flemings stretched their cramped legs, and washed the dust from their throats with long draughts of wine, while waiting for supper.

People crowding to the fair. (Medieval MS.) Flemish merchants will be foremost in supplying their needs for cloth. So much cloth was made in Flanders that many modern names for materials came from Flemish towns specializing in their manufacture; e.g. *cambric* from *Cambrai*, *lawn* from *Laon* (a French town near Flanders), *diaper*-patterned cloth called *d'Ypres* from *Ypres* (e′pr′). Flemish clothes were famous throughout all of Europe.

After supper they climbed a steep ladder to the one sleeping-room of the inn, a very crude sort of attic, where rows of beds lined the walls. Stripping to the skin and hanging their clothes on wooden poles that projected from the wall, the merchants tumbled in three or four to a bed. There were no sheets on the beds, for linen was far too expensive to be found in a public inn, and cotton was in those days almost unknown in Europe. Moreover, blankets or mattresses bore unmistakable signs of having been used before and were most uncomfortably full of lively fleas and lice; but that was to be expected by seasoned travelers, and after a half-hearted scratch or two, the Flemings were sound asleep. All night long rats and mice gamboled over the straw-covered floor, and one by one the other travelers stumbled noisily up the ladder and groped their way to bed. There was no air in the room, for the shutters were kept tightly closed, but the Flemings were accustomed to this and slept until the cocks crowed in the first blush of morning.

In the first days of July they arrived at last at Troyes to find the narrow crooked streets thronged with carts and animals, with merchants and visitors. Every tavern was full, and even the private houses had their quota of guests.

Though the fair was not yet opened, the Flemings unpacked their bales and began setting up their booths. Cloth-dealers occupied one public hall; grain-merchants another, and so with all the chief trades; and officers of the fair officially examined all the goods offered for sale. If they found a saddle badly made, a piece of cloth poorly woven, or a "silver" bowl made of tin, they fined the offending merchant or drove him from the fair.

By sunrise on the day for the formal opening of the fair, each merchant was in his place, and a herald with two attendants ceremoniously rode on horseback into the market-place where he blew a long blast on his trumpet while the sergeants rang shrill bells and loudly cried: "Haro! Haro!" It was the expected signal and trading began at once.

What a rushing from booth to booth! What a haggling over prices! Buy a Persian carpet! Look at my leather jackets! Here's where you get wines, armor, furs, or silk!

Booth of a merchant at a medieval fair. The people crowd about his display, anxious to buy. (Medieval MS.)

THE FEUDAL AGE

Dark-faced Syrians sold finger-bones of saints and bottles of Jordan water, sure-cure for the plague. Pilgrims and sea-faring men exhibited many strange objects; gaping country folk paid a penny to enter a tent and gaze on a real devil with long, hairy arms and a tail, and how were they to know that he was only an ape? They paid to see a plank from the hull of Noah's ark, or a genuine angel's feather, which looked remarkably like a quill from the geese, back home.

On all the street corners were stalls containing food and drink; in the open spaces, rope-dancers, acrobats, and jugglers went through their remarkable antics. Trick dogs and dancing bears collected crowds of onlookers; while light-fingered pick-pockets reaped a rich harvest among all those gaping crowds. So the business of the fair went on until the trading was done. Then once more the sergeants cried: "Haro! Haro!" and the fair was over. The visitors, high and low, went back to their castles or their huts, and the merchants counted their profits, packed up their stock, and set off for the next fair to be held many miles distant.

Scenes from a medieval fair. Acrobats balancing on swords, a performing dog, a hurdy-gurdy man and a drummer; and below, a dancing bear. (All from manuscripts in the British Museum.)

INDEX

INDEX

KEY TO PRONUNCIATION

ā as in māte   ä as in färm   ĭ as in ĭt   ū as in mūte
ă as in căt   ē as in ēve   ō as in mōte   ŭ as in cŭt
â as in câre   ĕ as in lĕt   ŏ as in nŏt   o͞o as in fo͞od
á as in ásk   ī as in mīnd   ô as in nôr   o͝o as in fo͝ot

Aachen (äch'en) or Aix-la-Chapelle, capital of Charlemagne, 172
Abbot, head of a monastery, 104, 189; *picture and note* 196, 200, 203
Abraham, patriarch, said to have founded the Kaaba, 121
Abu Bakr (ä-bo' bak'r), confidant and early follower of Mohammed, 128
   first caliph, 136
Acrobats, medieval fairs, 249; *picture and note* 249
Adrianople (ăd-rĭ-a-nō'pl), famous city n. w. of Constantinople
   Goths win famous victory over Valens, 65
Adventurers, Marcus Julius Paulus visits Roman provinces, 11–27
   Viking, 211–236
Aegir (ā'jir), in Norse mythology, god of the sea, 232
Aetius (a-ē'shĭ-us) (390?–454 A.D.), great Roman general, 69, 71, 80–84
   defeats Attila and his Huns, 80–83
   hostage of the Huns, 69–70
   murdered, 84
   rises to high posts, 71
   savior of Europe, 82
Africa, Mohammedans conquer Egypt, 136
   Vandals in, 66, 112
Agriculture, feudal system, 237–239
   in Charlemagne's day,
      royal family visits to consume produce, of royal farms, 172–174
   Middle Ages,
      monastic, 201; *picture and note* 201
         monks teach better methods, *note* 201
      ox team plowing, *picture and note* 238
      peasants harrowing and seeding, *picture and note* 239
Aix-la-Chapelle (ĕks-lȧ-shȧ-pĕl'), French name of Aachen, capital of Charlemagne, 172
Alaric (ăl'a-rĭk) (370?–410 A.D.), king of the Visigoths, 65–66; *picture and note* 65
   burial, 66
   sack of Rome, 66

Al'bion, king of the Lombards, 115–116; *picture and note* 115
Alcuin (alk'win) (735–804), English scholar and churchman
   head of Charlemagne's palace school, 171
Alemanni (ăl-ĕ-măn'ī), German tribes, 36; *note* 36
   driven back by Aurelian, 42
Alexander, bishop of Alexandria, Arian controversy, 56
Alexandria, patriarch of, 178
Alfheim (alf'hīm), in Norse mythology, home of elves, 231
Allah (ȧl-lä'), Mohammedan name for God, 128
Allah Akbar! (ȧl-lä' ak'bar), Mohammedan war cry, 153
Alpine race, in Alps and Central Gaul, 19, 117
Alps Mountains, Switzerland, *picture* 195
Alsace-Lorraine (ăl-sās' lŏ-rān'), territory in n. e. France, 209
Amalasun'tha, daughter of Theodoric the Great, died about 535 A.D., 89, 112; *picture and note* 113
Amphitheater, Roman in s. Gaul, *picture and note* 152
Amusements,
   Charlemagne's court, 174
   circus at Constantinople, *picture and note* 92
      Theodora, the circus-girl, 90–92; *picture and note* 91
   early Germanic tribes, 36
   Huns entertained by a dwarf, 78; *picture and note* 78
   Iberian, 16
   Middle Ages,
      falconry, 241; *picture and note* 241
      scenes from a medieval fair, 249; *picture and note* 249
Anasta'sius I (430?–518 A.D.), Byzantine emperor, 90
   honors King Clovis, 147
An'gles, German tribes, 36
   converted by St. Augustine, 184–187
   enter Britain, 68

INDEX

Animals,
  boar,
    hunted by Persian kings, *picture and note* 106
    sacred to the god Frey, 231; *picture and note* 29, 231
  camel, *picture and note* 106
    Arabian trade in, 122
    caravan of camels, 120; *picture and note* 120, 135
  cats,
    ice-giants' cat, 226; *picture and note* 226
    sacred to goddess Freya, 231; *picture and note* 231
  dogs, *picture* 175
    hunting dogs raised in Britain, 23; *picture and note* 25
  elephant,
    gift to Charlemagne, 170; *picture and note* 170
  horses, *picture* 15, 22, 31, 34, 38, 61, 62, 73, 75, 81, 82, 106, 118, 156, 161, 165, 222, 237, 239, 241, 246
    Arabian trade in, 122
  in the circus, *picture and note* 92
  lion,
    hunted by Persian kings, *picture and note* 39
  oxen, *picture* 65, 210, 238
Anthemius (an-thē'mi-us), of Tralles, famous 6th century Byzantine architecture
  glory of Sancta Sophia, 109–111; *picture and note* 110, 111
Antioch, patriarch of, 178
Antiquities,
  bronze model of Germanic sun chariot, *picture and note* 30
  Oseberg ship, *picture and note* 213; other objects from ship, *picture and note* 217, 220, 221
  Stonehenge, England, *picture and note* 24
Apse (ăps), in architecture, 109; *picture and note* 109
Aquitaine (ăk-wĭ-tān'), province in s. France, *map* 209
  Charlemagne wins subjects, 156
  duke keeps Moslems in check, 152
Arabia,
  Bedouin tribes, 122–123
  before Mohammed, 120
  commerce and trade, 122
  early religion: worship of idols, 121, 123, 129; *note* 121
  embraces Mohammedanism, 135
  Mecca, 120–121, 129, 131; *picture and note* 121, 122
  Medina, 131–133
  Mohammed, 120–135
  Mohammed's contribution, 135

Arabs, Semites from Arabia,
  civilization and culture, 170
  conquests, 136
  conquest of Spain, 138–141; war with Charlemagne, 160–168
  defeat in battle of Tours, 152–153
  gospel of the sword, 136
  Mohammed's contribution, 135
  nation of warriors, 137
  paradise, 129; *picture and note* 130
  worship of idols, i. e. early religion, 121, 129; *note* 129
Arca′dius (378–408 A.D.), Roman emperor, *note* 60, 71; *chart* 59
  of Constantine the Great, 50; *picture and note* 50
  Storied Column, *picture and note* 65
Arch,
  horse-shoe arch, *picture and note* 151
  Roman arch combined with Greek column, *picture and note* 41
Archaeology,
  Oseberg ship, *picture and note* 213; other objects from ship, *picture and note* 217, 220, 221
Archbishop, a chief bishop,
  in the medieval church, 178
  Turpin, 164, 166–168
Architecture,
  apse (ăps), 109; *picture and note* 109
  arch,
    horse-shoe arch, *picture and note* 151
    Roman arch combined with Greek column, *picture and note* 41
  basilicas, Roman law,
    form taken over by Byzantine churches, 109; *picture and note* 109
  Byzantine, 109–111,
    glory of Sancta Sophia, 57, 109–111; *picture and note* 110, 111
    Hippodrome, 57; *picture and note* 58
  capitals, Byzantine, *picture and note* 111
  columns,
    Byzantine, *picture and note* 111
    Corinthian, *picture and note* 175
    Greek combined with Roman arch, *picture and note* 41
    Storied, of Arcadius, *picture and note* 65
  dome,
    knowledge how to build lost in Italy, *picture and note* 89
    Sancta Sophia, 110–111; *picture and note* 111
  Franks, Charlemagne's villas, 174, *picture and note* 175
  houses, Middle Ages, 241, 244; *picture* 244
  Huns, Attila's capital in Hungary, 75–76; *picture and note* 75, 78

INDEX 255

Architecture—Continued
    huts of the Gauls, 20; *picture* 22
    hut-villages of the Germans, 33; *picture and note* 34
    interiors,
        Attila's wooden palace, 75–76; *picture and note* 78, 83
        furnishings in Charlemagne's villas, 174
        medieval castle, 241; table service, *picture* 240
        Sancta Sophia, *picture and note* 111
        Viking, *picture* 223
    Middle Ages,
        castle, 241; *picture and note* 239, 245
        choir loft, *picture and note* 190
        houses, 241; *picture* 244
        manor, *picture* 242
        monastery of St. Gall, *picture* 195
            cloister, 198; *picture and note* 198
        village, *picture* 194
    Mohammedan,
        horse-shoe arch, *picture and note* 151
        Kaaba, 121; *picture and note* 121, 122
        Mecca, *picture and note* 122
    palaces,
        Attila's wooden palace, 75–76; *picture and note* 78
        Theodoric, *picture and note* 87
    Palmyrenian, *picture and note* 41
    prehistoric,
        Stonehenge, *picture and note* 24
    Ravenna, *picture and note* 86, 87, 89
    Roman amphitheater in Gaul, *picture and note* 152
    stairways, Arab, *picture* 130, 131
    tomb of Theodoric at Ravenna, 89; *picture and note* 89
    towers of castles, 240; *picture* 239, 245
    Viking, *picture* 219, 223
    Visigothic, *picture and note* 137
    walls, around medieval castles and towns, 244; *picture* 239, 245

Ar′ianism,
    Burgundians, Arian Christians, 145
    heresy, 56–57
    Pope Gregory attempts to drive out, 184
    Theodoric and Ostrogoths Arians, 88, 180

A′ri-us (256–336 A.D.), a theologian of Alexandria
    founder of Arianism, 56–57

Armor,
    chain armor, early Middle Ages, *picture and note* 161; *picture* 163, 167, 175. *See also* Shields; Helmets

Arms. *See* Weapons

Army,
    Byzantine: mailed horsemen, 106
    lack of royal armies in Middle Ages, 237

Army—Continued
    Visigoths march to meet Moslems, 139–141; *picture and note* 139, 140
    warriors in chain armor, *picture and note* 161, 165

Ar′pad (died about 907), leads Magyars into Hungary, 210; *picture and note* 210

Art,
    book covers, *picture and note* 171, 181
    Britons, early, *picture and note* 24, 26
    Bronze Age, Germany, *picture and note* 32
    bronze work,
        Britons, *picture and note* 26
        Byzantine, *picture and note* 60
        Gallic, *picture and note* 19
        German or Teutonic tribes, *picture and note* 28, 29, 30, 32
        Iberian, *picture and note* 15
        of the Vandals, *picture and note* 85
    Burgundian, *picture and note* 144
    Byzantine, 94–96; *picture and note* 94, 95, 96
        bronze shield, *picture and note* 60
        fabric, *picture and note* 170
    Casket of Projecta, *picture and note* 54
    carving, Norse, *picture* 217, 220, 221
    chalice, Frankish, *picture and note* 155
    Christian,
        book cover, *picture and note* 181
        carvings on bishop's throne, *picture and note* 184
        change in Constantine's beliefs, *picture and note* 51
        dangerous to make pictures of Jesus, *picture and note* 52
        early representation of the Crucifixion, *picture and note* 55
        illuminated manuscript, 199; *picture and note* 182, 183, 186, 187, 189, 199, 200
        Madonna and Child, *picture and note* 57
        mixture of Christian and pagan, *picture and note* 54
        symbols, 49–50; *picture and note* 49, 51, 52, 53
    civilization arrested by barbarian invasions, 68; *picture and note* 68
    Coptic, *picture and note* 136
    crown of Charlemagne, *picture and note* 169
    design,
        applied to animal forms: East influences West, 96; *picture and note* 96
        Britons, *picture* 24, 26
        Byzantine, *picture* 94, 95, 108
        Celtic, *picture* 20, 21
        Coptic, *picture* 136
        Germanic, *picture* 28, 29, 32, 33, 35, 96, 155
        Iberian, *picture* 10, 11, 12, 13, 14
        illuminated initial-letters, *picture and note* 171; *picture* 110

Art—Continued
    influence of East on Teutonic and Celtic; 96; *picture and note* 96
    Lombardic, *picture* 116, 117, 157, 158, 159
    Persian textiles, *picture and note* 119, 120, 131
    Scythian, *picture* 72, 73
    Siberian, *picture* 72, 84, 118
    Vandals, *picture* 85
    Viking, *picture* 212, 213, 216, 217, 220, 223
  distinction between Greek and Byzantine, 95
  enamel work,
    of the Britons, 23; *picture and note* 23, 24, 26
  Frankish,
    bronze statue, *picture and note* 156
    buckles, *picture and note* 149
    chalice, *picture and note* 155
    engraved sword, *picture and note* 176
    illuminations, *picture and note* 171, 173
    Gallic, *pictures and notes* 20, 21
  Germanic tribes, *picture and note* 28, 29, 30, 32, 33, 35
  glass work, *picture and note* 52, 53
  gold work,
    Lombards, *picture and note* 116, 117, 158, 159
    Siberian gold ornaments, *picture and note* 72, 73, 84
    sun disk of the early Germans, *picture and note* 30
    Visigothic crown, *picture and note* 138
  Gosforth Cross, *picture and note* 235, 236
  Graeco-Syrian, *picture and note* 40, 43
  Iberian or early Spanish, 14–15; *picture and note* 11, 14; *picture* 12, 13, 15, 16, 17
    bust of the Lady of Elche, *picture and note* 14
  Iron Age, Germany, *picture and note* 33
  Iron Crown of Lombardy, 117; *picture and note* 117
  ivory carving, in monasteries, 199
    bishop's throne, *picture and note* 184
    chessmen, gift to Charlemagne, 170; *picture and note* 170
    diptych (two-leaved book of ivory, carved on the outside), *picture and note* 71, 92, 93
    diptych of Boethius, *picture and note* 88
    Madonna and Child, *picture and note* 57
    panel of Queen Amalasuntha, *picture and note* 113
  jewelry,
    buckle,
      Frankish, *picture and note* 149
      Germanic, *picture and note* 28
      Vandal, *picture and note* 85
    Charlemagne's jeweled crown, *picture and note* 169

Art—Continued
  Gallic, 21
  gold crown of Visigothic king, *picture and note* 138
  Iberian, 13; *picture* 10, 12, 13, 14
  jeweled book cover, *picture and note* 171
  of the early Britons, *picture and note* 24, 26; *picture* 23
  Lombard's *picture and note* 116, 117, 158, 159
  Magyars, *picture and note* 210
  manuscript illuminations, 199; *picture and note* 171, 199
    Byzantine, *picture and note* 110
    Frankish, *picture and note* 147, 148, 171
    medieval, *picture and note* 182, 186, 187, 189, 190, 191, 200, 201
    Persian, *picture and note* 121, 127, 134, 135
    Visigothic, *picture and note* 137
  miniatures, a small picture illustrating a manuscript, from the Latin word *miniare* to decorate with vermilion
    Frankish, *picture and note* 151
    Persian, *picture and note* 131
  mosaics,
    Byzantine, 95–96; *picture and note* 94, 95, 102
    Church of St. Demetrius, *picture and note* 102
    harbor and palace at Ravenna, *picture and note* 86, 87
    Sancta Sophia, *picture and note* 111
  Norse, *picture and note* 216, 217, 220, 221, 229, 232, 235, 236
  ornaments,
    of the early Britons, *picture and note* 26
    Siberian, *picture and note* 72, 73, 84
  painting,
    fresco, from Dura, *picture and note* 40
    Persian, *picture and note* 130
  Palmyrenian, *picture and note* 40, 43, 44
  Persian,
    miniatures, *picture and note* 131
    Sassanian, *picture and note* 38, 39, 106
    tapestry, *picture and note* 119, 120
  pottery,
    Iberian or early Spanish, 16; *picture and note* 16, 17
  Ravenna: mosaics of harbor and palace, *picture and note* 86, 87
  Sassanian Persia, *picture and note* 38, 39, 106
  sculpture,
    Franks: dedicatory, *picture and note* 172
    Persian: Sassanian, *picture and note* 38, 39
  sculpture, busts
    Roman, *picture and note* 37
  sculpture, gravestone,
    German, *pictures and notes* 35
    Palmyrenian, *picture and note* 43

INDEX 257

Art—Continued
 sculpture reliefs,
  Arch of Constantine, 50; *picture and note* 50
  Visigothic warrior, *picture and note* 140
 Scythian, *picture and note* 72, 73
 Siberian, *picture and note* 72, 73, 74
 silk cloth, *picture and note* 101, 105
 silver vase, Scythian, *picture and note* 72
 tapestries,
  Byzantine, *picture and note* 170
  Persian, *picture and note* 119, 120
 Teutons and Celts apply design to animal forms, 96; *picture and note* 96
 Vandals, *picture and note* 85
 Visigothic,
  crown, *picture and note* 138
  manuscript, *picture and note* 137
  wood-cut, *picture and note* 160
Arts and crafts,
 Britons, *picture and note* 26
 Iberian, 15; *picture and note* 15
 medieval monasteries, 199
 silk culture introduced into Constantinople, *note* 105
Asceticism, in the early Church, 102–105; *picture and note* 103
As′gard, in Norse mythology, the world of the gods, high above the earth, 219
 gods in, 227–232
 Twilight of the gods, 214, 233, 235–236
Assembly, among early Germans, 31–32; *picture and note* 31
Assyria, conquered by Mohammedans, 136
Athanasius (ath-an-ā′si-us), **Saint** (296–373 A.D.)
 defender of orthodox Christians, 56
Athletics, Iberian, 16. *See also* Sports
At′tila (died 453?), king of the Huns, known as "the scourge of God," 69–84
 alleged proposal to Honoria, 74, 80
 attack on Europe, 79
 becomes king, 72
 capital of the Huns, 75; *picture and note* 75
 defeated by Aetius, 80–81; *picture and note* 82
 described by Greek historian, Priscus, 75–78
 dreams of conquest, 70
 empire of Attila, *map and note* 70
 hostage at Ravenna, 69–70; *picture and note* 69
 marriage with Ildico, 83–84; *picture and note* 83
 sits at banquet, 77–78; *picture and note* 78
 wooden palace, 75–76; *picture and note* 78
Augustine, Saint (354–430 A.D.), bishop of Hippo in North Africa
 "City of God," 67; *picture and note* 67
Augustine, Saint (died about 613), sent as missionary to England by Pope Gregory, 185–187; *picture and note* 182, 187

Aurelian (aw-rē′lĭ-an) (died 275 A.D.), great Roman soldier-emperor, 42–44
 coin, *picture and note* 42
 Roman triumph, 44
 war against Queen Zenobia, 42–44
Aure′lius, Marcus (121–180 A.D.), Roman emperor, 37
 chart, 45
 scenes from column, *picture and note* 31, 34
Austrasia (âs-trā′sia), e. kingdom of Merovingian Franks
 rise, 148; Pippin, 151
A′vars, Tartars from Asia, akin to Huns threaten Eastern Empire, 117, 119
Axe,
 early Germans, *picture and note* 28
 battle, *picture and note* 28
 Franks, 142; *picture* 143
Ayesha (i′ē-sha), wife of Mohammed, 132

Babylon, conquered by Mohammedans, 136
Balder, in Norse mythology, god of light, 230
 beloved by the gods, 233
 death, 233–235; *picture and note* 234
Baltic Sea, Saxons live along shores, 159
Banners. *See* Standards and banners
Banquet scenes,
 Attila, the Hun, 77; *picture and note* 78
 Vikings in Valhalla, *picture and note* 223
Barbarian invasions, of the Western Empire, 61–89, 142
 Arabs, 139–141, 152–153
 effect on civilization, 68; *picture and note* 68
 Huns, 61–63, 69–84
 Magyars, 210; *picture and note* 210
 Scythians, 72–73; *picture and note* 72, 73
 Slavs, 117–118
 Teutonic,
  Burgundians, 36, 68
  Franks, 36, 65, 142–176
  Goths, 36, 61, 64–66
  Lombards, 36, 115–116
  Vandals, 65, 85
  Viking, 211–212
Baron, Middle Ages, 239
Barrack Emperors, 37; *chart* 45
Barter, practiced among Germanic tribes, 28
Basil (băz′il), **Saint** (329–379 A.D.), founder of Eastern monasticism, 104–105
Basil′icas or law courts, architecture taken over by Byzantine churches, 109; *picture and note* 109
Battle of Châlons (451 A.D.), 80–81
Battle of Milvian Bridge, 312 A.D., 50
Battle of Tours, 732 A.D., 152–153
Battle, Ordeal by, 242–243; *picture and note* 243
Beards,
 Germanic tribes, *picture and note* 27

INDEX

Beards—Continued
of the Lombards, 115; name, 115
Scythian, *picture* 72, 73
Bed, of Viking Queen, *picture and note* 221
Bede (beed) or **Baeda** (672?-735), a Saxon monk commonly called the Venerable Bede, *note* 185; *picture and note* 186
"Ecclesiastical History of the English Nation," *quoted* 101, 184-187
Bedouins (bĕd'ŏŏ-ins) (Arab Semites)
groom swords for conquest, 136
rough habits and customs, 122-123
Belgium, what is now Belgium, 208-209; *map and note* 209
Belisarius (bĕl-ĭ-sā'rĭ-ŭs) (born about 505 A.D.), famous Byzantine general
conquers Vandals in Africa, 112
discovered by Justinian, 106
Italy, won from the Goths, 112-114
subdues Nika rioters, 108-109
Benedict, Saint (480?-543), founder of the Benedictine Order, 188-189; *picture and note* 189
early life, 188
founds monasticism in the West, 189
Rule, 189
Benedictine monastery, life, 195-206
Bifrost (bē'frest), in Norse mythology, the rainbow bridge, 219, 222, 235; *picture* 219, 222
Bishop,
costume, *picture and note* 180; *picture* 196
emblems of office, *picture and note* 180
in the medieval church, 178
Bishop of Rome, 179
Bishop's throne, *picture and note* 184
Bleda, brother of Attila, 72
Boadicea (bō-à-dĭ-sē'a) (died 62? A.D.), fierce British warrior queen, 26
Boar,
hunted in Persia, *picture and note* 106
sacred to the god, Frey, 231; *picture and note* 29, 231
Boar-helmets, of the Germanic tribes, *picture and note* 29
Boats and ships,
St. Cuthbert's in England, *picture and note* 206. *See also* Transportation
Boethius (bō-ē'thĭ-ŭs) (480-524), Roman statesman and philosopher, 88; *picture and note* 88
"Consolations of Philosophy," 88; *note* 88
Book covers, *picture and note* 158, 171, 181
Books,
codex, 97; *note* 97
copied and preserved in monasteries, 199-200; *picture and note* 199
sent as gift to Charlemagne, 170
Bos'phorus, strait between Black Sea and Sea of Marmara. 57; *map* 18

Boys,
admission to manhood, among Germans, 32
life of a novice in a monastery, 195-206
Bragi (brä'gē), in Norse mythology, god of poetry and song, 228-229
men drink to health at Yule-tide, *note* 228
Breviary (brē'vĭ-ār-ĭ), 183
Britain, the English name for the Latin or Roman *Britannia*, 23-26
Angles, Jutes, and Saxons enter, 68
as a Roman province, 23-26
Boadicea resists Romans, 26
bronze and enamel work, 23; *picture and note* 23, 24, 26
Christianized, 184-187; *picture and note* 182, 187
Druids,
rite of plucking the mistletoe, 25
suppressed, 25-26
geography, 23
name, 24
Roman conquest, 26
ruled by Constantius, 45
Stonehenge, *picture and note* 24. *See* England
Britons (Mediterraneans and Celts), the people of early Britain, 23-26
enamel work, 23; *picture and note* 23, 24, 26
keep cattle, 23
mixture of races, 24; *picture and note* 23, 24
Brit'tany, ancient province in n. w. France, *map* 209
people raid Franks, 209
Bronze Age,
knives of the Germans, *picture and note* 32
Bronze work,
Britons, *picture and note* 26
Gallic, *picture and note* 19
German or Teutonic tribes, *picture and note* 28, 29, 30, 32
Iberian, *picture and note* 15
statue of Charlemagne the Warrior (?), *picture and note* 156
Vandals, *picture and note* 85
Brownies, 217
Bruges (brüzh), Belgium, old Flemish town
merchants, 245
Buckles,
Frankish, *picture and note* 149
Germanic, *picture and note* 28
Vandal, *picture and note* 85
Building materials,
of the early Germans, 33
stone, Theodoric's tomb, *picture and note* 89
stone, brick, and masonry, 174; *picture and note* 175
wood, 174, *note* 175
Attila's palace, 75-76; *picture and note* 78
Burgundy, founded along river Rhone, 148

INDEX

Burgundians, Germanic tribe, 36
  Arian Christians, 145
  art, *picture and note* 144
  establish kingdom in Gaul, 68
  subdued by Clovis, 147
Buri (bū′rē), in Norse mythology creation of, 216
Burial and funeral customs,
  early Germanic tribes, 36
  Viking, 221–223; *picture and note* 213, 220, 221
  funeral pyre on Ringhorn, Balder's ship, 234
Busts. *See* Sculpture, busts
Byzantine (bĭ-zăn′tĭn or bĭz′ăn-teen) **or Eastern or Greek Empire**, after the division of the Roman Empire, the eastern portion took the name of Eastern or Byzantine Empire, 90–119
  architecture, 109–111; *picture and note* 111
  art and life, 94–96; *picture and note* 94
  Christianity in days of Justinian, 98–105
  Constantinople or Byzantium chosen as capital by Constantine, 57–58
  decline after Justinian's reign, 115
  division of Roman Empire, 60, 90; *note* 60, 71
  emperors keep Germans at bay, 90
  Greek in civilization, 90
  Greek Orthodox or Eastern Church separation from Western or Latin Church, 179
  Heraclius saves empire from Persia, 118–119
  Justinian's reign, 90–114
    code, 97; *note* 97
    marries Theodora, the circus girl, 90–93
  Nika riot, 107–109; *picture and note* 107
  Sancta Sophia, 109–111; *picture and note* 111
  silk culture introduced, *note* 105
  threat of Lombards, Slavs, Avars, Persians, 115–119
Byzantium (bĭ-zan′shĭ-ŭm), Greek city in Asia Minor
  capital of Constantine the Great, 57–58
  changed to Constantinople, 58. *See also* Constantinople

Caesar, a title, 45–46
Caliph (kā′lĭf), civil and religious head of the Mohammedans, 136; *note* 136
Camel, *picture and note* 106
  Arabian trade in, 122
  caravan, 120; *picture and note* 120, 135
Canon, an ecclesiastic in the church, 191
Canopy, Attila's, *picture and note* 75
Canterbury, England, capital of Kent in Saxon times
  Christian missionary resides in, 187
Capitula′ries of Charlemagne, *note* 174; *quoted*, 174
Caracalla (kăr-á-kăl′á) (186–217 A.D.), infamous Roman emperor; (reign 211–217 A.D.), 37; *chart* 45

Carac′tacus, king of early Britain, 25
  opposes Romans, 25
Caravans,
  leave Mecca, 120
  Moslem pilgrims, 122, 135; *picture and note* 122, 135
Carcassone (kär-kä-sŏn), medieval fortress and city, *picture and note* 245
Carolin′gian line, Frankish rulers, the descendants of Charles Martel, 154–176
  Charlemagne, 156–176
  Pippin the Short, 154–155
Carthage, city and state in n. Africa seized by Vandals, 66, 112
Carts, ox-cart of the Magyars, *picture and note* 210. *See also* Transportation
Carving, Norse, *picture* 217, 220, 221
Casket of Projecta, *picture and note* 54
Castles, 240–241; *picture and note* 239, 245
Cath′edra, a seat or throne
  bishop's throne, *picture and note* 184
Cathedral, medieval
  cathedral school, 190
  services, 191
Cats,
  ice giants' cat, 226; *picture and note* 226
  sacred to goddess Freya, 231; *picture and note* 231
Celts (sĕlts or kĕlts)
  art, *picture and note* 20, 21
  in Gaul, 19–22; *picture and note* 20, 21
  term applied to language and culture, 19; *note* 21
Ceremonies and rites. *See* Rites and ceremonies
Cer′nunnus, Celtic god of abundance, 21; *picture and note* 21
Ceuta (sĭ-u′ta), province in Africa, 138
Chain-armor, *picture and note* 161; *picture* 167, 175
Chair
  Bede's, *picture* 186
  Frankish folding throne, *picture and note* 150
  Viking bench, *picture* 223
Chalice, Frankish, *picture and note* 155
Châlons (shä-lôn′), battle of (451 A.D.), 80–81; *picture and note* 82
Chariot,
  carruca, a modified Roman pleasure chariot, *picture and note* 148
  sun-chariot of the early Germans, *picture and note* 30. *See also* Transportation
Charlemagne (shar′le-main) or Charles the Great, king of the Franks, 156–176
  Aachen, 172
  administration of justice and the laws, 174–176
  appearance, 156
  architecture, 174; *picture and note* 175
  boyhood, 155

Charlemagne—Continued
  break-up of empire, 207–209; *map and note* 209
  capitularies, *note* 174
  coronation at St. Peter's, 169; crown, sandals, and robe, *picture and note* 169
  costume, *picture and note* 156, 162, 169, 172
  court, 172–174; *picture and note* 175
  could not read or write, 155
  emperor of the West, 169; *note* 169
  gifts from Haroun-al-Raschid, 170; *picture and note* 170
  government, 174–176; *missi regis* 176
  interest in education, 171
  name, 160
  royal procession, 172–174
  Saxons, wars, 159–160
  successors, 207–209
  villas, 174
  wars with Lombards, 157–159
  wars against Moors, 160–168
  wins over Aquitanians, 156
Charles I, the Bald (823–877), king of the Franks and emperor of the West (Holy Roman Empire), 207–208; *picture and note* 207, cover
  receives France and Belgium, 208–209; *map and note* 209
Charles III, the Simple (879–929), king of the Franks, 207
Charles Martel (mar-tel′) (688–741), great leader of the Franks, 151–154
  defeats Moslems in battle of Tours, 732 A.D., 152–153
  mayor of the palace, 151
  meaning of name, 151, 152
  never declared king, 154
Charles the Great. See Charlemagne
Charts,
  Roman emperors from Marcus Aurelius to Diocletian, 45
  Roman emperors after Diocletian, 59
Chess-men, ivory, gift to Charlemagne, 170; *picture and note* 170
Chil′deric, father of Clovis, *picture and note* 149
China,
  Great Wall, 63; *picture and note* 63
  silk culture introduced into Constantinople, *note* 105
Chin′deswinth (641–652), king of the Visigoths in Spain, *note* 137
Choir boys, in the medieval church, 190; *picture and note* 190
Chosroes I (koz′ro-eez) or **Khosru,** king of Persia 531–579 A.D.
  wars against Byzantine Empire, 106
Chosroes II (koz′ro-eez) or **Khosru,** king of Persia, 590–628 A.D.
  sweeps through Asia Minor, 118

Christianity,
  Arian heresy, 56–57
  becomes fashionable, 54–55
  Constantine, patron of Christianity, 47–58
  legalizes, 50
  conversion of Clovis and Franks, 145–147
  conversion of Norway, 232; *note* 214, 232
  council of Nicaea, 56
  council, general church, 98–99; *picture and note* 98
  early art, *pictures and notes* 52, 53
    change in Constantine's beliefs, *picture and note* 51
    early representation of the Crucifixion, *picture and note* 55
    labarum, *picture and note* 49
    Madonna and Child, *picture and note* 57
    mixture of Christian and pagan, 54–55; *picture and note* 54
  early Christians, 54–55
  England: St. Augustine, 185–187; *picture and note* 182, 187
  growth and spread, 53–54
  in days of Justinian, 98–105
  Nestorians, *note* 57
  pagan customs, festivals and rites given Christian meaning,
    Christmas Day, 102, 232
    Easter, 101; *note* 101
    Norse gods declared demons or witches, *note* 214, 231
  paganism in, 100–102, 193; *picture and note* 101
  persecutions, Licinius, 52
  restored after Julian the Apostate, 60
  St. Augustine's *City of God,* 67; *picture and note* 67
  symbols, 49–50; *picture and note* 49, 51, 52, 53
  under Julian the Apostate, 59–60. See also Church
Christmas Day, 232
  hanging tree with toys, 102
  origin, 102
  Yuletide customs transferred to Christmas, 232
Chrysostom (krĭs′os-tom), **Saint** (347?–407), famous Greek father, *quoted,* 100–101
Church, the
  asceticism, 102–105; *picture and note* 103
  civilizing influence, 206
  clergy, 178, 190–194
  division into Eastern and Western Church, 179, 187
  doctrine and heresies, 98–100; *picture and note* 98; Arian heresy, 56–57
  medieval, 177–206
    rise of the papacy, 177–180
    founding, 177–178

INDEX

Church—Continued
  missionary activity, 105; *note* 105
    Christianize England, 185–187; *picture and note* 182
  monasticism, 104–105, 195–206
  music, 183; *picture and note* 183
  organization
    the medieval church, 178
    under Constantine, 53
  services, 191–192
Church council,
  general council, *picture and note* 98
  Nicaea, 325 A.D., 56
  St. Demetrius, Salonika
    mosaics, *picture and note* 102
  S. Apollinare Nuovo, Ravenna
    mosaics, *picture and note* 86, 87
  S. Vitale, Ravenna
    mosaics, *picture and note* 94, 95
Church of Sancta Sophia, 109–111; *picture and note* 110, 111
Circus, in the Hippodrome, Constantinople
  Greens, party in the Circus, 91, 107
  riot of Blues and Greens, 107–108
  scenes from the circus, *picture and note* 92
  Theodora, the circus-girl, 90–92; *picture and note* 91
Cities, medieval, 244
  Carcassonne, *picture and note* 245
  distinguished from towns, 244
City of God, The, Saint Augustine's, 67; *picture and note* 67
Claudius II (214–270 A.D.), Roman emperor, 42; *chart* 45
Clergy, in the medieval church, 178, 190–194
  "regular" clergy, the monks were the regular clergy because they were subjected to *rule*, 190
  "secular" clergy ("belonging to the world"), were the ordinary clergy, because they were not subject to *rule*, 190
Cloister, monastery, 198; *picture and note* 198
Cloth,
  Flemish, *note* 247
  origin of name of materials, *note* 247
Clothing, of the early Germans, *picture and note* 34. *See also* Costume
Clotil'da, wife of Clovis, died about 544 A.D.
  Burgundian princess, 144
  converts Clovis to orthodox Christianity, 145–146; *picture and note* 146
Clovis, king of the Franks (481–511 A.D.)
  appearance, 143; *picture and note* 145
  conquers Gallo-Romans, 143
  conversion to orthodox Christianity, 145–146
  founds Lutetia (Paris), 147
  honored by Emperor Anastasius, 147
  seizes lands and slays relatives, 147

Code, a unified body of laws
  Justinian's, 97; *note* 97
Codex, meaning and origin, 97; *note* 97
Coins, *picture* 42, 46, 47, 48, 51, 68, 86, 112
Columns,
  Byzantine: Sancta Sophia, *picture and note* 111
  Corinthian, *picture and note* 175
  Greek combined with Roman arch, *picture and note* 41
  scenes from Column of Marcus Aurelius, *picture and note* 34
  Storied Column of Arcadius, *picture and note* 65
Commendation, vassalage in feudal times, 237–238; *note* 237
Commerce and trade,
  Arab, 122
  Arab or Moslem with Franks, 170
  development,
    roads and travel of medieval merchants, 245–247
  Flemish merchants, 245–249; *picture and note* 246, 247, 248, 249
  medieval fairs and markets, 245–249; *picture and note* 246, 247, 248, 249
Com'modus (161–192 A.D.), Roman emperor (180–192 A.D.), son of Marcus Aurelius
  bust, *picture and note* 37
  chart, 45
  cruel tyrant, 37; *note* 37
Common people,
  life in a medieval parish, 191–194
  Middle Ages, peasants, serfs, 237–239
Constans, Flavius Julius (320?–350 A.D.), Roman emperor, 58
  receives Italy, 58–59
Constantine I, the Great (288?–337 A.D.), Roman emperor, 47–58
  arch of Constantine, 50; *picture and note* 50
  battle of Milvian Bridge, 49–50; *picture and note* 50
  becomes a Christian, 49–51, 58; *note* 51
  "By this sign thou shalt conquer," 49
  Christianity, 51–57
    Arian controversy, 56
    Council of Nicaea (325 A.D.), 56
    growth and spread, 53–54
  civil war and claimants to the throne, 48–49
  coins showing change in Constantine's beliefs, 51; *picture and note* 51
  division of Empire upon death, 58
  founding and building of Constantinople, 57–58; *picture and note* 58
Constantine II (312–340 A.D.), Roman emperor and eldest son of Constantine the Great, 58–59
  chart, 59

INDEX

Constantinople, formerly **Byzantium,** now **Istanbul,** 57–58; *picture and note* 58
  art and life under Justinian, 94–96; *picture and note* 94, 95
  buildings and splendor, 57–58
    Hippodrome, 57; *picture and note* 58
    Sancta Sophia, 57, 109–111; *picture and note* 110, 111
  founded by Constantine, 57–58; *picture and note* 58
  Golden Horn, 57; *picture* 58
  Nika riots, 107–109; *picture and note* 107
  scenes from the circus, *picture and note* 92, 93
  silk culture introduced from China, *note* 105
  Theodora, the circus girl, 90–93; *picture and note* 91, 92
Constan'tius, Flavius Valerius (250?–306), commonly called Chlorus (the Pale) Roman emperor, 45–47; *picture and note* 46
  appointed "Caesar," 45–46
  protects Christians, 47
  rules Britain, 45–47
Constan'tius II (317–361 A.D.), Roman emperor, 3d son of Constantine the Great, 58–59
Consul, Byzantine, *picture and note* 93
Copts, native Egyptians, 136; *note* 136
  art, *picture and note* 136
Cor'dova, city in Spain, 160, 161
Costume,
  Amalasuntha, Ostrogothic queen, *picture* 113
  Arabs or Mohammedans, *picture* 123, 125, 127, 131, 134
  armor, early Middle Ages, *picture and note* 161; *picture* 163, 167, 175
  Byzantine, 94; *picture and note* 94, 95
  Chinese, *picture and note* 74
  ecclesiastical,
    abbot, *picture and note* 196, 200, 203
    bishop, *picture and note* 180, 196
    choir boys, *picture* 190
    churchmen, *picture and note* 102
    monks, *picture* 198, 199, 202
    monks: novices, *picture* 195, 198, 202
    officers in general council, *picture* 98
    pontifical robe of Pope Leo III, *picture and note* 178
    Pope Gregory the Great, *picture* 181, 182
    priest, *picture* 191, 194
    stole, *picture and note* 200
  Franks, 142; *picture and note* 143
    Charles the Bald, *picture* 207
    peasants, *picture and note* 173
    royalty, *picture and note* 145, 147, 154, 156, 162, 163, 169, 172, 175
    scribe, *picture and note* 151
    warriors, *picture and note* 143, 161, 165, 167, 175

Costume—Continued
  Gallic, 19, 20; *picture and note* 21; *picture* 22
  Germanic tribes, 34; *picture and note* 27, 28, 31, 34, 36
  gods and goddesses,
    Norse, *picture and note* 230, 231, 234, 235
      Odin, 220; *picture and note* 220, 223, 229
      Thor, *picture* 226; Thor's hammers, *picture and note* 224
      Skadi, 229; *picture* 230
  Goths, *picture and note* 64, 65
  Huns, *picture,* 61, 62, 75
    stolen finery, 74; *picture and note* 78
  Iberian or early Spanish, 13; *picture and note* 12, 13, 14; *picture* 10
  Lombards, *picture* 115, 157
  Magyars, *picture and note* 210
  Middle Ages,
    nobles and ladies, *picture* 238, 241, 242, 248
    peasants, *picture* 201, 237, 238, 239
  Norse or Viking, *picture* 223, 226, 230, 231, 232, 234
  Palmyrenian, *picture and note* 40, 43, 44
  peasants, *picture and note* 173, 201, 239
  Persian royalty, *picture and note* 38, 39, 106
  sandals, Charlemagne's coronation, *picture and note* 169
  Scythian, *picture and note* 72, 73
  serfs, *picture* 201, 238
  shoes, fur of the Magyars, *picture and note* 210
  Slavs, *note* 73
  Theodora, Empress, *picture* 91, 95
  trousers,
    costume of barbarians, 19; *picture and note* 20; *picture* 22
    worn by Germanic tribes, 34; *picture and note* 27, 28, 31, 34, 36
    worn by Nordic barbarians, *picture and note* 27
  Turkish noble, *picture and note* 74
  Visigothic, *picture and note* 141
Council meeting, of the early Germans, 31; *picture and note* 31
Councils, means of Church government, general, 98–99; *picture and note* 98
  Nicaea (325 A.D.), 56
Counts, Middle Ages, 239
Court-of-justice,
  Charlemagne, 174–175
  feudal, 242–243; *picture and note* 243
  trial by ordeal, 176, 242–243
  wergild, 174–175
Crafts, medieval monastery, 199
Creation story,
  Norse tales of creation and the gods, 215–236
Cross, a sacred symbol in many religions, especially Christianity
  Jesus nailed to cross, *picture and note* 55

INDEX 263

Cross—Continued
  Lombard gold cross, *picture* 159
  nail from True Cross, 159
Crown,
  Charlemagne's, *picture and note* 169
  Visigothic, King Reccenswinth, *picture and note* 138
Ctesiphon (těs'ĭ-fŏn), city on the Tigris River, stronghold of Parthians and of Persians
  capital, 38
  map, 18
Cu'ni-mund, king of the Gepidae, 115
Customs and manners,
  Bedouin, 122–123
  Byzantine life, 94–95
  Christmas Day
    hanging a tree with toys, 102
    why observed December 25, 102
    Yuletide customs transferred, 232
  exchange of Easter eggs: origin, 101; *note* 101
  Germans or Teutons, 28–36
  Huns, 62–63, 76–78
  Iberian, 12–16
  life of a feudal noble, 240–242; *picture and note* 240, 241
  of the Britons, 23–25
  of the Gauls, 20–23
  Scythian, *picture and note* 72, 73
  Viking,
    funeral pyre on Ringhorn, Balder's ship, 234
    Yuletide, 232; hanging tree with toys, 232
Cuthbert, Saint (died about 687), English bishop and hermit
  stories from Bede, 205–206; *picture and note* 205
Cyprian, Saint (200?–258), a leader in the early African church, *quoted,* 177

Dagger, early British, *picture and note* 26
Dagobert', king of the Franks, 622–638
  good reign, 150
  satirized in French nursery rhyme, 150; *picture and note* 150
Dancing, Iberian, 15, 16
Dark Ages, defined, 68
Days of the week, origin of names, *note* 227
Demons, devils, and witchcraft,
  medieval beliefs about, 193, 204–206; *picture and note* 193, 204
Denmark, Northmen, 212
Deside'rius, last king of the Lombards, 756–774 A.D.
  approach of Charlemagne, 157–158
Devils,
  medieval belief in, 204; *picture and note* 204
  said to torment man, *picture and note* 193
Dining table, medieval castle, *picture and note* 240

Diocle'tian (245–313 A.D.), Roman emperor 285–305 A.D.
  reorganizes Empire, 45–46
Divination, among early Germans, 30–31
Dogs, *picture* 175; raised in Britain, 23; *picture and note* 25
Dome,
  knowledge how to build lost in Italy, *picture and note* 109
  Sancta Sophia, 110–111; *picture and note* 111
Don'jon, of castle, 240
"Do-Nothing" kings, the successors of Clovis, 149–150
Doves, early Christian symbol, *picture and note* 52
Dragon-ship, Viking, 213; *picture and note* 211
Dragons, medieval belief in fire-breathing dragons, 197; *picture and note* 197
Dress. *See* Costume; Headdress
Druids, the priests and wise men of the Celts, 22
  offer human sacrifice, 22, 25; *picture and note* 20
  rite of plucking the mistletoe, 25
  suppressed, 25–26
Duke, Middle Ages, 239
Durendal', the sword of Roland, 168
Dwarfs, in Norse mythology, 217; *note* 217
Dwellings. *See* Houses

Eagle-helmet, of the Germanic tribes, *picture and note* 29
East, luxuries of, traded in Europe, 170
Easter, observance in early church, 101; *note* 101
Eastern Empire. *See* Byzantine Empire
East Goths. *See* Ostrogoths
Eddas, collections of early Scandinavian literature, *note* 214
Edict of Milan (313 A.D.), 50
Education and learning,
  Arab, 170
  Charlemagne's palace school, 171; subjects studied, 171
  civilizing influence of monasteries, 206; *note* 199
  monastery schools, 171, 197–200
  son of a feudal noble, 240; *picture and note* 240
  village priest teaches children, 192
Eginhard (ā'gin-hart) (770?–840?), secretary and chronicler of Charlemagne,
  describes Charlemagne, 156
  quoted 149
Egypt,
  conquered by Mohammedans, 136
  Coptic art, *picture and note* 136
  Copts, 136; *note* 136
Einhard. *See* Eginhard
Elephant,
  gift to Charlemagne, 170; *picture and note* 170

INDEX

Elli (el'lē), Thor wrestles with, 226–227
Eloi (ā-lwä), or **Eligius** (e-lij'ĭ-us), **Saint** (588–659), bishop of Noyon, 150
Elves, mischievous sprites, in Norse mythology, 218; *picture* 218
    light elves, 231
Enamel work, of the early Britons, 23; *picture and note* 23, 24, 26
England. For early history *see* Britain
    Bede's "Ecclesiastical History of the English Nation," 184–187; *picture and note* 186
    conversion to Christianity, 184–187; *picture and note* 182, 187
    early Britain, 23–26; *picture and note* 23, 24, 25
    Norsemen found colony, 213
    shores pillaged by Norsemen, 212
    Stonehenge, *picture and note* 24
Eskimo, Skadi's dog, 229
Estates,
    Charlemagne's royal, 172–174
    monastic, 201; *picture and note* 201
Eternal City (Rome), 67
Ethelbert, king of Kent in 6th century, 185
Explorations, of the Norsemen, 213

Fairies, in Norse mythology, 217–218
Fairs, medieval, 245–249; *picture and note* 246, 247, 248, 249
Falconry or **hawking,** 241; *picture and note* 241
Family, life, in a medieval castle, 241
Farming. *See* Agriculture
Fatimah (făt'ĭ-ma or fä'tĭ-mä) (born about 606 A.D.), daughter of Mohammed, 126
Fenris Wolf or **Fenris,** in Norse mythology, monster, child of the evil god Loki, 227
    shoe to defend Vidar against, 236; *picture and note* 236
Festivals,
    Easter, 101; *note* 101
    lack of in early Christian church, 100–101
Feudalism and the Feudal Age, 237–249
    agricultural system, 237–239
    castles, 239–241; *picture and note* 239, 245
    commendation, 237–238; *note* 237
    fairs and markets, 245–249; *picture and note* 246, 247, 248
    feudal court and trial by ordeal, 242–243; *picture and note* 242, 243
    fief, 239
    homage, 243
    land ownership, 238–239
    lords and vassals, 237–239
    nobles, 237–239
    product of anarchy, 237–238
    serfs, peasants, villeins, 237–239
    towns, 244; *picture and note* 245
    travel, 245–247

Feuds,
    Bedouin family feuds, 123
Fief (fēf), in feudal system, 239
Fish, early Christian symbol, *picture and note* 52
Flags. *See* Standards and banners.
Flanders, famous for cloth, *note* 247
Folk-lore, Norse trolls, fairies, goblins and elves, 217–218; *picture and note* 217
Food,
    Middle Ages, 241
    of the early Germans, 35
Forests,
    in Britain, 23
    in Germany, 27, 28
Fortifications, medieval towns and castles, 244; *picture and note* 239, 245
Fortresses, Carcassonne, *picture and note* 245
France,
    beginnings: treaty of Verdun, 208–209; *map and note* 209
    Clovis founds nation, 142–148
    early language, 208
    Gauls, ancestors of French, *note* 18
    name, 65; *note* 36
    Normandy settled by Northmen, 213
    pillaged by Norsemen, 212
Franks, yellow-haired, Germanic tribes, 36, 142–176
    appearance, 142; *picture and note* 143
    architecture, 174; *picture and note* 175
    art, *picture and note* 151, 155, 156, 161, 165, 171, 172, 173, 176
    Austrasia, 148, 151
    become orthodox Christians, 144
    Charlemagne, 156–176; break-up of empire, 207–209; *map and note* 209
    Charles Martel, 151–153
    Clovis, 143–148
    conquer Gallo-Romans, 142–143
    cross Rhine into Gaul, 65, 142
    give name to France, 65; *note* 36
    Mayfield, 160, 176
    Strassburg oath, 208
    treaty of Verdun, 208–209; *map and note* 209
    trial by ordeal, 176
    wergild, 174–175
Frey (frā), in Norse mythology, god of sunshine, 231; *picture and note* 231
Freya (frā'yä) or **Freyja,** in Norse mythology the goddess of love and increase, 231; *picture and note* 231
    Friday sacred to, 231
Friday,
    origin of name, *note* 227
    sacred to Freya, 231
Frigga (frig'ä), in Norse mythology, wife of Odin, and goddess of the atmosphere, 220, 233

INDEX

Frisians (frē′zhans), German barbarians, 151–152
Funeral pyre, in Norse mythology, 221
    pyre on Ringhorn, Balder's ship, 234
Furniture,
    Frankish, *picture and note* 150
    table, dining
        medieval castle, *picture* 240
        Norse: in Valhalla, *picture* 223
    thrones,
        bishop's, *picture and note* 184
        St. Augustine's, *picture and note* 185
    Viking queen's bed, *picture and note* 221

Gabriel, archangel, appears to Mohammed, *picture and note* 127
Gaiseric. *See* Genseric
Galę′rius (Galerius Valerius Maximus), Roman emperor, 305–306 A.D., 45, 48
    chart, 59
    intolerant toward Christians, 47
Gall, Saint (died about 640 A.D.), Irish monk and missionary, founded famous monastery at St. Gall, Switzerland
    life in a Benedictine monastery, 195–206
    story of Karl's (Charlemagne's) advance, *retold*, 158
Galla Placidia. *See* Placidia
Gallo-Romans, conquered by Franks, 142–143
Games, gladiatorial, etc.
    Christianity puts an end to, 60; *note* 92
Ganelon (gȧn-lôn′), officer of Charlemagne who out of jealousy betrayed him, 162–168; *picture and note* 163
Garden,
    in Charlemagne's villa, 174; *picture and note* 175
    Moslem, *picture and note* 130
Gaul (gôl), or **Gallia**, now modern France and Belgium with parts of Holland, Germany and Switzerland
    as a Roman province, 18–22
    barbarians in, 142
    Druids in, 22, 25
    early civilization, 18–22; *picture and note* 19, 20, 21, 22
    Franks conquer, 142–143
    map and note, 18
    races of people, 19, 142; *note* 143
Gauls, a Celtic speaking people, 19, 142; *note* 143
    art, *pictures and notes* 20, 21
    costume, 19, 20; *picture and note* 21; *picture* 22
    gods, 21; *picture and note* 21
    jewelry, 21
    language, 19, 21; *note* 21
    villages, 22; *picture and note* 22
    warriors, 20–21; *picture and note* 22

Genseric (gĕn′ser-ĭk) or **Gaiseric** (390?–477 A.D.), Vandal king
    takes and plunders Rome, 85
Geography,
    scenery,
        Alps, Switzerland, *picture and note* 195
        Mecca, *picture* 122
Gep′i-dae, 115
German or Teutonic tribes,
    Angles, Jutes and Saxons enter Britain, 68
    art, *picture and note* 28, 29, 30, 32, 33, 35, 155
        Teutons apply art to animal forms, 96; *picture and note* 96
    barter, 28
    Bronze Age knives, *picture and note* 32
    bronze work, *picture and note* 28, 29, 30, 32
    burial and funeral customs, 36
    clothing, 34
    costume, 34; *picture and note* 27, 28, 31, 34, 36
    customs and manners, 27–36
    described by Tacitus, 28–36
    division into tribes, 36. *See also* under name of each of these tribes
    divination, 30–31
    government: assembly and council meeting, 31; *picture and note* 31
    hut-villages, 33; *picture and note* 34
    invade Roman Empire, 38, 42, 61–89
    marriage ties, 35
    map, 18
    meaning of name, 27
    physical appearance, 27, 28; *picture and note* 27
    religion, 30; *picture and note* 30
        Woden worship, 21, 30; *note* 21
    warfare, 29
    women: position, 29, 35
German language, early, 208
"Germania" of Tacitus, 27; *quoted* 28–36
Germany, beginnings: treaty of Verdun, 208–209; *map and note* 209
Giants,
    in Norse mythology, 215–216, 225–236
    Thor attempts to wipe out, 225–227; *picture and note* 226
Gibralt′ar, meaning of name, *note* 139
Ginnungagap (gĭn′nōōn-gä-gap′), in Norse mythology, the gaping abyss, 215; *picture and note* 215
Girls, of the early Germans, 35
Gladiatorial shows,
    Christianity puts an end to, 60; *note* 92
Glasswork, *picture and note* 52, 53
Gnomes, 217
Goblins, grotesque fairies,
    Norse, 217; *picture and note* 217
Gods and goddesses,
    Graeco-Syrian in Palmyra, *picture and note* 40

Gods and goddesses—Continued
  Iberian war-god, 15; *picture and note* 15
  Norse, 215–236. Their abode was in Asgard, heavenly Hall of the Chosen Slain; others were gods of the ocean and of cruel and destructive powers
    Aegir (ā′jir), god of the sea, 232
    Balder, god of light, 230, 233–235; *picture and note* 234
    Bragi (brä′gē), god of poetry and song, 228–229; *note* 228
    Frey (frā), god of sunshine, 231; *picture and note* 231
    Freya (frā′yä), goddess of love, 231; *picture and note* 231
    Frigga (frig′ä), goddess of the atmosphere, 220, 233
    Heimdall (hām-däl′), guardian of the Rainbow Bridge, 235; *picture and note* 236
    Hel, goddess of death, 221
    Her′mod, messenger of the gods, 234
    Hodur (hō′der), god of darkness, 233–234; *picture and note* 234
    Hoenir (hee′neer), one of the gods of creation, 228
    Iduna (ē-don′a), goddess of youth and spring, 228–229
    Loki (lō′kē), god of mischief and evil, 225–236
    Niörd (nyerd), god of the summer sea, 230; *picture and note* 230
    Odin or Woden, chief of the gods, and ruler of the Universe, 216–236; *picture and note* 220, 223, 229
      worshiped by Germanic Nordics, 21, 30; *note* 21; *picture and note* 35
    Ran, goddess of the shipwreck, 232
    Sigyn (sē′gēn), Loki's faithful wife, 235; *picture and note* 235
    Skadi (skä′dē), goddess of winter, 229–230; *picture and note* 230
    Thor, god of thunder, eldest son of Odin, 224, 226, 236; *picture and note* 226
      hammers, *picture and note* 224
    Twilight of the gods, a time when the world of gods was to be destroyed, 214, 216, 235–236
    Vidar (vē′där), god of primeval forests, 233, 236; *picture and note* 236
  of the Gauls: adore Cernunnus, 21; *picture and note* 21
  Saxon, 159–160; *picture and note* 160
  Slavic, 117
  Syrian, *note* 40
Golden Horn, harbor of Constantinople, 57; *picture* 58
Gold work,
  Lombards', *picture and note* 116, 117, 158, 159

Gold work—Continued
  Siberian ornaments, *picture and note* 72, 73, 84
  sun disk of Germans, *picture and note* 30
  Visigothic crown, *picture and note* 138
Gosforth Cross, scenes from, *picture and note* 235, 236
Goths, 36, 61, 64–65; *picture and note* 64, 65
  cross the Danube, 64
  home beyond the Danube, 61
  invade Roman Empire, 38, 64–65
  Ostrogoths or East Goths,
    Arians, 88, 180
    conquered by Narses, 114
    lose Italy, 112–113
    under Theodoric the Great, 86–89
  Visigoths,
    Alaric, 65–66; *picture and note* 66
    kingdom in Spain, 66, 138–140
      architecture, *picture and note* 137
      art, *picture and note* 138, 141
      Roderick, last of the Visigoths, 138–141
    sack of Rome, 66
Gott′land, island in Baltic
  ships on the Stenkyrka stone, *picture and note* 212
Government,
  administered by Charlemagne, 174–176
  assembly and council meeting of Germanic tribes, 31; *picture and note* 31
  Justinian's code, 97; *note* 97
Gravestone, sculpture,
  German, scenes from, *picture and note* 35
  Palmyrenian, *picture and note* 43
Great Wall of China,
  built to keep out Huns, 63; *picture and note* 63
Greek Empire. *See* Byzantine Empire
Greek or Eastern Church,
  separation from Western or Latin, 179
Greenland, discovered and colonized by Norsemen, 213
Gregorian chants, 183
Gregory I, the Great (540?–604), pope from 590–604 A.D., 181–187; *picture and note* 181, 182
  church music, 183; *picture and note* 183
  earnestness and humility, 181–182
  sends St. Augustine and missionaries to England, 185–187; *picture and note* 182, 187
Gregory, bishop of Tours (538–594)
  "History of the Franks," quoted 145–146; *note* 146
Gund′o-bald, leader of Burgundians, 68
Gun powder, invented, *note* 239

Hammers, of Thor, 224; *picture and note* 224
Harbors and ports,
  Golden Horn, harbor of Constantinople, 57; *picture* 58

INDEX

Haroun-al-Raschid (ha′roon al rash′id) (born about 765), famous caliph of Bagdad
 Arab civilization, 170
 hero of "Arabian Nights," 170
 sends gifts to Charlemagne, 170; *picture and note* 170
Harp, Viking, *picture* 223
Hawking, or falconry, 241; *picture and note* 241
Headdress,
 Arab or Mohammedan, *picture* 123, 125, 127, 134
 bishop's mitre, *picture and note* 180; *picture* 196
 Frankish: long hair, sign of nobility, 143; *picture*, 143; *picture and note* 149
 Iberian or early Spanish, 13; *picture and note* 13, 14; *picture* 10
 Lombard, *picture and note* 158
 Persian dome-shaped crown, *picture and note* 38
 Scythian, *picture* 72, 73
 tonsure, *picture* 190, 194, 198, 202. *See also* Helmets
Heaven
 Augustine's "City of God," *picture and note* 67
 Mohammedan, 129; *picture and note* 130
Hegira (he-jī-rä or hĕg′ĭ-ra), Mohammed's flight from Mecca, 622 A.D., 131
Heimdall (hām-däl′), in Norse mythology, guardian of the Rainbow Bridge, 219
 horn blown by, 235; *picture and note* 236
Hel, in Norse mythology, goddess of death, 221
Hel′e-na (247?–327?), wife of the Emperor Constantius, and mother of Constantine the Great, 47; *picture and note* 47
Hell, Mohammedan, 129; *note* 130, 131
Hel′lespont, strait separating Europe from Asia, now the Dardanelles, 57; *map* 18
Helmets,
 Britons, *picture* 23
 Franks, *picture* 143, 161, 165
 Gallic, 21: *picture and note* 20, 21, 22
 Germanic tribes, 29; *picture and note* 29
 Visigothic, *picture and note* 139, 140
Heraclius (he-ra′klĭ-us) (575–641), Byzantine emperor
 saves empire from Persians, 118–119
Heresy, Arian, 56–57
Hermits, 104
Her′mod, messenger of the gods, 234
Hippodrome, famous for circus and chariot racing course at Constantinople, 57
 building, 57; *picture and note* 58
 circus during Justinian's time: Theodora, 90–92; *picture and note* 91, 92
 riot of Blues and Greens, 107–108; *picture and note* 107

History and historians,
 Bede's "Ecclesiastical History of the English Nation," *note* 185; *quoted* 184–187, *note* 205
 Charlemagne's Capitularies, *note* 174; *quoted* 174
 Gregory of Tours, "History of the Franks," *quoted* 145–146; *note* 146
 Lecky "History of European Morals," *quoted*, *note* 99
 Paul the Deacon (Lombard historian), *quoted* 115–116; *note* 115
 Priscus (Greek historian), describes Attila, 75–78
 Procopius (Byzantine historian), describes Sancta Sophia, 110
 records preserved by monasteries, 199; *picture and note* 199
 Socrates, 5th century church historian, *quoted* 101; *note* 99
Hodur (hō′der), god of darkness
 slays Balder, 233–234; *picture and note* 234
Hoenir (hee′neer) in old Norse mythology, one of the three gods who created the first man and woman,
 visits earth, 228
Holland, treaty of Verdun, 209; *map and note* 209
Homage, a feudal ceremony, 243
Hono′ria (Gratia Justa Honoria), sister of Valentinian III
 alleged proposal of marriage to Attila, 74
Hono′rius, Flavius (384–423 A.D.), Roman emperor of the West
 chart, 59
 empire permanently divided, *note* 60
 retires to Ravenna, 66
 successor, 71; *note* 71
Horses, *picture* 15, 22, 31, 34, 38, 61, 62, 73, 75, 81, 82, 106, 118, 156, 161, 165, 222, 237, 239, 241, 246
 Arabian trade in, 122
 sacred to early Germans, 30–31
Hospitals, medieval monastery, 203
Houris (ho′rēz), beautiful winged angels who attend good Moslems at death, *picture and note* 130
House furnishings,
 Charlemagne's villas, 174
 Middle Ages, 241; *picture* 240
Houses, Middle Ages, 241, 244; *picture* 244
Hrim- faxi, in Norse mythology, the steed of night, 217
Hungary, Magyars enter, 210; *picture and note* 210
Huns, barbaric, Turko-Mongolian people of Farther Asia, invaded Europe in 4th and 5th centuries, 61–63, 69–84
 attack Goths, 61, 63–65

INDEX

Huns—Continued
    Attila, "the scourge of God," 69–84
    bogey-men of Europe, 61; *picture and note* 62
    Châlons, 80–81
    costume, *picture* 61, 62, 75; stolen finery, 74; *picture and note* 78
    defeated by Aetius, 80–83
    described by the historian, Priscus, 75–78
    empire of Attila, *map and note* 70
    live on horseback, 61–63; *picture and note* 61, 62
    nomadic character, 63
    Rugila, king of the Huns, 69, 70, 72
Hunt, the
    boar, hunted in Persia, *picture and note* 106
    lions, hunted in Persia, *picture and note* 39
Huts,
    hut villages of the Germans, 33; *picture and note* 34
    of the Gauls, 20; *picture* 22
Hypatia (hy-pay′shee-a) (died 415 A.D.) head of school of Neo-Platonic philosophers, *note* 99

Ibe′rians (dark Mediterraneans), people in ancient Spain, 12
    art, 14–15; *picture and note* 11, 14; *picture* 12, 13, 15
    civilization, 11–17. *See also* Spain
    costume, 13; *picture and note* 12, 13, 14; *picture* 10
Iceland, early Norse literature, *note* 214
Idols,
    Bedouin, before conversion, 121; *note* 121
    Saxon, 160; *picture and note* 160
Iduna (ē-don′a), in Norse mythology, goddess of youth and spring, 228–229
Ildico, bride of Attila, 83–84; *picture and note* 83
Illuminations. *See* Manuscript illuminations
Industry,
    Flemish cloth, *note* 247
    Iberian or early Spain
        mining, 12
        pottery making, 16
    medieval monasteries, 199
    silk culture introduced into Constantinople, *note* 105
Inns, Middle Ages, 246–247
Interiors,
    Attila's wooden palace, 75–76; *picture and note* 78, 83
    furnishings in Charlemagne's villas, 174
    medieval castle, 241; table service, *picture* 240
    Sancta Sophia, *picture and note* 111
    Viking, *picture* 223
Ireland,
    missionaries from monasteries convert North England, 186

Ireland—Continued
    monastery: Bede writes history, *picture and note* 186
    Norsemen found colony, 213
    shores pillaged by Norsemen, 212
Iron,
    scarcity in early Germany, 28
    urns, *picture and note* 33
    weapons, *picture and note* 26
Iron Age,
    urns from Germany, *picture and note* 33
Iron Crown, of Lombardy, 117; *picture and note* 117
    Charlemagne crowned with, 159
Isido′rus of Mile′tus, famous 6th century Byzantine architect, *note* 111
Is′lam, another name for Mohammedanism. *See* Mohammedanism
Italy,
    barbarian invasions,
        Huns, 82–84
        Lombards, 115–117; *picture and note* 115
        Theodoric the Ostrogoth, 86–89
        Vandals capture Rome, 85
    kingdom of Lothair, 208–209; *map and note* 209
    power of popes, 180
Ivory carving,
    bishop's throne, *picture and note* 184
    chessmen, gift to Charlemagne, 170; *picture and note* 170
    diptych (two-leaved book of ivory, carved on the outside), *picture and note* 71, 92, 93
    diptych of Boethius, *picture and note* 88
    Madonna and Child, *picture and note* 57
    medieval monasteries, 199
    panel of Queen Amalasuntha, *picture and note* 113

Jack and Jill, in Norse mythology, *note* 216
Jarrow, Ireland, monastery
    Bede writes history, *picture and note* 186
Jerusalem, patriarch of, 178
Jesus, founding of medieval church, 178–179; *picture and note* 179
Jewelry,
    buckles,
        Germanic, *picture and note* 28
        Frankish, *picture and note* 149
        Vandal, *picture and note* 85
    Charlemagne's crown, *picture and note* 169
    Gallic, 21
    gold crown of Visigoths, *picture and note* 138
    Iberian, 13; *picture* 10, 12, 13, 14
    jewel encrusted book cover, *picture and note* 171
    of the early Britons, *picture and note* 24, 26; *picture* 23

INDEX

Jotunheim. *See* Yotunheim
Julian, Flavius Claudius Julianus (331–363 A.D.), Roman emperor called the Apostate, 59
  despises Christians, 59
  respects teachings of Jesus, 59
Justice,
  administered by Charlemagne, 174–175
  among tribal Germans, 31
  feudal court, 242–243; *picture and note* 243
  Justinian's code, 97; *note* 97
  trial by ordeal, 176, 242–243; *picture and note* 243
  wergild, 174–175
Justin'ian I, the Great (483–565 A.D.), Byzantine emperor, 90–114
  Byzantine life and art, 94–96; *picture and note* 94, 95
  character, 93
  Christianity, 98–102
  codification of laws, 97; *note* 97
  marries Theodora, the circus girl, 90–93; *picture and note* 91
  Nika riot, 107–109; *picture and note* 107
  Sancta Sophia, 109–111; *picture and note* 111
  silk culture introduced, *note* 105
  wars with Ostrogoths and Vandals, 112–114
Jutes, German tribes, 36; enter Britain, 68

Kaaba (kä'ä-bá or kä'bá), or Kaba, famous Mohammedan shrine at Mecca
  Black Stone, 122; *picture and note* 125
  description, 121; *picture and note* 121
  pilgrimages, 122, 135; *picture and note* 122, 135
  said to have been founded by Abraham, 121
Kelts. *See* Celts
Khadija (kä-dē'ja), wife of Mohammed
  companion and inspiration of Mohammed, 127–129
  marriage with Mohammed, 125–126
  rich widow, 123; *picture and note* 123
Khosru. *See* Chosroes
Knights, Middle Ages, 239. *See also* index in Vol. VI
Knives,
  German, *picture and note* 32
Kobad (kö-bâd'), Persian king in the 6th century, declares war on Justinian, 106
Koran', sacred book of the Mohammedans
  opening Sura, *picture and note* 133
  quoted 124; *note* 124, 133
  sayings of Mohammed collected, 136

Labarum (lăb'a-rŭm), the standard adopted by Emperor Constantine after his conversion to Christianity, *picture and note* 49
Labor. *See* Peasants; Serfs
Labrador, visited by Norsemen, 213

Lady of Elche, bust, Iberian art, *picture and note* 14
Laity, or the people, 178
Land ownership,
  feudalism, 238–239
  monasteries, 201
Languages,
  Celtic language in Gaul, 19
  Frankish tongue, 174
  French and German, 208; early examples, quoted 208
  French separated from German, *note* 227
  Latin, language of the church, 197
  of the Gauls as distinguished from the Germanic Nordics, 21; *note* 21
Laws,
  Franks,
    administered by Charlemagne, 174–175
    capitularies of Charlemagne, *note* 174
    Justinian code, 97; *note* 97
Leather work, Scythian, *picture and note* 73
Lecky's "History of European Morals," *quoted, note* 99
Leo I, Byzantine emperor 457–474 A.D., 90
Leo III, Pope (died 816)
  crowns Charlemagne, 169
  pontifical robe, *picture and note* 178
Libraries, medieval monasteries, 200
Licin'ius, Flavius Galerius Valerius, Roman emperor (307–323 A.D.)
  Constantine defeats, 52
  persecutes Christians, 52
Lion hunt, sport of Persian kings, *picture and note* 39
Literature,
  Augustine's "City of God," 67; *picture and note* 67
  "Consolations of Philosophy" by Boethius, 88; *note* 88
  folk-lore, Norse, 217–218; *picture and note* 217
  history and historians,
    Bede's "Ecclesiastical History of the English Nation," *note* 185; *quoted* 184–187; *note* 205
    Gregory of Tours, "History of the Franks," *quoted* 145–146; *note* 146
    Lecky's "History of European Morals," *quoted, note* 99
    Paul the Deacon (Lombard historian) *quoted* 115–116; *note* 115
    Priscus (Greek historian) describes Attila, 75–78
    Procopius (Byzantine historian) describes Sancta Sophia, 110
    Socrates, 5th century church historian, *quoted* 101; *note* 99
  Latin,
    Tacitus, "Germania," 27; *quoted* 28–36

Literature—Continued
  Mohammedan,
    Koran,
      opening Sura, *picture and note* 133
      quoted, 124; *note* 124, 133
      sayings of Mohammed collected, 136
  mythology,
    Norse, tales of creation and the gods, 215–236; *pictures and notes* 215–236
  Norse,
    Elder Edda, a precious relic, *note* 214
    sagas, *quoted* 212; *note* 214
    tales of creation and the gods, 215–236
  nursery rhymes, French
    "On the bridge of Avignon," *picture and note* 246
    satirizing King Dagobert, 150; *note* 150
  Song of Roland, *retold* 161–168
  Southey's "Roderick, Last of the Goths," 139 *note* 139
Loki (lō′kē), in Norse mythology, god of mischief and evil, 225–236
  banished from heaven, 235
  eating wager, 225–227
  jealousy of, 233–234
Lombards or Langobards, Germanic tribes which settled in n. Italy, 36, 115–116
  Albion, 115–116; *picture and note* 115
  art, *picture and note* 116, 117, 158, 159
  costume shows Byzantine influence, *picture and note* 157; *picture* 159
  defeat by Franks, 157–159
  Desiderius, last king, 157–158
  driven out of Rome and Ravenna, 155
  Iron Crown, 117; *picture and note* 117
    Charlemagne crowned with, 159
  Paul the Deacon, *quoted* 115–116; *note* 115
  threaten the Pope, 154–155, 157
  women, *picture and note* 157
Lorraine (lō-rān), also **Lotharingia,** 208–209; *map and note* 209
Lothair′ I (795–855), emperor of the West, grandson of Charlemagne, 208–209; *map and note* 209
Lotharin′gia, also **Lorraine,** district in n. e. France, *map and note* 209
  bone of contention, 208–209
Louis I, the Pious (778–840), king of the Franks and emperor of the Franks, 207–208; *map and note* 209
Lutetia (lū-tē′shĭ-a), early name of Paris, France residence of King Clovis, 147

Madonna and child, *picture and note* 57
Magyars (măg′yärs), Ural-Altaic, later the Hungarians, 210; *picture and note* 210
  Arpád, 210
  settle in Hungary, 210

Mahomet. *See* Mohammed
Major Domus. *See* Mayor of the Palace
Mani (man′e), in Norse mythology the moon, 216; *note* 216
Manners. *See* Customs and manners
Manor, the estate of a lord in feudal times, 241–242; *picture* 242
Manufacturing, cloth, Flanders, *note* 247
Manuscript illuminations, 199; *picture and note* 171, 199
  Byzantine, *picture and note* 110
  copied and preserved in monasteries, 171, 199–200; *picture and note* 199
  Frankish, *picture and note* 147, 148, 171
  medieval, *picture and note* 182, 186, 187, 189, 190, 191, 200, 201
  Persian, *picture and note* 121, 127, 134, 135
  Visigothic, *picture and note* 137
Maps,
  Breaking Up of the Roman Empire, 18
  Divisions of Charlemagne's Empire, 209
  Empire of Attila, 70. *See also* Charts
Marcian (390?–457 A.D.) emperor of the East 450–457 A.D., 90
  refuses tribute, 79; *picture and note* 79
Markets and fairs, medieval, 245–249; *picture and note* 246, 247, 248, 249
Marriage,
  among early Germans, 35
  Mohammed's ideas, 132, 135
Martyrs, martyrdom of a saint, *picture and note* 99
Mary, madonna and child, *picture and note* 57
Maxen′tius, Marcus Aurelius Valerius (died 312 A.D.), Roman emperor of the West, 48–50; *picture and note* 48
  defeated by Constantine, 48–50; *pictures and notes* 50
  Milvian Bridge battle, 50; *picture and note* 50
Max-im′ian, also **Maximianus,** Roman co-emperor 286–305 A.D., 45–48; *chart* 59
Mayfield, annual gathering of the Franks, 160, 176
Mayors of the Palace, 149–150
  become kings of Frankland, 155
Mec′ca, holy city of the Mohammedans
  description, 120–121
  Kaaba, 121; *picture and note* 121, 122
  opposes Mohammed, 129–131
  pilgrimages, 122, 135; *picture and note* 122, 135
  religious center of Mohammedanism, 135; *picture and note* 135
Medi′na or **Yathrib,** Mohammedan holy city
  Mohammed flees to from Mecca, 131–133
Medicine,
  doctors and hospitals in monastery, 203
  medieval superstitions and practices, 193

INDEX

Merchants,
  Flemish, 245–249; *picture and note* 247
  Middle Ages,
    fairs and markets, 245–249; *picture and note* 246, 247, 248, 249
  Mohammed, 120–126
Merovin'gians, Frankish line of kings founded by Clovis, 142–154
  Charles Martel, 151–154
  Clovis becomes chief, 143
  Do-Nothing kings, 149–150
  Mayors of the palace, 149; become kings of Frankland, 155
Middle Ages,
  agriculture,
    feudal system, 237–239
    ox team plowing, *picture and note* 238
    peasants harrowing and seeding, *picture and note* 239
  armor, chain
    early Middle Ages: Frankish, *picture and note* 161; *picture* 163, 167, 175
  art. *See* Art
  arts and crafts: in monasteries, 199
  books copied and preserved, 199; *picture and note* 199
  castles, 240–241; *picture and note* 239, 245
  Charlemagne, 156–176
  Christian church, 177–206
  cities and towns, 244; *picture and note* 244, 245
  commerce and trade,
    Arab with Franks, 170
    Flemish, 245–249
  costume. *See* Costume
  Dark Ages, 68
  education and learning,
    Charlemagne's palace school, 171
    civilizing influence of monasteries, 206; *note* 199
    education of a noble youth, 240; *picture and note* 241
    monastery schools, 171, 197–200
  fairs and markets, 245–249; *picture and note* 246, 247, 248, 249
  falconry, 241; *picture and note* 241
  feudalism, 237–243
  food, 241
  house furnishings, 241
    kitchen utensils in Charlemagne's villas, 174
    table utensils, *picture* 240
  inns, 246–247
  justice: feudal court, 242–243; *picture and note* 243
  land ownership: feudalism, 238–239
  libraries in monasteries, 200
  manuscript illuminations, 199; *picture and note* 171, 199

Middle Ages—Continued
  medicine,
    doctors and hospitals in monastery, 203
    medieval superstitions and practices, 193
  monks and monasticism,
    in the East, 104–105
    in the West, 188–206
  ordeals and trials, 176, 242–243; *picture and note* 243
  pilgrims and palmers, 202; *picture and note* 202
  roads, 245–246; *picture and note* 246
  rule of the road, *note* 245
  serfdom, 238–239; *picture and note* 201, 238
  Song of Roland, *retold* 161–168. *See also* Literature
  windows, 241, 242
Middle Classes,
  life in a medieval parish, 191–194
Mid'gard, in Norse mythology, the Earth, 216, 218
Mid'gard snake, in Norse mythology, serpent encircling the earth, 235–236; *picture and note* 236
  child of the evil god Loki, 227
  Thor slays, 236
Midnight sun, in land of the Northmen, 214
Milan, Edict (313 A.D.), 50
Military art and science. *See* Warfare
Milvian Bridge, bridge over Tiber on Flaminian Way
  battle, 312 A.D., 50; *picture and note* 50
Miniature, a small picture illustrating a manuscript, from the Latin word *miniare*, to decorate with vermilion
  Frankish, *picture and note* 151
  Persian, *picture and note* 131. *See also* Manuscript illuminations
Mining, in Spain, 12
Missal, book containing service and music of the mass, 183
Missi Regis (mĭs'sĭ Rēg'ĭs) or king's messengers, 176
Missionaries,
  early, 105; *note* 105
  introduce silk culture into Constantinople, *note* 105
  sent to England by Pope Gregory, 185–187; *picture and note* 182, 187
Mistletoe,
  Balder legend, 233–234, *picture and note* 234
  Druid rite of plucking, 25
Mithra (mĭt'ra), Persian god of sun and truth people cling to worship, 100
Mitre, bishop's, *picture and note* 180; *picture* 196
Moat (mōt), around a castle, 240; *picture* 239
Moham'med or **Mahomet** (570?–632 A.D.), founder of the Mohammedan religion, 120–135

272 INDEX

Mohammed—Continued
  angel Gabriel appears, *picture and note* 127
  boyhood and early years, 120–124
  children, 126; adopted, 128
  commands of Mohammedanism, 128–129
  contact with other religions, 124
  first converts, 128–129
  gospel of the sword, *picture and note* 134
  Hegira, 622 A.D., 131
  ideas about marriage, divorce and position of women, 132–133, 135
  meditations in cave, 126
  marriage with Khadija, 123, 125–126
  opposed by Meccans, 129–131
  persecutions, 129–131
  sacredness of Mohammed, *picture and note* 131
  takes up sword in self-defense, 133–135
  teachings, 135
Mohammedanism, religion founded by Mohammed
  Allah, 128
  becomes a gospel of the sword, 133–134, 136; *picture and note* 134
  commands of Mohammedanism, 128–129
  first converts, 128–129
  heaven and hell, 129; *picture and note* 130
  Hegira, 622 A.D., 131
  Koran
    opening Sura, *picture and note* 133
    quoted, *note* 124
    sayings of Mohammed collected, 136
  Mecca,
  Kaaba and pilgrimages, 121–122, 135; *picture and note* 121, 122, 135
  Mohammed's ideas about marriage, divorce, and position of women, 132–133, 135
  persecutions, 129–131
  prayer, 132
  teachings of Mohammed, 135. *See also* Mohammed; Mohammedans
Mohammedans or **Saracens** or **Moslems** also **Islam**
  caliphs, 136
  commerce and trade, 170
  conquests extended, 136–137
  defeated in battle of Tours, 152–153
  destroy Visigothic kingdom, 138–141
  gospel of the sword, 136; *picture and note* 134
  paradise, 129, 136; *picture and note* 130
  universities, 170
  wars of Charlemagne against: "Minstrel's Song of Roland," 160–168
Mona, the ancient name of Anglesey, an island north of Wales
  seat of Druidism, 25
Monasteries,
  agriculture, 201; *picture and note* 201
  teach better methods, *note* 201

Monasteries—Continued
  arts and crafts, 199; *picture and note* 199
  beginnings of monasticism,
    in the East, 104–105
    in the West, 188–189
  books and libraries, 199–200; *picture and note* 199
  charitable institutions and hospitals, 202–203
  Charlemagne and court visit, 173
  civilizing influence and guardians of learning, 199–200, 206; *picture and note* 199
  daily life in a Benedictine monastery, 195–206
  founded by St. Benedict, 189
  Ireland: missionaries, 184
    Jarrow: Bede writes history, *picture and note* 186
  pilgrims and palmers, 202; *picture and note* 202
  schools, 171, 197–198
  scriptorium, 199; *picture and note* 199
  wealth, 201
Monasticism,
  beginnings,
    in the East, 104–105
    in the West, 188–189
  Basil's Rule, 105
  Benedict's Rule, 189
  ideals, 188
  monks,
    costume, *picture* 198, 199, 202
    novices, *picture* 195, 198, 202
    position explained, 190
  rules for novices, 197
Mon'za, city in n. Italy
  beautiful relics of Queen Theodelinda, *picture and note* 158, 159
Mosaics,
  Byzantine, 95–96; *picture and note* 94, 95, 102
  Sancta Sophia, *picture and note* 111
  Church of St. Demetrius, *picture and note* 102
  harbor and palace at Ravenna, *picture and note* 86, 87
Mos'lems, name applied to the followers of Mohammed. *See* Mohammedans; Mohammedanism
Mosque, Mohammedan place of worship
  Mohammed's, 132
Music and song,
  choir boys, 190; *picture and note* 190
  Gregorian chants and rise of church music, 183; *picture and note* 183
  strolling minstrels, 174; *picture and note* 175
  taught in monastery schools, 197
Musical instruments,
  animal-mouthed horns of the Gauls, *picture and note* 20
  harp, Viking, *picture* 223
  made in monasteries, 199
  of wandering Viking, *picture* 175

INDEX 273

Musket-bearing people, rule of the road; *note* 245
Muspellsheim (mōōs'pels-hĭm), in Norse mythology home of fire, 215, 216; *picture and note* 215
Mythology,
  Norse, 214-236
    climate effects, 214; *note* 214
    Fenris wolf, 227, 236; *picture and note* 236
    importance, *note* 214
    Midgard snake, 227, 235-236; *picture and note* 236
    tales of creation and the gods, 215-236; *pictures and notes* 215-236
    Valhalla, 221-223; *picture and note* 223
    Valkyries, 222-223; *picture and note* 223

Nanna (nän'nả), in Norse mythology, Balder's wife, 234
  dies of grief on funeral pyre, 234
Narses (när'sez) (478?-573), general of Justinian, 114
Nations, Western Europe,
  contain Germanic and Roman ideas, 206
  division of Charlemagne's Empire by Treaty of Verdun, 208-209; *map and note* 209
Nesto′rians, Christian sect named after Nestorius (died about 440 A.D.), *note* 57
Neus′tria, w. kingdom of the Franks,
  pleasure chariot, *picture and note* 148
  Pippin of London, 150-151
  rise, 148
Newfoundland, visited by Northmen, 213
Nicaea (ni-sē'a), city in Asia Minor
  council, 325 A.D., 56
Nicomedia (nĭk-ō-mē'dia), Asia Minor
  seat of Diocletian's rule, 45
Nidhug (nē'dhōōg), in Norse mythology dragon who gnaws root of Yggdrasil, 219, 235
Niflheim (nĭf'l-hīm), in Norse mythology, the land of mist, 215; *picture and note* 215
  root of Yggdrasil in, 219
Nika riot, 107-109; *picture and note* 107
Niörd (nyerd), god of the summer seas, 230; *picture and note* 230
Nobles, 238-243
  Middle Ages,
    feudalism, 237-239
    life, 240-242; *picture and note* 238, 241
Normandy, settled by Northmen, 213
Norns, in Norse mythology, three goddesses corresponding to the Greek Fates, 219, 236
Northmen or **Norsemen** or **Vikings** (blond, blue-eyed Nordics), 211-236
  architecture,
    interior of hall of Valhalla, *picture* 223
  art, *picture and note* 216, 217, 220, 221, 229, 232, 235, 236

Northmen—Continued
  burial and funeral customs, 221-223
  converted to Christianity about 1030 A.D., 232; *note* 214, 232
  costume, *picture* 223, 226, 230, 231, 232, 234
  explorations, 213
  found colonies, 213
  harry and pillage shores of Europe and England, 211-212
  Norse mythology, 214-236
    climate affects, 214; *note* 214
    importance, *note* 214
    tales of creation and the gods, 215-236; *pictures and notes* 215-236
  origin of the name "Viking," 212
  St. Olaf, 232; *picture and note* 232
  ships,
    ancient ship and warriors; *picture and note* 212
    dragon ship, 213; *picture and note* 211
    Oseberg ship, *picture and note* 213
    Viking Queen's sledge, bed and wagon, *picture and note* 220-221
Norsemen. *See* Northmen
Norway, home of the Northmen or Vikings, 211-236
  description, climate, etc., 214
  fall of St. Olaf, *picture and note* 232
Nursery rhyme and song,
  "On the bridge of Avignon," *picture and note* 246
  satirizing King Dagobert, 150; *note* 150

Oath of Strassburg, 208
Odena′thus (died about 270 A.D.), general and ruler of Palmyra, 39-41
O′din or **Woden,** in Norse mythology, the chief of the gods, 216-236, *picture and note* 220, 223, 229
  creation tale, 216-219
  excursion to earth, 228
  Freya his wife, 220, 224
  Fenris wolf, 236; *picture and note* 236
  Sleipnir, Odin's steed, 236
  Thor, eldest son, 224
  twin sons, 233
  Valhalla, 221-223; *picture and note* 223
  Valkyries attend, 222-223
  Wednesday sacred to, 220
  worshipped by Germanic Nordics, 21, 30; *note* 21; *picture and note* 35
  worshipped by early Franks, 144
  worshipped by Saxons, 159
Odoacer (ō-dō-ā'ser) (434?-493 A.D.), German leader who deposed Romulus Augustus, 85; *note* 71
  defeated and killed by Theodoric, 87
  overthrows Western Roman Empire, 85

INDEX

Olaf II (995–1030), king and patron saint of Norway
conversion of Norway, 232; *picture and note* 232; *note* 214
Ol'iphant, the wonderful horn of Roland, 166–168; *picture and note* 167
Olive branch, early Christian symbol, *picture and note* 52
Oliver, comrade of Roland, 162–166
Omar (ō'mar) (581?–644), second Mohammedan caliph
organizes Mohammedans for conquest, 136–137
Ordeals and trials, medieval, 176, 242–243; *picture and note* 243
Ork'ney Islands, off the coast of Scotland
Norsemen colonize, 213
Orléans (ôr-lā-än'), city in France
siege of, 80
Ornaments,
ancient Britons, *picture and note* 26
Siberian gold, *picture and note* 72, 73, 84
Orthodox Christians, 56
Arians vs. Orthodox, 98–99; *picture and note* 98, 99
Ose'berg, near Oslo, Norway
other objects from Oseberg ship, *picture and note* 217, 220, 221
ship, *picture and note* 213
Oslo (ôs'lô), Norway
Oseberg ship and other objects, *picture and note* 213, 217, 220, 221
Os'trogoths or **East Goths**,
Arians, 88, 180
conquered by Norses, 114
home beyond the Danube, 61
lose Italy, 112–113
under Theodoric the Great, 86–89
Oxen, *picture* 65, 210, 238

Painting,
fresco from temple at Dura, *picture and note* 40
Persian, *picture and note* 130
Pal'estine, southern part of Syria conquered by Mohammedans, 136
Palmyra (păl-mī'ra), magnificent city and kingdom in Syria in an oasis of the desert, 120 miles n. e. of Damascus, 39–44
architecture, *picture and note* 41
art, *picture and note* 40, 43
costume, *picture and note* 40, 43, 44
description, 39
map and note 18
worshipers, *picture and note* 40
Zenobia, Queen of the East, 40–44
Pannonia (pă-nō'nĭ-a), Roman province s. and w. of the Danube River.
stronghold of Slavs and Gothic tribes, 210

Papacy, rise of, 177–180
Paradise, Moslem, 129, 136; *picture and note* 130
Paris, France, beginnings: residence of King Clovis, 147
Parish village, life in, 191–194
Patriarch, in the Roman Catholic church the term means a bishop of the highest rank, and in the Greek church it means a high dignitary, 178
in the Eastern Empire, 178
Paul the Deacon (720–790), Lombard historian
"History of the Lombards," *quoted* 115–116; *note* 115
teaches in Charlemagne's school, 171
Paulus, Marcus Julius, adventures in Roman provinces, 11–27
Pavia, Lombard city in n. Italy
taken by Charlemagne, 158
Peacock, *picture* 175
Peasants,
in Charlemagne's time, *picture and note* 173
Middle Ages, 237–239; *picture and note* 237, 238, 239
work for monks, 201; *picture and note* 201. *See also* Serfs
Pepin. *See* Pippin
Perfume, gift to Charlemagne from Haroun-al-Raschid, 170
Persia,
history, *note* 38
map and note 18
Sassanian or Sassanid dynasty
art, *picture and note* 38, 39, 106
Chosroes I, 106
Chosroes II sweeps Asia Minor, 118
New Persia, *note* 38
Sapor overthrows Rome, 38; *picture and note* 38
Peter and Paul, *picture and note* 52
Peter, St., regarded as first bishop of Rome, 179
"Phantom Emperors," *chart* 45
Philosophy, Boethius "Consolations of Philosophy," 88; *note* 88
Picts, people of disputed origin, St. Cuthbert establishes church; *picture and note* 206
Pillars. *See* Columns
Pillar saints, 103–104; *picture and note* 103
Pillars of Hercules, the two promontories, Gibraltor in Europe and Abyla in Africa, 11
Pip'pin I or **Pepin** (pep'in) (died 639), Pippin of Landen, 150–151
Pip'pin II or **Pepin** (pep'in) (died 714)
Mayor of Austrasia and Neustria, 151
Pip'pin III or **Pepin the Short** (died 768), first Carolingian king of the Franks, 154–155
becomes king of Frankland, 155
drives Lombards from Rome and Ravenna, 154–155

INDEX

Placidia (pla-sĭd'ĭ-ä), **Galla** (388?–450?), 71; *picture and note* 71
Plow, Middle Ages, *picture and note* 238
Polygamy (pō-lĭg'a-mi), Mohammed's ideas about, 132, 135
Poor relief, work of the monasteries, 202; *picture and note* 202
Pope,
   meaning of word, 180
   origin of office, 180
   pontifical robe of Pope Leo III, *picture and note* 178
Port. See Harbors and ports
Pottery, Iberian, 16; *picture and note* 16, 17
Praetorian (prĕ-tō'rĭ-ăn) **Guard**, imperial bodyguard founded by Augustus made and unmade emperors, 37
Presbyters, in the medieval church, 178
Priest,
   Iberian, *picture and note* 15
   in the medieval church, 178, 190
   of the early Germans, *picture and note* 30
   Palmyrenian: Greco-Syrian, *picture and note* 40
Priscus, Greek historian, middle of fifth century A.D.
   envoy to Attila: reception, etc., 75–79
Pro'bus, Marcus Aurelius (230?–282 A.D.), Roman emperor, 45; *chart* 45
Proco'pius (born close of 5th cent. A.D.), Byzantine historian, *quoted* 110
Pulcheria (pul-kē'rĭ-ä) (399–453), empress marries Marcian, 79, *note* 79
Pyrenees Mountains, Arabs cross, 141

Races of mankind,
   Alpines, 19, 117
   Britons (Mediterraneans and Celts), 24; *picture and note* 23
   Burgundians (yellow haired Teutonic Nordics), 36, 68
   Celts, term applied to language and culture, 19; *note* 21
   Franks (yellow haired Nordics), 142; *picture and note* 143
   Gauls, a Celtic speaking people, 19; *note* 21
   Germans or Teutons, 27, 28; *picture and note* 27
   Huns (barbaric Turko-Mongolians), 61–63; *picture and note* 61, 62
   Iberians or early Spaniards, 12; *picture* 10, 12, 13, 14
   Lombards (yellow-haired Germanics), 115
   Magyars (Slavs, later the Hungarians), 210; *picture and note* 210
   Mediterraneans, 12, 19
   Nordics, 19
   Scythians (blue-eyed Nordics), *picture* 72, 73

Races of mankind—Continued
   Silures, swarthy peoples along borders of Wales, 24
   Slavs (brown-haired Alpines), 117; *picture and note* 118
   Visigoths, *note* 139
Ragnarok (rag'na-rŭk), twilight of the gods, 234
Ran, in Norse mythology, goddess of the shipwrecks, 232
Raven'na, Italy, emperors lived there during barbarian invasions because it could more easily be defended, 404 A.D.
   art, harbor and palace in mosaic, *picture and note* 86, 87
   Attila, a hostage, 69–70
   bishop's throne, *picture and note* 184
   capital of Odoacer, 87
   Emperor Honorius retires to, 66
   mosaics, in Church of San Apollinare Nuovo, *picture and note* 86, 87
   Placidia and court, 71
   tomb of Theodoric, 89; *picture and note* 89
Reading,
   taught in Charlemagne's palace school, 171
   taught in monastery schools, 197
Reccens'winth (649–672), king of the Visigoths bejeweled golden crown, *picture and note* 138
Religion,
   Arab-Bedouin, before conversion, 121–123
   Christians,
     Constantine, 47–58
     in Justinian's day, 98–105. *See also* Christianity
   early German, 30; *picture and note* 30
   Iberian or early Spaniards, 12, 15
   medieval belief in fire breathing monsters, 197; *picture and note* 197
   Mohammed and Mohammedanism, 120–141
   Norsemen,
     converted to Christianity, *note* 214, 232
     tales of creation and the gods, 214–236
   paganism in Christianity, 100–102; *picture and note* 101
   medieval Christians, 193
   worshipers in a Palmyrenian temple, *picture and note* 40
   Zoroastrianism, 124
Remi (rŭ-mē') or **Remigius** (re-mij'i-us), bishop of Rheims
   baptizes Clovis, 146; *picture and note* 146
Rents, paid in kind by peasants to monasteries, 201
Rheims (rēmz, in French răns), baptism of Clovis, 146; *picture and note* 146
Rik'imer, Count, a German general deposes puppet emperors of Rome, 85
Ringhorn, in Norse mythology
   Balder's funeral pyre, 234

INDEX

Riots, Nika, 107–109; *picture and note* 107
Rites and ceremonies,
  Druid rite of plucking the mistletoe, 25
  Iberian, 15–16
Roads,
  Middle Ages, 245–246; *picture and note* 246
  rule of the road, *note* 245
Rock of Gebel Tarik (Gibraltar), 139; *note* 139
Roderick, last Visigothic king in Spain (710–711), 138–141
  defeated by Moslems, 139–141; *picture and note* 139
  legend, 140
Ro'land, hero of Charlemagne's army in fight against Saracens, 160–168
  "Minstrel's Song of Roland," 161–168; *picture and note* 167
Roman Catholic or Western Church,
  separation from Greek church, 179. *See also* Church, medieval
Romance languages, French, 208; *note* 227
Romances, "Song of Roland," *retold* 161–168
Rome and the Romans,
  captured by Vandals and fall of Rome, 85
  medieval church, 177–180
  "Phantom Emperors," *chart* 45
  provinces, *map and note* 18
    Britain, 23–26
    Gaul, 18–22
    German or Teutonic tribes, 27–36
    Spain, 11–17; *pictures and notes* 11–17
  Roman Empire,
    barbarians threaten, 38, 59
    barbarian invasions, 61–89; *pictures and notes* 61–89. *See also* under name of each group
    "barrack" emperors, 37
    break-up, 37–60
    capital in the East: Nicomedia, 48; Constantinople, 57
    decline, 37, 59–60
    division, 60, 90; *note* 60, 71
    Christianity in, 46–60
    decay of life, 70
    Rome ceases to be capital, 48
    reorganized by Diocletian, 45–46
    Western Empire overthrown, 85
  triumphs and processions
    Aurelian's, 44. *See also* Byzantine Empire
Romulus Augustulus, 85; *note* 71
Roncesvalles (rons-val', Spanish ron-thes-val' yays), pass in n. Spain
  defeat of Charlemagne's guard, 165–167; *picture and note* 167
Rosamund, Lombard queen, 115–116; *picture and note* 115
Rugila, king of the Huns, 69–70, 72
Rule of the road, *note* 245

Russia,
  Norsemen found colony, 213
  steppes, 72–73; *pictures and notes* 72, 73

Sabbath, Mohammedan, 132
Sacrifice, human, Druids, 22, 25
Sa'gas, old Scandinavian prose tales, *quoted* 212; *note* 214
Sagus, woolen cloak of the Gauls, 20; *picture and note* 21
St. Gall (san-gal'), Switzerland, named after the monk of St. Gall, *picture and note* 195
  life in a Benedictine monastery, 195–206
St. Peter's, church in Rome
  coronation of Charlemagne, 169; *picture and note* 169
  sacked by Saracens, 210
Sanc'ta Sophia (sō-fē'a), famous church built by Constantine at Constantinople, 57
  burned, 108
  glory of Sancta Sophia, under Justinian, 109–111; *picture and note* 110, 111
Sandals, Charlemagne's coronation, *picture and note* 169
Sa'por I, Sassanian king, (240–309 A.D.), 38
  takes Emperor Valerian prisoner, 38; *picture and note* 38
Saracens, name applied to Mohammedans during Middle Ages. *See* Mohammedans
Sarma'tians,
  costume, *note* 73
  occupy Russian steppes, 73
Sassanians (sa-sā'nians) or Sassanid dynasty, last native dynasty of ancient Persia (226–637 A.D.), 38
  art, *picture and note* 38, 39, 106
  Chosroes I, 106
  Chosroes II sweeps Asia Minor, 118
  Rome overthrown, 38; *picture and note* 38
Satan,
  Loki, counterpart of, 227
  watches Mohammed, *picture and note* 131
Saxons, German tribes, 36, 159–160
  Charlemagne's attempt at conquest, 160
  enter Britain, 68
  gods and idols, 159–160
  home around the Baltic, 159; *map* 18
Scandinavians. *See* Northmen
Schools,
  cathedral, 190
  Charlemagne founds, 170–171
  monastery schools, 171, 197–198
    civilizing influence, 206; *note* 199
  none in Frankland, 155. *See also* Education and learning
  universities of the Arabs, 170
Scissors, of the early Franks, 142; *picture and note* 142

INDEX

Scotland,
  Norsemen found colony, 213
  shores pillaged by Norsemen, 212
Scribe, Frankish, *picture and note* 151
Scripto′rium, writing room in medieval monastery, 199; *picture and note* 199
Sculpture,
  Franks: dedicatory, *picture and note* 172
  Persian: Sassanian, *picture and note* 38, 39
Sculpture, busts,
  Roman, Commodus, *picture and note* 37
Sculpture reliefs,
  Arch of Constantine, 50; *picture and note* 50
  Visigothic warrior, *picture and note* 140
Scythians (blond blue-eyed Nordics)
  art, *picture and note* 72, 73
  costume, *picture and note* 72, 73
  occupy Russian steppes, 73; *note* 72
Sea-faring,
  Vikings, 211–213; *picture and note* 211, 212
Serfs,
  feudal, 238–239; *picture and note* 238; *note* 237
  medieval, *picture and note* 201. *See also* Peasants
Severus (sĕ-vē′rŭs), **Lucius Septimius** (146–211 A.D.), Roman soldier-emperor, 37; *chart* 45
Shetland Island, colonized by Norsemen, 213
Shields,
  Franks, *picture* 143
  Gallic, *picture and note* 20
  German tribes, 29; *picture* 27, 29, 35
  Iberian, 17; *picture and note* 11, 16, 17
  of the early Britons, *picture and note* 23
  Viking, on sides of ships, 213; *picture and note* 211, 212
  Visigothic, *picture and note* 139, 140
Ships. *See* Boats and ships; Transportation
Shoes, fur of the Magyars, *picture and note* 210
Shops, medieval, 244; *picture and note* 244
Siberia, art, *picture and note* 72, 73, 84
Sigyn (sē′gēn), in Norse mythology, Loki's faithful wife, 235; *picture and note* 235
Silk, silk culture introduced, *note* 105
Sil′ures, powerful and warlike tribe along borders of Wales, 24
Simeon Stylites (stī-lī′tēz), famous "pillar-saint," 103–104; *picture and note* 103
Skadi (skä′dē), in Norse mythology, goddess of Winter, 229–230; *picture and note* 230
Skrymir (skrim′ir), Thor's encounter, 224–227
Slaves, among Germanic tribes, 36
Slavs (slavz), important branch of Alpine race living in eastern and central Europe, 117; *picture and note* 118
  costume, *note* 73
  gods, 117
  invade Balkan Peninsula, 117–118
  occupy Russian steppes, 73

Sledge, Viking, *picture and note* 220
Sleipnir (slĭp′nir), Odin's steed, 236; *picture and note* 35
Socrates, famous 5th century church historian, quoted 101; *note* 99
Soissons (swä-son′), battle of, 482 A.D., 143
Sol, in Norse mythology, the sun maid, 216; *note* 216
Soldiers. *See* Warriors
Song of Roland, *retold* 161–168
Songs. *See* Music and Song
Spain,
  as a Roman province, 11, 17
  Charlemagne wars with the Saracens, 160–168
  early settlements, 14
  geography, 11, 16; *map* 18
  Iberian civilization, 11–17
    art, 14–15; *picture and note* 11, 14; *picture* 12, 13, 15, 16, 17
    costume, 13; *picture and note* 12, 13, 14; *picture* 10
    dances, 15, 16
    gods and goddesses, 15; *picture and note* 15
    mining, 12
    warriors, 17; *picture and note* 11, 16
  Mohammedans in, 139–141; *picture and note* 139
  Vandal settlers, 66
  Visigoths, 66
    art, *picture and note* 138, 140, 141
    costume, *picture* 137, 140, 141
    end of kingdom, 138–141
Spears, *picture* 22, 23, 27, 29, 35, 72, 79, 107, 139, 143, 161, 165
Spinning and weaving, Charlemagne's time, 174
Sports,
  hunt, the, *picture and note* 39, 106
  Iberian, 16
  Middle Ages,
    falconry, 241; *picture and note* 241
Spur, Lombard gold, *picture and note* 116
Stairways, Arab, *picture* 130, 131
Standards and banners,
  banners of the Visigoths, *picture* 139
  fish standards, *picture and note* 165
  labarum, *picture and note* 49
  Saxon, *picture* 160
  Viking banner, *picture* 211
Statues,
  Charlemagne, *picture and note* 156
  Clovis, *picture and note* 145
  Iberian, *picture* 12, 13
Steppes (stĕps), Russia: people, 72–73; *pictures and notes* 72, 73
Stonehenge (stōn′-hĕnj), prehistoric monument on Salisbury Plain, England, *picture and note* 24
Story-time, in a monastery, 203–206

278 INDEX

Strabo (strā'bo) (born about 63 B.C.), Roman geographer and historian
describes Iberian civilization, *note* 15
Strassburg, Oath of, 208
Streets, medieval, 244; *picture and note* 244
Stylites (stī-lī'tēz), **Simeon,** famous "pillar-saint," 103–104; *picture and note* 103
Sue-to'ni-us, Roman governor of Britain, 25–26
Sun, in Norse mythology, 216; *picture and note* 216
Sun chariot, *picture and note* 30
Sun-worship, of the early Germans, *picture and note* 30
Superstitions,
medieval, 193; *picture and note* 193
why cats accompany witches, *note* 231
Surtr (soor't'r), in Norse mythology, the flame giant, 235–236
Sweden. *See* Northmen
Swords, rule of the road, *note* 245
Symbols,
Christian, 49–50; *picture and note* 49, 51, 52, 53
doves, fish, etc., *picture and note* 52
"XP," *picture and note* 49, 51, 52, 53, 79
Syria, conquered by Mohammedans, 136–137

Table manners, Middle Ages, 241
Table service, Middle Ages, *picture and note* 240
Tacitus (tas'ĭ-tŭs), Cornelius (55?–120? A.D.), Roman historian
describes Germans or Teutons, *quoted* 28–36
Tapestries,
Byzantine, *picture and note* 170
Persian, *picture and note* 119, 120
Tarik (died about 720), Mohammedan general, leader of invasion into Spain, 138–139
Taxes, collected by feudal noble, 239
Teutonic language, 21; *note* 21
Teutons. *See* German or Teutonic tribes
Textiles,
cotton scarce in Middle Ages, 247
Flemish cloth, *note* 247
German cloth, *picture and note* 36
linen, expensive, 247
origin of names of materials, *note* 247
silk culture introduced into Constantinople, *note* 105
Textile design,
Byzantine, *picture and note* 170
Persian, *picture* 120
silk cloth, *picture* 101
The-od'a-had, nephew of Theodoric the Great, 89; *picture and note* 112
loses kingdom and life, 112–113
Theod'elinda, Lombard queen
book cover, *picture and note* 158
donates Monza treasure, *picture and note* 159

Theodo'ra (died about 547 A.D.), wife of the emperor Justinian, *picture and note* 95
circus-girl, 90–93; *picture and note* 91, 92
Empress of the East, 93
Theodoric (thē-ŏd'o-rik) the Great, king of the Ostrogoths, 488–526 A.D., 86–89; *picture and note* 86
Arian, 88
execution of Boethius, *picture and note* 88
hostage at Constantinople, 86
just and beneficent government, 88
palace, *picture and note* 87
religious toleration, 88
tomb, 89; *picture and note* 89
Theodo'sius the Great (346?–395), Roman emperor, 60; *picture and note* 60
abolishes Olympic games, 60
closes pagan temples, etc., 60
empire divided permanently, 60; *note* 71
Theodosius II (401?–450 A.D.), emperor of the East, 79; *chart* 59
Thialfi (te-älf'e), in Norse mythology a young attendant, 225
defeated in race by a giant, 226
Thiasse (te-äs'se), in Norse mythology, one of the storm giants
Loki's adventure with, 228–229
Thor, in Norse mythology, god of Thunder, 224
appearance, 224
drinking wager, 226
hammer, 224; *picture and note* 224
slays Midgard snake, 236
Thursday named for, *note* 227
visits Utgard-Loki, 225–227
worshiped by Franks, 144
Yule, month sacred to, 232
Thrones,
bishop's or ivory cathedra, *picture and note* 184
St. Augustine's, *picture and note* 185
Thrymheim (trim'hīm), in Norse mythology, home of Thiassi, 230
Thursday, origin of name, *note* 227
Tithe, tenth part, in the medieval church, 194
Tivoli (tē-vō-lē), Italy
Queen Zenobia spends last days, 44
Toilet articles, of the Franks, 142
Tonsure, *picture* 190, 194, 198, 202
Totila (tŏt'ĭ-lä), Ostrogothic king, 114
Tours, Battle of, 732 A.D., 152–153
Tours, Gregory, bishop of
"History of the Franks," *quoted* 145–146; *note* 146
Towns,
early Iberian or Spanish, 16
medieval, 244
Toys, custom of hanging tree with, 102
Trade. *See* Commerce and trade

INDEX

Transportation,
  boats and ships,
    St. Cuthbert's, *picture and note* 206
    Viking,
      dragon ship, 213; *picture and note* 211
      Oseberg ship, *picture and note* 213
  carts, Magyar, *picture and note* 210
  chariots,
    carruca, *picture and note* 148
    German sun-chariot, *picture and note* 30
  sledge, *picture and note* 220
  wagons,
    bronze wagon from Gaul, *picture and note* 19
    Gallic wagon, *picture and note* 21
    Middle Ages, 245, 247; *picture and note* 246, 247
    Viking, *picture and note* 221
Travel,
  Middle Ages, 245–247; *picture and note* 246, 247
  rule of the road, *note* 245
Treasure of Monza, *picture and note* 159
Treaty of Verdun, 208–209; *map and note* 209
Tree of life, in Norse mythology, 219, 235
Trial by ordeal, 176, 242–243; *picture and note* 243
Triumphs and processions, Aurelian's, 44
Troll, in Norse mythology, mischievous underground elves, 217; *picture and note* 217
Troyes (trwä), France, medieval fair, 245–249
Turkish nobleman, *picture and note* 74
Twilight of the Gods, in Norse mythology a time when the world of gods was to be destroyed, 214, 216
  last days, 235–236

Underworld, in Norse mythology, the dark realms of Hel, the goddess of death, 221
Universities, Arab, 170. *See also* Education and learning
Urns,
  iron, German, *picture and note* 33
  yellow ware, early British, *picture and note* 25
Utensils, in Charlemagne's villas, 174
Utgard-Loki (ōōt′gard lō′kē), castle of, 225

Valentin′ian I (321–375 A.D.), Roman emperor, 60; *chart* 59
Valentin′ian III (419?–455), Roman boy emperor, 71; *picture and note* 71
  decree, 179
  murdered, 85
Va′lens (328?–378 A.D.), Roman emperor of the East, 61; *chart* 59
  Goths invade empire, 64, 65
Vale′rian, Roman emperor, 252–260 A.D.
  defeated and imprisoned by Persians, 38; *picture and note* 38

Valhalla (väl-häl′ä), in Norse mythology, home and paradise for the souls of heroes slain in battle, 221–223; *picture and note* 223
  warriors welcome summons, 213, 222, 223; *note* 211
Valkyries (val-kĭr′ēz), in Norse mythology the battle-maidens of Odin who bring back the slain heroes to Valhalla, 222–223; *picture and note* 223
Valpurgis (väl-pōōr′gēs) **Night,** witches hold revels, *note* 231
Vandals, barbaric German tribe which overran Europe in 5th century
  art, *picture and note* 85
  cross into Africa, 66
  division of Germans into tribes, 36
  Genseric, 85
  in Spain, 65
  seize Carthage, 66
  take and plunder Rome, 85
Vassal, subject of a feudal lord, 239
"Venerable Bede, The." *See* Bede
Venice, Italy, city built on small islands, 82
Verdun (vêr-dŭn), Treaty of, 208–209; *map and note* 209
Vidar (vē′där), in Norse mythology, god of primeval forests, 233
  braces shoe in mouth of Fenris wolf, 236; *picture and note* 236
Viking dragon-ship, 213; *picture and note* 211
Vikings (vī′kings). *See* Northmen
Villages,
  Gallic, 22; *picture and note* 22
  life in medieval village, 191–194
  of the Germans, 33; *picture and note* 34
Vili (vē′lē), in Norse mythology, in creation story, 216
Villein (vĭl′ĭn) or serf, under feudalism, 237–239
Vis′igoths or West Goths,
  Alaric, king of the Visigoths, 65–66; *picture and note* 66; burial, 66
  home beyond the Danube, 61
  kingdom in Spain, 66, 138–140
    architecture, *picture and note* 137
    art, *picture and note* 138, 141
    gold crown, *picture and note* 138
  Roderick, last of the Visigoths, 138–141
  sack of Rome, 66
Vitiges (vit′i-jez), Ostrogothic warrior of the 6th century, 113

Wagons,
  bronze wagon from Gaul, *picture and note* 19
  Gallic two-wheeled wagon, *picture and note* 21
  Middle Ages, *picture and note* 237, 247
  Viking, *picture and note* 221
Wales, Silures, ancient people, 24
Wall of China, Great, 63; *picture and note* 63

INDEX

War-god, Iberian, 15; *picture and note* 15
Warfare,
  battle of Milvian bridge, *picture and note* 50
  German tribes, 29; *picture and note* 34
  gun powder invented, *note* 239
  Huns, 61–62; *picture and note* 62
  Mohammedan gospel of the sword, *picture and note* 134
  Viking, 211–212
Warriors,
  Britons, *picture and note* 23
  Frankish, 142; *picture and note* 142, 161, 165
  Gallic, 20–21; *picture and note* 22
  German, 29; *picture and note* 27, 29, 34, 35
  Huns, 61–62; *picture and note* 62; Attila, *picture* 82
  Iberians, 17; *picture and note* 11, 16
  Mohammedan, *picture and note* 134
  Scythian, *picture* 72, 73
  Viking, 211–212; *picture and note* 211, 212
  Visigothic, *picture and note* 139, 140
Weapons,
  battle-axe, 142; *picture* 143; *picture and note* 28
  dagger, *picture and note* 26
  Franks, *picture* 143; *picture and note* 142, 147
  Gallic, 21; *picture* 22
  Germans or Teutons, 29; *picture and note* 27, 28, 29, 32, 35
  Hunnic, *picture* 62, 82
  Iberian, *picture and note* 11
  Mohammedan, *picture* 134, 167
  of the Britons, *picture and note* 26; *picture* 23
  scramasax or sword-knife, *picture and note* 147
  Scythian, *picture* 72, 73
  spears, *picture* 22, 23, 27, 29, 35, 72, 79, 107, 139, 143, 161, 165
  Visigothic, *picture* 139, 140
Weaving, Charlemagne's time, 174
Wednesday,
  origin of name, *note* 227
  sacred to Odin, 220
Week, origin of names of days, *note* 227
Wergild (wer'gild) or man money in Anglo-Saxon and Teutonic law, 174
West Goths. *See* Visigoths.
Windows, unglazed, in Middle Ages, 241–242
Witchcraft, demons, and devils,
  cure for witches, 193
  medieval beliefs about, 193, 204–206; *picture and note* 193, 204
  why witches are accompanied by cats, *note* 231
Woden. *See* Odin
Women,
  Amalasuntha, Ostrogothic queen, 89, 112; *picture and note* 113

Women—Continued
  Khadija, wife of Mohammed, 123, 125–129; *picture and note* 123
  Lombard, *picture and note* 157
  Middle Ages, 241
  Mohammed's ideas about marriage, divorce, and position of women, 132–133, 135
  position among early Germanic tribes, 29
  sacredness of marriage tie among Germans, 35
  Theodora, Byzantine circus-girl and empress, 90–93; *picture and note* 91, 92
  Visigothic, *picture and note* 141
  Zenobia, queen of Palmyra, 40–44; *picture and note* 42, 44
Wood-cut, *picture and note* 160
Writing,
  capital letters illuminated, 171; *picture and note* 171
  Frankish scribe, *picture and note* 151
  monks copy and illuminate manuscripts, 171, 199; *picture and note* 171, 199
  music written down, *picture and note* 183
  studied in Charlemagne's palace school, 171
  studied in monastery schools, 197

"XP," the first two letters of the name of Christ in its Greek form, *picture and note* 49, 51, 52, 53; *picture* 79

Yathrib. *See* Medina
Yggdrasill (ĭg'drah-sĭl), in Norse mythology, the tree of life, 219, 235
Ymer (ü'mer) or **Ymir,** in Norse mythology, the ice-giant from whose body the world was created, 215–218; *picture and note* 215
Yotunheim (yĕ'tōōn-hīm), in Norse mythology, home of the giants, 216
Ypres (e'pr), Belgium
  diaper-patterned cloth named, *note* 247
Yule tide customs,
  feast, 232
  in Norse mythology, *note* 228
  meaning of word, 232
  observance transferred to Christmas Day, 232

Zeno, emperor of the East or Byzantine Empire (474–491 A.D.), 85, 86, 87, 90
Zenobia (ze-nō'bia), queen of Palmyra in third cent. A.D., 40–44
  assumes title of Queen of the East, 41
  coin, *picture and note* 42
  meets Emperor Aurelian in battle, 42–43
  statue, *picture and note* 44
  walks as a captive in Aurelius' triumph, 44
Zoroast'er, founder of Zoroastrianism, the religion of ancient Persia, 124